STRAIGHT TALK

Discourses on Practice

Rangjung Yeshe Books • *www.rangjung.com*

Padmasambhava • *Treasures from Juniper Ridge* • *Advice from the Lotus-Born, Dakini Teachings*

Padmasambhava and Jamgön Kongtrül • *The Light of Wisdom, Vol. 1, & Vol. 2, Vol. 3, Secret, Vol. 4 & Vol. 5*

Padmasambhava, Chokgyur Lingpa, Jamyang Khyentse Wangpo, Tulku Urgyen Rinpoche, Orgyen Tobgyal Rinpoche, & others • *Dispeller of Obstacles* • *The Tara Compendium* • *Powerful Transformation* • *Dakini Activity*

Yeshe Tsogyal • *The Lotus-Born*

Dakpo Tashi Namgyal • *Clarifying the Natural State*

Tsele Natsok Rangdröl • *Mirror of Mindfulness* • *Heart Lamp*

Chokgyur Lingpa • *Ocean of Amrita* • *The Great Gate* • *Skillful Grace* • *Great Accomplishment* • *Guru Heart Practices*

Traktung Dudjom Lingpa • *A Clear Mirror*

Jamgön Mipham Rinpoche • *Gateway to Knowledge, Vol. 1, Vol. 2, Vol. 3, & Vol. 4*

Tulku Urgyen Rinpoche • *Blazing Splendor* • *Rainbow Painting* • *As It Is, Vol. 1 & Vol. 2* • *Vajra Speech* • *Repeating the Words of the Buddha* • *Dzogchen Deity Practice*

Adeu Rinpoche • *Freedom in Bondage*

Khenchen Thrangu Rinpoche • *King of Samadhi* • *Crystal Clear*

Chökyi Nyima Rinpoche • *Present Fresh Wakefulness* • *Bardo Guidebook*

Tulku Thondup • *Enlightened Living*

Orgyen Tobgyal Rinpoche • *Life & Teachings of Chokgyur Lingpa*

Dzigar Kongtrül Rinpoche • *Uncommon Happiness*

Tsoknyi Rinpoche • *Fearless Simplicity* • *Carefree Dignity*

Marcia Binder Schmidt • *Dzogchen Primer* • *Dzogchen Essentials* • *Quintessential Dzogchen* • *Confessions of a Gypsy Yogini* • *Precious Songs of Awakening Compilation*

Erik Pema Kunsang • *Wellsprings of the Great Perfection* • *A Tibetan Buddhist Companion* • *The Rangjung Yeshe Tibetan-English Dictionary of Buddhist Culture & Perfect Clarity*

STRAIGHT TALK

Discourses on Practice

Orgyen Tobgyal Rinpoche

Translated by Erik Pema Kunsang,
Gyurme Avertin, and Marcia Binder Schmidt

Compiled and Edited by Marcia Binder Schmidt

Rangjung Yeshe Publications
55 Mitchell Blvd, Suite 20
San Rafael, CA 94903 USA

Address emails to:
Rangjung Yeshe Publications
C/O Above

www.rangjung.com
www.lotustreasure.com

1 3 5 7 9 8 6 4 2

First paperback edition published in 2019

Printed in the United States of America

Distributed to the book trade by:
Perseus Books/Ingram

Publication data: ISBN13: 978-0-9977162-9-0 (pbk)

Title: Straight Talk: Discourses on Practice
Padmasambhava, Chokgyur Lingpa, Orgyen Tobgyal Rinpoche
1. Vajrayana/Yidam—Tradition of Pith Instructions
2. Buddhism—Tibet

Photos courtesy of Boon Ngoei

First Edition

CONTENTS

FOREWORD

Dzongsar Khyentse Rinpoche

Orgyen Tobgyal Rinpoche is known for not being the easiest person to approach, simply because he isn't burdened by being politically correct. He just says what he thinks. So even among Tibetans, some think of him as being rude and arrogant.

Orgyen Tobgyal Rinpoche is also famous for his photographic memory and his ability to recount accurately the life stories, conversations, and teachings of some of the most eminent and revered teachers of our time. I've tested him on this myself, by asking him the same questions at different times with long gaps of a year or more in between. Sure enough, he will say exactly the same thing, just like rewinding and playing back a tape.

But beneath all that is Orgyen Tobgyal Rinpoche's deep dedication to the study and practice of the Dharma, and his profound gratitude to these masters for all they have taught and given him. And that's really why Orgyen Tobgyal Rinpoche has become a true treasury of knowledge, in particular for the Vajrayana teachings and, most importantly, for everything connected with Guru Padmasambhava. He is especially loyal in fiercely guarding the teachings of the three supreme Jamgöns—Khyentse Wangpo, Jamgön Kongtrül, and Chokgyur Lingpa.

In the years to come, people will gradually realize how incredibly important are the footprints left by Orgyen Tobgyal Rinpoche. This collection of his teachings is not only remarkably informative and educational but also very precious. In fact, Tibetans should also make these teachings available in Tibetan.

PREFACE

Marcia Binder Schmidt

How do you describe a sublime being like Orgyen Tobgyal Rinpoche? The simile of his being like a diamond, with its different qualities, comes closest to fulfilling that difficult task. As is stated, "The quality and value of a diamond are judged on five fundamental criteria: carat, color, clarity, cut, and confidence." *Confidence* here means having a certificate of value. OT, as we fondly call him, has several of these: he's a recognized incarnate lama, the son of a great master and powerful dakini in human form, and a supremely experienced vajra master in his own right.

As his younger brother Jigme Kongtrul Rinpoche explained, "Orgyen Tobgyal Rinpoche is a reincarnation of Jetson Tulku from Jetson Monastery, which I believe was established by Taksham Nuden Dorje, 'Powerful Tiger-skirted Vajra,' born in the late part of the seventeenth century. Taksham Nuden Dorje was an incarnation of Atsara Sale, the Nepali consort of Yeshe Tsogyal, and a disciple of both Yeshe Tsogyal and Padmasambhava. Taksham Nuden Dorje discovered the hidden treasure of Yeshe Tsogyal's biography, *The Secret Life and Liberated Song Thread of Yeshe Tsogyal,* among other treasures. I do not know how many tulkus have been found since the first. When the previous Jetson Tulku passed away, the monastery asked Jamyang Khyentse Chökyi Lodrö to find the incarnation, and he recognized Orgyen Tobgyal Rinpoche.

"I heard that his predecessor was even more amazing than this current incarnation, my eldest brother. For example, Jetson Tulku hardly ate or slept; he was always meditating. There was once a drubchen in Jetson Gonpa. However, Jetsun Tulku almost never came out of his room, where he remained naked on his bed. That time he did come down, and everyone saw him in the doorway, but they had no idea how he got immediately from the doorway to his throne. He sat there for seven days and nights, without eating, sleeping, or talking to anyone. At the end, when the accomplishments were to be received, all the tormas melted into nectar, and the other substances showed marvelous signs as well.

"I have been told he was really an accomplished siddha of some sort. I went to his monastery in Dorshu, in Riwoche, eastern Tibet, and stayed there for a few days. The older monks recounted to me how great the previous incarnation was. He did not do any PR or cultivate any relationships, but he was a fully realized being. So, OT Rinpoche is similar to that."

Whenever I am in the presence of OT Rinpoche, I experience him as a heruka, strolling through our realm with the stride of such a powerful being—in the diamond mode, displaying his high carat quality, or in his regular form. The first time I ever met him was in Dordogne, France, but his reputation preceded him, as someone to skirt cautiously, unless you wanted to be mowed down. He was brandishing a raksha seed mala, chanting something scary. So, I secretly named him *Raksha Totreng*, a wrathful emanation of Padmasambhava, and subsequently referred to him that way. Of course, I later came to realize that in the case of siddhas like OT, they show anger out of great compassion; his secret side is really so kind.

The qualities of cut and clarity are evident in his teachings and conduct: he cuts through all misconceptions and doubts and clearly explains all aspects of practice and ritual with a precision of detail that is almost unequalled by any living master today. As for color, I can only repeat, a bit shyly, what my Mexican psychic Yolanda says whenever she looks at him: she only sees pure light, which makes her feel really good the whole rest of that day! In a more practical vein, I can say that most of these things will become evident in reading the contents of this book. OT never waters it down or makes the dharma more palatable for any audience. He clearly tells it like it is, straight and unfiltered, with full knowledge that this will not gather disciples or sponsors, which he cares little about. It is almost as if he were born in the wrong age, a character from eastern Tibet's past, an old Khampa lama born anew in the modern world. However, he is able to give the most relevant, current advice, all the while adhering to tradition with scriptural resources. Please, sit back and read these precious teachings and make the aspiration to meet him in this present life. Even though you may be completely afraid when you do, it will be an unforgettable experience. I guarantee it.

It is always an enriching experience working with diverse, talented people to produce a book. *Straight Talk* is the outcome of such an exciting endeavor. To get such practical, unadulterated advice—especially in these troubled times—makes the project even more precious, pertinent, and sorely needed. Much appreciation and devotion go to both Dzongsar Khyentse Rinpoche, for his amazing foreword, and to Dzigar Kongtrul Rinpoche, for his elucidating information on Orgyen Tobgyal Rinpoche's past incarnation.

Incredible thanks are due to Maha Lotsawa Erik Pema Kunsang, who translated all the texts—except for the *Drubchen Framework,* translated by Ryan Conlon—and was the oral interpreter for most of these talks. Other talks were initially interpreted by Gyurme Avertin and were retranslated by me, with enormous help from Sean Price, as an on-the-spot translation is never as accurate as we would like it to be. The talks primarily took place at different Rigpa locations around the world, including Oakland and San Francisco, California; Lerab Ling, France; Asura Cave, Nepal; Bodhgaya, India; and Gomde USA, Leggett, California. In addition to having sincere gratitude to the translators and interpreters, I cannot thank enough my trusted editor, Anne Paniagua; my patient book designer, Joan Olson; the diligent proofreaders, Lynn Schroeder and Michael Yockey; the gifted cover artist, my horse-riding sister Jane Hicks; the cover designer, Mary Sweet; and my generous production sponsor, Richard Gere.

May this work clear away confusion and bring students closer to realizing the essential aspects of the Dharma.

Orgyen Tobgyal Rinpoce

Lamrim Yeshe Nyingpo and The Nyingma Tradition

It is said that one should always explain the historical origin of a teaching, where it comes from; otherwise, people won't feel certain about it. They won't have trust in it, and without trust, it is hard to receive blessings. Therefore, before beginning the teachings, one always starts with explaining the historical origin.

The teaching of *Lamrim Yeshe Nyingpo, The Gradual Path of the Wisdom Essence,* belongs to the Nyingma School. In the Nyingma tradition, there are three main kinds of teachings, called the "three great transmissions": the extensive oral tradition, called Kama; the profound treasure transmission, called Terma; and the short lineage of the Pure Vision. Those three together are called Nyingma.

Rongzom Pandita said that six types of superiority distinguish the Early Translations, the Nyingma School. It is awkward to state these six, because I am a Nyingmapa follower myself, but still there is the tradition of mentioning them. According to the view of the Rongzom Pandita, Rongzom Chökyi Sangpo, the Early Translation school possesses these six superior qualities: the greatness of the benefactors who made the invitations, the greatness of the site where the teachings were translated, the greatness of the lotsawas who made the translations, the greatness of the panditas who clarified the translations, the greatness of the offerings and gifts, and, finally, the greatness of the translated teachings. The Nyingma School of Secret Mantra, exalted by these six special qualities, also possesses the three special qualities of transmission.

Nyingma is one of the Tibetan Dharma's names. There were many Dharma traditions in Tibet, and apart from Bonpos, they were all Buddhist. The Buddhists teachings that flourished in Tibet were brought from India. The first and oldest tradition was called Nyingma, which literally means "old" in English. Right now, in many countries, the Buddhist tradition of Tibet is called Lamaism, noted as separate from Buddhism. This is completely incorrect, because the Buddhist schools of Dharma in Tibet were all very pure teachings of Buddha.

Buddhism was first brought to Tibet at the time of King Songtsen Gampo [seventh century]. During this period, Tonmi Sambhota was sent to India, where he constructed the Tibetan alphabet. Written Tibetan, that is still used today, was developed by Tonmi Sambhota.

Later, the main practice of the Buddhist teaching was instigated during the reign of King Trisong Deützen [eighth century]. At this time, a great argument was aroused between the Bonpos and the Buddhists. The king held councils and, according to historical narrations, the Bonpos were banned. It was never stated that the Tibetan Buddhist tradition was modeled on the Bonpo. After this, during the time of King Ralpachen [ninth century], the teaching of the Buddha was firmly established.

Regarding the first superiority of Nyingma, the greatness of the benefactors who made invitations, the great kings were Songtsen Gampo, Trisong Deütsen, and King Jah.[1] It didn't happen later that kings of such might and domain invited Buddhist teachers.

The second is the greatness of the site where the teachings were translated. There are great, important places in India, there were important places in Tibet; there were also important times. The time was after the Buddha, when the dynasty of the Gupta kings had subsided. In other words, the Buddhist teachings were still alive and well in India during the time when the Nyingma teachings were brought to Tibet, and they were highly valued during that period. It was a time when the teachings of the Buddha were flourishing in Bodhgaya, Varanasi, Shravasti, Vikramashila, and so forth. The site was extremely significant, in that it was the spontaneously perfected great temple complex, or Samye, the fulfillment of great aspirations. This was where 108 great panditas met together in one single place to translate the teachings. India is regarded as the mother of the Dharma, but there probably isn't any other place in history where great masters like Padmasambhava, Shantarakshita, and Vimalamitra met together at the same time. Besides these sublime masters, 108 of the greatest panditas from India were invited and traveled up to Tibet and converged in one sole location. I feel that it probably never happened before or after that anyone had the ability to invite such a number of masters at the same time.

These days, everything is very easy; you can fly around the world in a matter of hours, and masters are invited to all parts of the world. Benefactors invite them and they teach. There is a lot of prosperity and progress in many parts of the world, also here in the West. But you don't hear about 108 great masters being invited to the same place at the same time—not to France or anywhere in Europe, not to America. You don't even hear that ten great masters are meeting at the same time.

Regarding, the greatness of the lotsawas who made the translations and the greatness of the panditas who clarified them, the king—particularly King Trisong Deütsen—fostered many thousands of intelligent young Tibetans, educating them from an early age in Indian languages, especially Sanskrit. When they were old enough, they were given all the expenses they needed and sent to the study centers of Nalanda and Vikramashila and to places in present-day Pakistan and Indonesia to study other prominent Buddhist traditions under learned masters.

The young Tibetans recorded all the teachings they received from these various male and female great masters and scholars. They wrote them down on palm leaves, translated them, and brought them back to Tibet. The translation of both words and meanings were always edited and checked three times, after which the translated script was offered to the king. With great attention to detail, the king would verify the correctness of both words and meaning. Indian scholars would review and approve the translation. If it was completely approved, the king would give his permission for publication. The Indian originals, written on the palm leaves, were kept in the library of the monastery of Samye.

Another style of translation was that many learned panditas were invited into Tibet from the countries now called India, Pakistan, Burma, and Indonesia. Some of these panditas were very great; therefore, they had to first obtain the local Indian king's permission to leave India, as in the case of Vimalamitra. When they arrived in Tibet, the Buddha's words in the Tripitaka, together with the commentaries upon them composed by learned panditas, were translated into Tibetan with great care, as were the other translations. The teachings given by Indian scholars were spoken in Indian languages. The Tibetans who knew both tongues perfectly would translate them and, subsequently, establish them in writing. The Tibetan lotsawas would then reread the translated text aloud for the panditas. If the panditas approved it, a clear statement was added, which included the Indian title, the names of the panditas and lotsawas, and the number of chapters or verses the scripture contained.

As I mentioned, at this time, the teaching of Lord Buddha was still a living tradition in India. All the panditas who visited Tibet were of a very high standard. Among them were the masters Padmasambhava, Vimalamitra, and Shantarakshita. Even nowadays, these masters are highly respected in India. The preceptor Shantarakshita had arrived in Tibet to spread the monastic tradition, and ten bhikshus were invited from Bengal to aid in giving ordination. Shantarakshita and these monks then conducted the first ordination of monks in Tibet. First, only seven men were ordained in order to test whether Tibetans were suited to monastic life. As they were successful, the number of bhikshus gradually increased to several hundred thousand. Within the scriptures called *Nyingma Kama, Oral Teachings of the Nyingma,* the history of the lineage of the precept transmission is written, tracing it from Shakyamuni and Shariputra down until Trulshik, Taklung Tsetrul, and Penor Rinpoches.

The teachings that were translated in that period are contained in the *Kangyur, The Words of the Buddha,* and in the *Nyingma Gyubum, The Hundred Thousand Nyingma Tantras.* Moreover, most of the collections of the *Tengyur,* the commentaries of the Indian panditas, were translated at that time.

The teachings of the Secret Mantra were also taught, translated, and established in writing during this period, but in great secrecy. In particular, Guru Rinpoche stayed in person in Tibet for 120 years, during which time he taught the Secret Mantra and Maha Ati to his main twenty-five disciples, headed by King Trisong Deütsen, his companion Yeshe Tsogyal, and his subject Vairochana. Likewise, Vimalamitra extensively taught the teachings of *Gyutrul, The Illusory Creation,* and *Nyingtig, The Heart Essence.*

Most of these teachings of the Secret Mantra were concealed as treasures for the sake of reversing the future degeneration of the Dharma. In addition, the oral teaching lineage was continually transmitted, without being hidden as treasures. It is called the Kama tradition, as previously mentioned. The teachings later spread by treasure revealers, tertöns, make up the Terma tradition. During this early period of Buddhism in Tibet, the teachings of Maha Ati were kept extremely secret. Three great masters taught Maha Ati in Tibet: Guru Rinpoche, Vimalamitra, and Vairochana. Among these, the Lotus Born Guru and Vimalamitra were Indian mahasiddhas, who had accomplished the great transformation rainbow body. At present, they are residing in the parts of this world called Sangdok Palri, the Glorious Copper-Colored Mountain, and Wu Tai Shan, the Five-peaked Mountain in China. Vairochana, a native Tibetan, was learned in 120 languages. He received, especially from Shri Singha, the three sections of Maha Ati known as mind section, space section, and instruction section, which he passed on to Pang Mipham Gonpo. The lineages of these three masters are contained within both the Kama and Terma scriptures.[2]

To further explain the word *tertön,* it literally means "secret treasure revealer." While Guru Rinpoche physically stayed in Tibet, he accepted and taught many disciples who practiced and then attained accomplishment. For the benefit of the disciples of future generations, these accomplished people made aspirations to be tertöns, at specific times in the future. Due to the maturation of these aspirations, many tertöns, beginning with Sangye Lama, have appeared up to the present time.

These days, some people say there is no lineage for Maha Ati and for the treasure teachings. That is incorrect. Without depending on education and scholarship within that very life, the tertön reawakens the karmic potential of his former lives and receives the list of treasures or a command from Guru Rinpoche with consort, who appear in person to him. Due to various circumstances, the tertön reveals the three main treasure teachings of Guru Sadhana, Maha Ati, and Avalokiteshvara. Thereafter, he practices these himself until he has an actual vision of the guru with consort and the yidam deity, receives the blessings in his being, and becomes inseparable from the wisdom mind of the deity. Since the tertön then passes on the empowerment to his disciples, there is definitely a lineage. In general, there are seven different kinds of terma treasures, which I will explain in a bit.

Concerning the Maha Ati instructions, the lineage was passed down from Samantabhadra Buddha through Guru Rinpoche, Vimalamitra, and Vairochana until today. This is the long lineage. The lineage of Maha Ati is especially a mind transmission and realization is therefore paramount. A mere lineage of explanation is not sufficient; it is a lineage of realization. Since the first tertön, Sangye Lama, there has been an uninterrupted appearance of great tertöns. The great tertöns are inseparable from Guru Rinpoche and are able to communicate with him as one person does with another. They learned not only the methods of meditation and instructions but even the tunes of chanting and music directly from Guru Rinpoche himself, so there is no mistake in them. Even in these bad times, there are people who attain accomplishment and the rainbow light body.

There is one rule within Nyingma that was made by King Trisong Deütsen. In general, Buddhists are followers of the Truly and Completely

Awakened One. Yet, in particular—among all the numerous enlightened masters who appeared in India and spread his word—future followers of the teachings translated during the reign of Trisong Deütsen, should adhere to the conduct according to the tradition of the preceptor Shantarakshita, the philosophical view according to Arya Nagarjuna, the meditation according to Vimalamitra, and the oral instructions according to Padmasambhava. Three of these masters went in person to Tibet and turned the wheel of Dharma. There were also many other masters who spread the Dharma in Tibet, and they are called the twenty-five disciples. Later on, there appeared Zurchen, Zurchung, Sangdak Trophukpa, Rongsom Pandita, Kunkhyen Longchenpa, Ngari Panchen Pema Wangyal, the two brothers of Mindroling, Jigme Lingpa, the three Jamgöns—Khyentse, Chokling, and Kongtrül—and Mipham Rinpoche. These and innumerable others, such as the 108 great tertöns, appeared to uphold, protect, and spread the doctrine so that it would last, as it has, until the present day.

In Tibet, there were more than seven thousand monasteries practicing the Nyingma tradition. Among these were the six major ones: Mindroling, Dorje Trak, Shechen, Dzogchen, Payül, and Katok. These were not especially impressive to look at from outside or very rich, because Nyingma masters were not known historically to engage in politics. For this reason, the Nyingma tradition in Tibet was not politically strong. Yet due to the kindness of the lineage holders, the Nyingma tradition of scriptures and realization has remained unbroken until the present day.

Recently, there have been many great lineage holders, such as Kyabje Dilgo Khyentse Rinpoche and Kyabje Dudjom Rinpoche. If you consider their life examples, from an early age they followed many learned and accomplished masters, and just within the five general sciences, they were unrivaled among the people of Tibet. Concerning the Dharma, both of them studied and learned their whole life and never stopped, up until their passing. When you consider that they had established their learning through contemplation and then practiced it, you will be amazed. When you consider that their activities of upholding the Buddha's teachings were without self-interest and solely for the sake of others, you will realize they were totally unrivaled in this world. They were both authentic tertöns, prophesied by Guru Rinpoche himself.

They had great appreciation of all other Buddhist schools and had great faith in the teachers of them. Thinking of the previous lives and deeds of tulkus who did not possess even the slightest learning, they still paid respect, by offering prostrations. They were without the slightest concern for position and power. Looking at these two, when you think of Dilgo Khyentse Rinpoche, you encounter a mind that did not contain the merest speck of partiality towards any of the Buddhist schools. He was a master who was most learned in the various views and practices of the eight great schools of the Tibetan Buddhist tradition. The Nyingma tradition flourishes greatly throughout many countries in the world.

The Buddha's teachings mainly keep to his words and to the treatises. The sublime words from the Buddha have been spoken either directly by the Buddha or in one of three ways: with his permission, through his blessings, or through his inspiration. The treatises have come from Buddha giving permission to write to certain people, both male and female, who have the capacity to be great scholars endowed with the ten specific qualifications. The *Lamrim Yeshe Nyingpo* belongs to the sublime words of the treatises, because Padmasambhava's realization is indivisible from that of the Buddha. Some people ask, "When did the Buddha go to Tibet?" Well, he didn't, but the Buddha's state of realization and that of Padmasambhava are indivisible, no difference. The dharmakaya buddha, out of the immense vastness of original wakefulness, expounds the Dharma that infuses the sublime words. Likewise, so do the sambhogakaya buddhas, who teach through the great displays of the peaceful and wrathful buddhas, in the time of unceasing eternity to a retinue that is not different from the central figure, the Buddha himself. Those teachings of dharmakaya and sambhogakaya also belong with the sacred words, the sublime words. For this reason, the *Lamrim Yeshe Nyingpo* is no different, in essence, from the tantras of the new schools and old school.

Chokgyur Lingpa, the revealer of this teaching, was a direct incarnation of the second of King Trisong Deütsen's sons, called Prince Murub Tseypo. His name was also Lhasey Damdzin, Prince Damdzin. He was incarnated as a great treasure revealer, totally indisputable, trusted by everyone. This is one of his revealed treasures, among forty volumes of scriptures that belong within these teachings, called the new treasures of Chokgyur Lingpa. The lineage of these teachings is unbroken to this very day.

Some people think that when speaking of the great masters of the past, it is either mythology or some fairy tale. Well, it isn't. Chokgyur Lingpa actually lived; he was born in a place in eastern Tibet, grew up there, studied, and performed many miracles. The places where he did those miracles still exist; people can go there. Also his teachings are kept to this day, through the lineages. His family line has continued. He had a daughter called Könchok Paldrön and her son Chimey Dorje was Tulku Urgyen

Rinpoche's father. Also the incarnation lineage of Chokgyur Lingpa has continued. There are two main incarnations alive this very day.

Chokgyur Lingpa revealed thirty-six different termas, and this is one of them. It was discovered at a place in eastern Tibet called Rongmey Karmo Taktsang, the Tiger's Nest of Rongmey. That cave, the Tiger's Nest, is still there. Even though nobody took photos, the imprint where it was taken out of the rock in the cave is still visible. Other things were taken out together with this terma: There is one statue of the wrathful guru, Guru Drakpo, that is in the possession of Pewa Tulku, who lives in Derge, in eastern Tibet. There is a thangka with the inscriptions and the signature and so forth of Jamyang Khyentse Wangpo, Jamgön Kongtrül, and Chokgyur Lingpa, which was made right after; I have this. There are other things as well; we still have them today.

There are many tertöns, treasure revealers, but Chokgyur Lingpa was definitely an authentic one. Not everyone who has the name tertön is at all the same as an authentic tertön. One does not become a tertön, a treasure revealer, by just showing some writings that one puts down on paper for others, saying it is a terma, without having even one single yellow scroll of parchment with inscription, without having even one single treasure article that one revealed.

In this terma itself, in the teaching here, there is a prediction of who will take care of this teaching, one who is described as the reincarnation of the king, the great king of Tibet, Trisong Deütsen. That was Jamyang Khyentse Wangpo, who is world-famous today. If you think about Jamyang Khyentse's life—for example, if you read his biography, how learned he was, how accomplished he was in practice—then I feel you will conclude that there was probably no one like him in the whole Tibetan history. Honestly speaking, he was totally unique.

The *Lamrim Yeshe Nyingpo* is the backbone of support for the Five Great Treasures. Actually, this terma is what is called an earth treasure, and it was brought forth in unison by Chokgyur Lingpa and Jamyang Khyentse. After it was brought forth and Jamyang Khyentse expounded it for the first time, then the one who gave the clarification was the incarnation of the great translator Vairochana, who appeared in human form known as Jamgön Kongtrül the Great. The very fruit, or the quintessential extract, of the activity and blessing of these three great masters is known as the *Five Great Treasures.* There is one text found in the very back of these *Five Treasures* that is like the support upon which all of these *Five Treasures* rest—and that is the *Lamrim Yeshe Nyingpo.*

The chief disciples of these three masters all regarded the *Lamrim Yeshe Nyingpo* as the core of their practice. They treated it as something incredibly precious. I heard from my own father, the incarnation of Chokgyur Lingpa, Neten Chokling, who said, "Even though I didn't study a lot of scriptures, I feel that if you learned well the root text and the commentary from the *Lamrim Yeshe Nyingpo,* you would lack nothing for reaching complete enlightenment." Tulku Urgyen said similar words. Tulku Urgyen Rinpoche was someone who spent the majority of his life practicing meditation and did not spend a great amount of time on studies, on scholarship. However, he did learn the *Lamrim Yeshe Nyingpo* in great detail, to the best of his ability. Dilgo Khyentse Rinpoche did the same. This is one of the most precious teachings, and it was a great mistake that I agreed to teach this.[3]

Starting with Padmasambhava, all the way down through the lineage, not including myself, all the masters attained the wisdom body. Even though they didn't manifest the rainbow body at the time of death, still their minds were at the level of the wisdom body, the embodiment of original wakefulness. They were definitely great beings, who had attained high levels of enlightenment. The transmission of this teaching has passed through these masters. Therefore, I feel that all of them, not including myself, have been such great masters. If you can receive the reading transmission, which means the transmission where you hear the root text read out loud, then this meeting together will have already been meaningful.

As it is said about terma teachings, if the opportunity allows for the greatest detail to be conveyed, you receive the extensive explanations; if it's a medium-level opportunity, you at least receive the reading transmission; if it's not even that, you at least receive the scripture at the top of your head, from someone who has the authentic lineage of transmission. Then you have the blessings to do the practice.

Terma teachings are not constructed by intellectual reasoning, by someone who accepts and rejects, saying, "It shouldn't be like this; maybe it should be like that. This is not good; this sounds better." There is no kind of consideration of that type involved here. How, then, is it possible that a terma teaching is in accordance with the words spoken through the Buddha's permission? It is so, because termas are totally arising out of the wisdom mind of Guru Padmasambhava. Also, the tertön who reveals them has already reached a level of realization in which his mind and Padmasambhava's mind are indivisible—then the teaching manifests. Therefore, there is no place for even one ordinary word.

There is a letter introducing Chokgyur Lingpa to Jamyang Khyentse for the first time. In this, Jamgön Kongtrül says that this person here, called Chokgyur Lingpa, doesn't even have the ability to write a letter on his own. He has no education. Yet if you look at this terma teaching he has revealed, called the *Pema Tsuktor, The Lotus Protuberance,* you will find it is nothing but vajra words, totally flawless and impeccable. So, for that reason, I entrust him as an authentic tertön.

Even if a hundred or a thousand learned writers stayed together for hundreds of years and combined their efforts, they would never be able to compose something as concise and perfect and beautiful as a terma teaching, not at all. Therefore, termas are not the words of common or ordinary people. Not only are they not the words of common people, they are also not adulterated by words ordinary people put in, as gold is adulterated when mixed with copper.

Also, a terma is not a repetition of what others have said. It is so easy to write a thick book, copying a little bit from here and there and piecing it together. Termas are never like that. When a tertön writes down a teaching, he does it without looking at anything else. From a state of samadhi, the words flow out, totally unblocked and perfect. That is why they are vajra words. Vajra speech is not constructed by intellectual reasoning, not corrupted by ordinary words, and not a repetition of what others have said. Termas are graced with the splendor of great blessings. What kind of blessing have I been talking about? By simply seeing a terma teaching, you are benefited; by hearing it and thinking about the meaning, you have experiences, some realization, and insight; and by actually training in the meaning of the words, your stream of being is being liberated into the state of original wakefulness. This is the kind of terma teaching that Jamgön Kongtrül says he will explain here; it is one that liberates through seeing, hearing, touching, and reflecting.

In the transmission of teachings, there are various types of lineages from the great vajra-holder, Vajradhara, down to your own root guru. The teaching can be transmitted in various ways: from mind to mind, through symbolic gestures, orally, through yellow parchment, and so forth. These teachings are also contained, to some extent, in the sublime words of the victorious ones and the treatises. Also, there are the tantras, both of the old school, the Nyingma, and the new schools, the Sarma, as well as the transmission of empowerments and the transmission of the explanations, and of instructions, all of which have continued uninterruptedly to this very day. Please understand that when these transmission lineages remain intact, unbroken, then the Buddhadharma is still present in our world. When the lineages of transmission are broken, there is no more teaching present. Please understand this difference!

Among these different types of transmission, there is the transmission of blessings and the transmission for practice, where you bring the meaning into your own experience. That takes place when you connect with an authentic master, who is the holder of the lineage, and you receive the ripening and liberating transmission, which ripens your mind and brings you to maturity and liberation. When applying this personally, in your own practice, then as an ordinary person, you can discover the state of original wakefulness. When that happens, you have received the transmission of blessings.

A person endowed with the karmic continuation and destiny will, by means of a profound coincidence of place, time, and aspiration, be able to decode the symbolic meaning of these treasure letters— which are nirmanakayas, the vajra forms endowed with all eminent aspects—and establish them correctly in writing. To indicate this, seven symbolic letters have been placed at the beginning of this book.

In the text, the second main heading is called "Explaining the Sign Script and the Homage." This gives the reason for the sign script and the meaning of paying homage. Here's a quote from *The Tantra of Secrets*:

> Dakinis make use of symbols.
> They are skilled in symbols and symbolic replies.
> They link the ultimate essence to symbolism.
> Dakinis are the life force of symbols.

The dakini script that makes use of symbols is impossible to decipher by anyone other than a person who is of equal status to the dakinis. Furthermore, since most of the profound teachings existing as terma treasures are encoded in symbolic script, and therefore originate from the secret treasury of the dakinis, they do not lie within the reach of experience of the ordinary learned or accomplished masters of India and Tibet.

This means the person has to have an extraordinarily special mandate, a transmission directly from Padmasambhava, in order to understand what is within the dakini script. No one else can do that, no matter how learned he or she may be. If you showed the dakini script to Tsongkhapa Lobsang Drakpa, or to Sakya Pandita, or to the Indian great panditas, like Jnanakirti, they probably wouldn't understand. In addition, the dakini script differs from tertön to tertön. You have to have the specific mandate for that. Unless you have the karmic destiny to reveal that, you won't be able to decode it. Thus, one tertön won't necessarily be able to decipher another tertön's dakini script.

Only the tertön can really comprehend the meaning of the dakini script. As this quote states here:

> Treasure letters are the body of magical creation.
> They are also speech to understand sounds and words.[4]

Actually, the symbolic writing is a form of the nirmanakaya, and when a person has the right karmic destiny, he or she will, by means of a profound coincidence of place, time, and aspiration, be able to decode it. So, these letters are born in the nirmanakaya, and from them—even if there are only seven—many volumes of scriptures can be written down, because the tertön is able to hear the sound and comprehend the meaning. They are also speech.

As I mentioned earlier, the person endowed with the karmic continuation will be able to decode the symbolic meaning of these nirmanakaya treasure letters, the vajra forms endowed with all eminent aspects, and establish them correctly in writing. To indicate this, seven symbolic letters have been placed at the beginning of this book.

There are three reasons for putting dakini script at the beginning of a text: First, these treasure letters are the seal of command of the Second Buddha, the Master of Uddiyana. Symbolic signs directly represent his seal, indicating that ordinary people have not corrupted the transmission; thus, the source is authentic. It's the same as when a king's decree has his seal at the bottom, showing that it is the bona fide word of the king to be heeded. In the same way, the terma signs at the beginning of a scripture show that it is the authentic speech of Padmasambhava.

The second reason relates to the teaching, which translates the secret code of the dakinis, without altering the symbols, mistaking the words, or confusing the meaning. This indicates that the profound instruction and great blessing of the original scripture remain potent and unblemished, as the terma text has not been altered, mistaken, or confused in any way. Who can actually witness that? Jamyang Khyentse Wangpo, the most important of the five tertön kings, witnessed that. Among all 108 major tertöns that appeared in Tibet, the two later ones, Jamyang Khyentse and Chokgyur Lingpa, both possessed what is called the "seven transmissions." In the past, no one was said to have these seven transmissions.

The first of these seven is the oral tradition of Kama, which both of these masters received. This is a transmission mandate originating from Padmasambhava and Vimalamitra. It has been passed down through empowerment, reading transmission, explanation of tantras, and the authorization to be "indivisible from me." Therefore, this first one is called the "four rivers of transmission" given by Padmasambhava and Vimalamitra. Together, they form the first transmission, called the "oral tradition of Kama." The second is the earth treasure revelation, such as *Lama Tennyi Korsum,* and many other earth treasures. At one point, Jamyang Khyentse Wangpo saw in a pure vision that the entire land of Tibet had buried treasures, terma teachings, everywhere. He saw all of them clearly, as though placed in the palm of his own hand. Concerning many of the termas that Chokgyur Lingpa revealed, Jamyang Khyentse first received the "address" of where they were located, and then he sent Chokgyur Lingpa out to fetch them. Jamyang Khyentse didn't always write down the addresses, which sometimes came on little scrolls, as they were simply too secret, and he was afraid that some tertön thief would reveal them at the wrong time. For example, Yeshe Tsogyal immediately wrote down the *Dzogchen Desum, The Three Sections of the Great Perfection,* and handed it to Jamyang Khyentse Wangpo, putting it exactly in the rice bowl in front of him.

Some tertöns only reveal articles, ritual articles, and the like, or precious substances. Some only reveal teachings and no material things. Jamyang Khyentse and Chokgyur Lingpa, however, revealed both teachings and articles, as if taking them out from a huge treasury. Jamgön Kongtrül once sent a letter to Jamyang Khyentse, saying, "I need a little statue to put in the heart center of Dorje Sempa, a huge Vajrasattva statue that I'm building. Can you please give me a really special one?" Then Jamyang Khyentse invoked the dharma protector Dorje Yudrönma, and she went to a place in India called Palri, the site of the stupa remains of King Jah, one of the great kings of India. She brought a small Vajrasattva statue from there and placed it right on his desk, instantaneously. So, these two masters also had power over earth treasures.

They also had what is called *yangter,* rediscovered treasures. For example, Jamyang Khyentse revealed *Tsasum Drildrub,* which had been discovered in the past; he rediscovered it. He also had mind treasures, such as the *Chimey Phagma Nyingtig*. Furthermore, he had many types of transmissions, such as *Phurba* and *Yangdak,* which belong to the hearing lineage. Jamyang Khyentse also had the transmission of pure vision. For instance, after Chokgyur Lingpa passed away, he manifested in the sambhogakaya pure land where Chokgyur Lingpa took the form of the buddha called Pema Nyugu. Jamyang Khyentse wrote down a teaching called *Kusum Rikdü Zabtig,* which is based on that pure vision.

In addition, he had what is called "recollection of a former life," wherein he had total recall of being tertön Chökyi Wangchük,[5] [one of the five tertön kings]. Thus, he revealed the *Chetsün Nyingtig,* the heart essence of that great tertön. This happened when Jamyang Khyentse was near Chimphu, in the upper part of a valley in Reding. All the phenomena of this world dissolved. He had a recollection of his past life as Chetsün Senge Wangchük and revealed *Chetsün Nyingtig, The Heart Essence of the Great Chetsün,* which is like the quintessence of all the Dzogchen teachings.

Since these two masters possessed the seven great transmissions, and they were both there, looking at each other, when this text [*Lamrim Yeshe Nyingpo*] was revealed, I feel confident that it is free from mistakes and confusion. Such a teaching has great blessing.

The third reason to place the sign script at the beginning pertains to potential recipients. Just as someone born blind cannot adequately examine an elephant, people lacking the right fortune cannot even partially comprehend the symbolic script, no matter how sharp-minded they may be. You can therefore trust that the treasure master transcends the scope of common people.

Someone like me wouldn't even see one single syllable to write down, even if I soaked the dakini script in water for a hundred days and stared at it. The way to decode yellow parchment with dakini script is to soak it in water mixed with the five nectars and perform a ganachakra, a feast offering. Miraculously, the writing will then start to appear. The paper doesn't sink in the water; it doesn't dissolve either, but the script will start to appear.

Even though I am not a tertön, myself, I know about tertöns. You don't have to write the revelation down immediately once the magical writing manifests. As a matter of fact, it is better not to write it down immediately. It's much better to supplicate one-pointedly to Padmasambhava and mingle your minds together, so that they are indivisible. And then, within that state of samadhi, whatever manifests will be exactly the appropriate amount and meaning to influence people. Then you write that down correctly. Once it is recorded on paper, the previous script vanishes, and the next will appear. This is not within the reach of normal people, right? No one can make that up. It is something to trust in; it's trustworthy. That was an explanation of the reason why the *Lamrim Yeshe Nyingpo* begins with some sign script [as do other treasure texts].

The Precious representation of the Guru Dorje Draktsal terma revealed at Meshod Rongmey, Karmo Taktsang, in Derge, Kham by the Great Treasure Revealer Chokgyur Lingpa.

Short Biography of Guru Rinpoche

There is a lot of discussion about a qualified master, and we will examine that in more detail later on. I am not talking about someone like myself. Some people, when they hear the virtues of the masters of Tibet extolled, one lama talking about another, think, "They are talking about themselves. They are praising themselves." Also this statement, "The guru is superior to the buddha," doesn't fit within the comprehension of most of the Buddhists in this world. But, honestly, when you think about it, although the qualities of a master may not be the same as the Buddha's, when it comes down to you, personally, then your own teacher is more kind to you than the Buddha. Both Guru Rinpoche and Gampopa have said that even if you connect with someone who doesn't have all the specific qualifications as mentioned in the scriptures—of realization, great experience, and so forth—if he or she has the words of the teachings, you still regard that person as being Padmasambhava in person. Both Padmasambhava and Vimalamitra have promised that they will issue forth from their wisdom body into that person in order to bestow the blessings. That's why, when you do the practices, in many of the texts you see the sentence that states, "the one who in essence is your root guru, but appears in the form of so-and-so," like Padmasambhava and Vajrasattva, and so forth.

In particular, Guru Rinpoche is the natural form of indestructible wakefulness, the embodiment of all buddhas. Guru Rinpoche, himself, has said in his vajra words:

> Meditate upon me, and you will accomplish
> all buddhas.

> See me, and you will behold all buddhas.
> I am the embodiment of all the sugatas.

There are countless such statements.

The *Lamrim Yeshe Nyingpo* identifies who the perfect teacher is:

> The essence of all the buddhas of the three times . . . Mahaguru Padmasambhava.

He is mentioned as being the king of the victorious ones. "Victorious ones" is the name for buddhas, meaning those who are victorious over the four maras. Guru Rinpoche is like the king among all of them. He's called Padmakara because it means "originated from a lotus flower." He's the lotus-born master. As the *Lamrim* states:

> He is not an ordinary person, who progressed through a path, but he is Buddha Amitabha and the Matchless King of the Shakyas, Buddha Shakyamuni, manifesting in the form of a vajra master for the sake of beings who are difficult to tame.

He is equal to all the buddhas of the past, the buddhas of the present, and the buddhas of the future through three kinds of equality. This threefold equality denotes three ways of being equal to all buddhas:

- He is equal in having perfected the accumulations of merit and so forth.
- He is equal in being enlightened.
- He is equal in accomplishing the welfare of beings and in acting for the sake of all sentient beings.

He is equal in these three regards: in being enlightened, in having perfected the accumulations, and helping all sentient beings. He is not necessarily equal to other buddhas in terms of life span, body height, and so forth. It has been established that he is indivisible from all other awakened ones. Just as you cannot differentiate space, or say that space in one place is different from space in another place, in the same way, the nature of Padmasambhava is totally indivisible from the nature of all other buddhas.[6]

However, when speaking of Padmasambhava, as perceived by beings, there is a difference in that he appeared as a nirmanakaya and attained enlightenment, as perceived by others. In this regard, we have to learn from his life story how this happened.[7]

> When he took birth in a lotus flower in the Northwest of Uddiyana, in the milky lake, and was accepted as son of the king of Uddiyana and enthroned as the regent of that country, that corresponds to attaining the vidyadhara level of Full Maturation.

Later on, after abandoning the kingdom, he went to the kingdom of Zahor. After his meeting with Mandarava, he was burned alive in a great fire but remained unharmed.

> He miraculously transformed the mass of fire into a lake [and] he established that kingdom in the Dharma. [Later on he went to] do a longevity sadhana in the Maratika cave, together with Mandarava, who was his consort on this path [of practicing longevity. In actuality,] he received the empowerments of immortality from Buddha Amitayus. And at that time, he manifested the vidyadhara level of Life Mastery.

Some people believe that Zahor is the kingdom of Mandi in India, but actually in some of the life stories it says that Zahor kingdom is to the east of Bodhgaya and the place he was burned is even further to the east of that. That corresponds to places in Bangladesh. In Chokgyur Lingpa's life story, he had visions that correspond very closely to that description.

When you identify a sacred place, which is actually in this world right now, it is very nice if it can be substantiated with some story that is written down from the past. If they coincide, you can say that it is well-based and authentic. However, if it is only hearsay, such as, "this is probably the place where such and such happened," it is not really based in history.

As for these two vidyadhara levels,

> The vidyadhara level of Full Maturation and the vidyadhara level of Life Mastery correspond to the path of seeing.

Later on, in the kingdom of Nepal, in the place called Yangleshö, in order to overcome obstacles, Padmasambhava extracted the sadhana from the Kilaya tantra called *the Vidyottama*. Together with the Nepalese princess Shakya Devi, he manifested the vidyadhara level of Mahamudra, overcoming all obstacles by means of the Phurba practice of Vajrakilaya. That place is in Pharping, where the water is coming out of the rock and off the cliff. Jigme Lingpa identifies Yangleshö as being where both the cliff and the water are coming out; that's the place where Padmasambhava manifested the vidyadhara level of Mahamudra.

For a follower of the Nyingma tradition, who has faith in Padmasambhava and supplicates him at this site in Yangleshö, there is no difference between being there and going to Bodhgaya. It is the place where Padmasambhava manifested the state of complete enlightenment. That corresponds to realizing the path of cultivation.

From that point onward, Padmasambhava was invited to Tibet by King Trisong Deütsen, and he remained as a vidyadhara of Mahamudra throughout his whole time there. When he left, he went to the Palace of Lotus Light on the southwestern continent of Chamara, where he still remains:

> As the Regent of Vajradhara, the vidyadhara level of Spontaneous Presence of the path of consummation, where his realization equals the Lords of the Three Families.

In this way, throughout his life, Padmasambhava mastered the realization of the four vidyadhara levels. Right now he remains, still in actuality, as a vidyadhara of Spontaneous Presence or Spontaneous Perfection. His state of realization is equal to that of the Lords of the Three Families, who are Avalokiteshvara, Manjushri, and Vajrapani. This is according to the oral tradition of Jamyang Khyentse Wangpo.

It is said that Padmasambhava received the eight great transmissions from vidyadharas of India. These great masters were the holders of the *Kabgye, The Eight Sadhana Teachings,* all of which he received.[8] He also received the four rivers of empowerment as direct transmissions from the following masters:

- The first empowerment of the yidam from Garab Dorje.
- The transmission of being a spiritual teacher from Buddhaguhya.
- The empowerment for the expression of rigpa awareness from Shri Singha.
- The river of empowerment of tantric scriptures from King Jah.

> Therefore, even the eight great vidyadhara receivers bowed at his feet. Thus, he remains in the position of the supreme sovereign of all masters who have attained the vidyadhara levels and wield great power of wisdom.

Moreover,

> The aggregates, elements, and sense-bases, as well as the actions, faculties, and objects, are by nature completely pure and self-manifest as the display of dharmadhatu, the deity circle of the great Spontaneous Presence.[9]

What does this mean? It means that, in their pure nature, the five elements and five aggregates are the five male and female buddhas. In their pure nature, the sense spaces, the sense objects, and the faculties are the eight male and female bodhisattvas. The faculties, objects, and actions are the male and female gatekeepers. Furthermore, Padmasambhava is also the all-encompassing lord, who emanates and absorbs the peaceful and wrathful deities, such as the Vajradhatu mandala of peaceful deities and also the Great Assemblage, theTsokchen Düpa of wrathful deities, such as Chemchok Heruka with the twenty-one heads, and all the surrounding wrathful yidam deities.

Regarding the inner mastery of Padmasambhava, the text says:

> He mastered all the inner places comprised of the structuring channels, moving winds, and essences of bodhichitta . . .[10]

About the channels, winds, and essences: First, the channels are being described as the structure; they form the structure inside the body. We have 72,000 major channels and 40 million minor channels in our body. That's how they can be counted. The moving winds, or pranas, are within these structuring channels. If you want to count those, there are 21,600 movements or winds.

Within these channels and the energy currents, or winds, something is circulating—these are the essences, or the bindus, which are of the white and red types. They totally permeate the entire body. These essences have some potency, or capability, which is called the bodhichitta, the awakened mind. As it is noted here:

> Padmasambhava had purified these essences of bodhichitta within the sphere of the great wisdom of luminosity.

That was the inner mastery. By the power of this inner mastery over the channels, energies, and essences, some outward manifestation of mastery automatically takes place. This is described here as follows:

> By the power of that, Padmasambhava, he is . . . moves through the skies.[11]

The sacred places in different countries are traditionally called the twenty-four major places, the thirty-two major countries, and the eight charnel grounds; altogether they number sixty-four. At will, Padmasambhava was able to enjoy and partake in the ganachakra of coemergent great bliss with all the dakas and dakinis—which is something unimaginable. As for the ganachakra, the "wheel of gathering," the one who presides over that is called the "chief of the gathering," the *tsokpön* in Tibetan.

Padmasambhava was someone who was able to master and control all the dakinis: the celestial dakinis above, the terrestrial dakinis in the middle, and the sub-terrestrial dakinis below; thus, all the dakinis belonging to devas, humans, and nagas. He controlled them in not just one or two places, but in all the sixty-four places: the twenty-four major places, the thirty-two major countries, and the eight charnel grounds. This is very difficult. It is difficult to control even five dakinis. But Padmasambhava was someone who could master all of them, which is kind of inconceivable.

When you mention the word *dakini,* or *khandroma,* to Tibetans, they understand it to be a pretty woman, someone with a very light skin that has a rouge color from within. In India, the word *dhaki* or *dakini,* which in Tibetan is *khandroma,* means non-human, someone who is beyond this world: maybe a flesh-eating spirit, someone who has the power of mantra, who can kill you and eat you. It's someone who can fly in the sky and go through solid matter. Gendün Chöpel said, "When you tell a Tibetan lady that she is really a dakini, she is flattered. But when you say that to an Indian woman, she will start a fight with you."

Padmasambhava was the tsokpön, the ganachakra lord or chief, of hundreds of thousands—millions—of dakinis. He was able to engage in yogic discipline with them, which is something unusual.

> Since his expression manifests as the great display of kayas and wisdoms, he is the great being whose majestic splendor, the awesome bodily form of the Great Blazing Heruka, has the power to outshine all the Dharma protectors and guardians upholding the vajra samaya and functioning as the wisdom,[12]

These three classes of Dharma protectors are the male class, called jungpo; the female class, called lhamo or devi; and the neutral class, called maning.

> Likewise, he also outshines all the haughty forces, who are filled with the arrogance of being the great elemental spirits of appearance and existence, such as Palgön.[13]

There are seventy-two types of Palgön, which means "glorious protectors" as well as the guardians of the directions. The power and splendor of Padmasambhava is such that he totally outshines all the protectors, all of these types called "haughty forces," or drekpas, who are filled with the arrogance of being great. They always think they're very special and something powerful. Still, when they hear the name of Padmasambhava in the form of Guru Dorje Drakpo Tsal, they don't dare disobey him or transgress his command. This is the same terror that deer in the mountains feel when they hear the roar of the lion; they all get intimidated.

Padmasambhava, the Lotus-Born, is one name that pervades the realms in the ten directions, the infinite buddhafields. Yet, within each realm, each buddhafield, he is known under countless other names as well. There is one supplication to Padmasambhava, called *Clearing the Obstacles from the Path, Barchey Lamsel,* which is chanted quite a lot. One of the verses states that he has various names:

> One was Padmasambhava,
> One was Padmakara,
> One was Lake-Born Vajra,
> The secret name was Dorje Drakpo Tsal.

This verse corresponds to the four cycles of Guru Sadhana: *The Barchey Künsel* outer guru is called Padmakara. In the inner practice, *Sampa Lhündrub,* he is called Padmasambhava. According to the secret sadhana, *Tsokye Nyingtig,* he is called Tsokye Dorje, or Lake-Born Vajra. According to the innermost sadhana of *Dorje Drakpo,* he is called Dorje Drakpo Tsal, the wrathful guru.

He is also known as the eight manifestations. The eight manifestations of Guru Rinpoche are in countless buddha realms. These are famous as well. But these eight manifestations are mainly known within this realm. There is one tantra called the *Magical Net of Manjushri,* which is the *Manjushri Namo Sangirti.* A quote from that tantra says:

> Glorious Buddha Lotus-Born . . . knowledge mantras.

That refers to the eight manifestations. The first of these four lines reads, *Glorious Buddha Lotus-Born.*

> That first line clearly indicates . . . King of the Shakyas. The second line, which is "Bearer of the treasure of omniscient wisdom" indicates Loden Choksey . . . The third line, "King and master of various miracles" indicates Padma Gyalpo . . . The fourth line, "Great Buddha, retainer of knowledge mantras," indicates Senge Dradrok . . . knowledge mantras.[14]

These are the eight manifestations. It is also said that Padmasambhava:

> Manifested as the regent . . . ocean of mandalas.

How is it possible to be a single figure who encompasses all other buddha families? You can understand it from this example: when the full moon shines in the sky, and there are millions of ponds of water, the single moon can be present in all of them simultaneously. That's a good example.

Also, he is the one who embodies all buddhas and all buddha families within one single form. Yet he is chiefly the lord of the lotus family, padma family:

> Of supreme speech. And he demonstrated . . . Lotus-Born.

In the dharmakaya realm, he has a name as well:

> Dharmakaya realm called Luminous Vajra Essence,
> Padmasambhava is known as . . . liberation.

On the sambhogakaya level, he is what is called:

> The self-manifest sambhogakaya realm of Thunder . . . five certainties.

Out of Sambhogakaya is projected or manifested . . . first what is called the semi-apparent nirmanakaya, which is the outward manifestation. This is called:

> Natural nirmanakaya realms . . . All-Holding Lotus, Padma Küntu Chang.

In particular, it is taught that simply within our world, called the Sahaloka:

> The Saha realm, he illuminates . . . with definite names.

You can find these one hundred names of Padmasambhava in the *Katang, The Chronicles of Padma*. In this way, he acts as the lamp, the torch of Dharma to illuminate fifty world systems simultaneously. We take the example of just one of these world systems, our world. There are the eight manifestations through which he acts for the welfare of sentient beings, to tame them in these places, in these worlds. Padmasambhava assumes different forms in order to influence the different types of beings.

Yeshe Tsogyal had a vision once in which she saw one form of Padmasambhava, called the Vajra Guru Immense Ocean, in the eastern direction of five. She saw one billion realms in each of the pores of his body. In each of these one billion realms, she saw one billion world systems. In each of those world systems, she saw one billion forms of Guru Padmasambhava, each of which had one billion emanations. Each of these one billion emanations had one billion disciples. That was according to her vision. At the same time, she saw that King Trisong Deütsen and Yeshe Tsogyal were in each of these billions and billions and billions of world systems. That was just in the eastern direction. In the same way, she saw that in the central direction and the other directions, it was exactly the same.

This world we are in now, which is called the Jambu continent, has gotten its name from the sound of the fruit from the Jambubriksha tree. When it falls into a certain river, it makes a certain splash, which is called the "jambu." That's why it is called the Jambu continent. And just in our world:

> Here on the Jambu continent alone, in terms of merely one fraction of the nirmanakayas that tame beings, he was seen to appear in different ways, corresponding to the different types of fortune and faculties to be tamed.[15]

Jamgön Kongtrül quotes the biography of Padmasambhava called the *Wish-Fulfilling Tree*. It is found in the Tersar. At the time when Jamgön Kongtrül compiled this, the Tersar, or "new treasures," referred to Chokgyur Lingpa's termas. These days, when you say Tersar, you think of something else, but at that time, Tersar referred to Chokgyur Lingpa. To quote that biography:

> As perceived by some people, I appeared in the land of Uddiyana, in Danakosha from the top of a lotus flower. As perceived by some, I was the son of Uddiyana's king. As perceived by some, I appeared as a lightning bolt on the Peak of Meteoric Iron—thus, there were different versions.[16]

In this way, most of the terma traditions explain that Padmasambhava was born miraculously from a lotus. As this life story of Padmasambhava, which comes from the *Zabdün* cycle of termas of Chokgyur Lingpa, continues:

> Although there are those different versions, twenty-one years after Buddha Shakyamuni passed away, the letter HRIH was emanated from Buddha Amitabha, which dissolved into the Lake Danakosha, and from its miraculous transformation, I was born from a lotus flower.

He did not just appear there, but also in an inconceivable number of other worlds, in all of these that we just mentioned. In billions and billions of other world systems, Padmasambhava miraculously appeared in different forms in all those places.

The oral tradition of Vajrakilaya as well as the many histories of India chiefly mention that Padmasambhava was born as a son of one of the ministers of Uddiyana. However, there are also other stories explaining that Padmasambhava appeared at the summit of Mount Malaya, like a flash of a thunderbolt, a flash of lightening. Nobody knew where he came from, but all of a sudden, he appeared. That fits very well with the quotation from this life story.

The people have always been uncertain about the exact location of Mount Malaya, which is also called the "Peak of Meteoric Iron"—but it is in Sri Lanka. Some people say that Malaya Mountain is in Mysore, in southern India, but that's not the place of the Peak of Meteoric Iron, which is in Sri Lanka. If you look into Chokgyur Lingpa's life story, you will see that in the vision where he flew to this Malaya Peak of Meteoric Iron, it fits exactly with the geographical position of Sri Lanka.

Visions at best should be fitting exactly with the geography of the world. In some of his visions, Chokgyur Lingpa, while not moving out of his retreat hut—the door was closed—travelled to all different places and wrote down what he saw. These accounts fit exactly with the maps of the world that we have right now. That's the best way.

We should go on pilgrimage to Mount Malaya. For people who practice Vajrayana, it is an extremely important place; I myself went. I feel it is one of the most astounding places within this world. Even Christians and Muslims go there on pilgrimage; of course, Buddhists do. The Western name for this mountain is Adam's Peak.

There are different styles of biographies of Padmasambhava, which varyingly recount that he was miraculously born from a lotus, born from a womb, or born like a lightening bolt. All of them are marvelous, amazing. Guru Rinpoche himself said:

> For the sake of future people with pure samaya,
> I wrote and concealed ten thousand nine hundred biographies.

Chokgyur Lingpa had the opportunity to reveal an extremely extensive version of Padmasambhava's life story, in three volumes, but it didn't work out; it didn't appear. Jamyang Khyentse revealed one terma that describes the life of Padmasambhava according to the Bönpo tradition, where Padmasambhava was born from a womb; his father was called Tsewang Rigdzin, and his mother some other name. That's included in the Rinchen Terdzö. The Bönpos say that Padmasambhava was actually born from a mother, afterwards he was placed in a big lotus and sent down the river; the people who found him then believed that he was born from a lotus. "So, you Buddhists believe that he was miraculously born from a lotus, but we have the real life story," they would say.

These life stories of Padmasambhava actually transcend the scope of any ordinary person by far.

> Padmasambhava's great qualities actually described here represent merely a fraction of what the intelligence of an immature being may understand, demonstrating the exaltedness of this master, who is the lord of the teachings.[17]

An immature being can only understand this much. Nobody can really grasp the full extent of how Padmasambhava manifested in the world. The imagination of immature beings is like a collection of information based on hearsay—trying to picture how it really is based on that. Therefore, we can try to figure and grasp Padmasambhava's life exactly, to the full extent, but it is impossible. A normal person cannot do it. The reason to now mention who Padmasambhava was—his special qualities, how amazing he is, the qualities of his greatness—is to explain who composed the *Lamrim Yeshe Nyingpo* text that we are going to study. That person, Padmasambhava is like a buddha, someone amazing.

How to Follow a Spiritual Guide

The Compendium declares:[18]

> The Victorious One, who possesses the supreme of all virtues,
> Has taught that you should follow a spiritual guide [to attain]
> enlightened qualities.

Generally, in the world, we need to know what to adopt and what to reject, and there are many scriptures that refer to this. That is why Buddha Shakyamuni, who is the fourth of the thousand and two buddhas of this time, manifested and taught the three turnings of the wheel of Dharma. He gave teachings showing clearly what to adopt and what to reject. First, he taught about the suffering in this world, but he didn't leave it at that; he showed how we can free ourselves from this suffering. Buddha Shakyamuni came into this world and stayed a long time. The teachings he gave were very much in accordance with reality. This is not a new teaching that the Buddha created. He did not create a religion. He was describing the situation, the reality, as it is and showed us within that context what is good to adopt and what is good to reject. The perfect Buddha showed how we can reach liberation and free ourselves from samsara. The teachers, the spiritual friends, represent the Buddha. Up till now, there are teachers who hold these pith instructions and manifest to continue these teachings.

The spiritual friend is so important, because he or she holds the students with the words and presents the meaning of what needs to be practiced. On a larger scale, if the words and meaning are connected, the student can reach the state of buddhahood. On a lesser scale, the student makes a connection to the Dharma and can be freed from the suffering of samsara and the three lower realms and, gradually, by following the path, reach enlightenment. That is how powerful the teachings are. If you do not have a teacher, a spiritual friend, or vajra master, no matter how much you have studied by yourself, even though you are very learned in words, in knowledge, you lack the true meaning and the power of the blessings of the lineage. All the great and realized masters of India and Tibet had qualified lineage-holding teachers themselves. We have records of who had such and such teacher, who was the teacher of whom and who was the student of whom. Based on this, the doctrine of the Buddha has remained until this present day.

Every spiritual friend has received the Buddhadharma based on words and has a word lineage. Within this, there is the extraordinary Vajrayana vehicle, and within Vajrayana, in particular, there is the extraordinary luminosity, Dzogchen instruction, which has both the lineages of words and of meaning. There is the lineage of words, which is extremely important and the lineage of realization, which is considered to be even more precious than the words. The transmission of realization can only be received from one master to the next; no other way of transmission exists.

To receive the lineage of realization is not that easy. When we talk about teachers, there is the root teacher. The root teacher is not somebody that you choose among many different masters because he or she is physically attractive or because he or she gives high teachings. It's the teacher that you had connection with from many previous lifetimes. There is the teacher endowed with the three kindnesses, the teacher endowed with the two kindnesses, and the teacher with the one kindness. There are many different types of teachers, but the root teacher is the one who has introduced you to the nature of your mind. Not only were you introduced to the ultimate meaning of the Great Perfection, but you also recognized the nature of your mind. You individually acknowledged this recognition of your mind's nature. That is the incredible kindness of what is called your root teacher. There is no greater kindness within the ocean of suffering of samsara than that of the one person who can temporarily show you the state of realization of the Buddha and temporarily guide you there. It's not the lama who bestowed the vows on you. It is the master through whom you recognized [mind's nature] once you received the vows; that is your root guru.

For example, the great master Jamyang Khyentse Wangpo had more than one hundred and fifty different teachers. Of those, he had four main root teachers, and among them was Tate Namkha Chimey Sempa Kundu

Tenzin, his main root teacher. Tertön Chögyur Lingpa also had different teachers. He received the outer vows from Ta Long Maitröl and the bodhisattva vows from Takdrol Tenpey Namkey. He received the inner vows of Vajrayana from Jamgön Kongtrül Lodrö Thaye. But the one who was most important for him was Jamyang Khyentse Wangpo, from whom he received the Dzogchen introduction to the nature of mind. That is your root teacher, the one from whom you've received the introduction to nature of mind and recognized it.

Nowadays people have so many teachers and go around to hear many Dharma talks. It is like they are going to different restaurants to eat different kinds of foods. When you ask, "Who is your teacher?" the reply is, "I have so many masters. I have received Dzogchen teachings so many times." Then you ask, "But who did you receive the pointing-out instruction from, *the rigpa'i tsal wang,* the direct introduction?" "Oh, I received it so many times," they say. If they cannot even state who their root teacher is, it is a sign that those people haven't received the introduction to nature of mind and have no root guru, even though they have sat in many Dzogchen teachings.

When you receive the introduction to the nature of mind, you decide that for yourself. First you are introduced to your nature, next you decide upon that one thing, and then you gain confidence in liberation. After being introduced, that decision on one thing is what determines who your root guru is and with whom you are connected, for good or bad. It's not, as I said earlier, about somebody whom you like based on him or her wearing good clothes.

The *Lamrim Yeshe Nyingpo* commentary by Jamgön Kongtrül Rinpoche explains very clearly why you need to follow a spiritual friend from the beginning of the path and what characterizes a qualified master. To illustrate this, many textual quotations are given:

> Although all the sutras, tantras, and instructions have extensively discussed the characteristics of a master, they are, in short, as follows: His being should be perfectly pure. He has abandoned wrongdoing, because he is untainted by flaws or downfalls in the conduct or whatever samaya vow he has taken among the three sets of precepts, which are the foundation of all good qualities.
>
> [A master should be] beautified by not being ignorant about anything, and by his lifestyle, which is free from falling into

> extremes, due to his great learning in the sutra system and in the tantras, statements, and instructions of Mantrayana.[19]

> A master should be learned in the six limits and four modes.[20]

The four modes are: First, to explain just in general the word-for-word meaning by means of the sense, grammar, and implication of the term. Second, to explain the general intent common to the sutras. Third, to explain the hidden and uncommon profound meaning of the unexcelled Anuttara. Fourth, to explain in the manner of being able to combine the ultimate meaning with the unified level of training and beyond training.

Jokyab Rinpoche's statement in the notes[21] that each word of the tantras should be understood according to the literal meaning, general meaning, direct meaning, and indirect meaning corresponds fairly well to what is meant in the *Lamrim*. Without possessing these oral instructions, you will not be able to gain true knowledge, no matter how detailed the analysis of your reflection may be. However, when you possess the oral instructions, you will give rise to the flawless knowledge resulting from reflection, when examining the ways of the sutras and tantras.

You may wonder why Jokyab Rinpoche goes on so long about these six limits and four modes. The reason is that a true, genuine vajra master is someone who is totally familiar with explaining and unravelling the intent of the tantras through these six limits and four modes. Therefore, if a vajra master is learned in these points, then he is a learned vajra master, a skilled vajra master. And if not, then he isn't.

The master should have a compassionate heart. To condense down the true qualities of a vajra master, the essence, in short, is having a superior motivation, a pure motivation, and also a truly altruistic frame of mind. In other words, the master is motivated by compassion and by genuinely wanting to help the students. Of course, a qualified master should possess the other virtues of being learned, having reflected, and having meditated and practiced. Also, key aspects are keeping pure vows, pure discipline, as well as having gone through the training—but the most important is the altruistic heart, the pure motivation of wanting to help. Such a teacher, when he or she is primarily concerned with the welfare of the student, the disciple, will not misuse or abuse that power, by manipulating or trying to take advantage of the followers at all. Rather, such a teacher will try to guide with a true, sincere attitude. Therefore, the pure motivation and good heart are the most crucial things to look for in a spiritual teacher.

The important thing concerns attitude, or mind. When you look for a teacher, you don't have to look for whether the teacher is rich or not rich; whether he is a smart talker, a crowd pleaser, or not a crowd pleaser; or whether he or she has a nice face or not. These are not the important points. The real thing to look for is the spiritual qualities. If a spiritual teacher has these true inner qualities, which are on a mental level, then that is what makes such a person authentic or genuine. It's not about an outward display of that, because in general, Dharma practice is not about making a display of yourself, making an image. That is not what it is about. It all has to do with the training, or changing your frame of mind, your attitude. You should practice in improving or changing your attitude. Then you can train all the time, every day, and you will make progress all the time. That's a really important point.

True, pure motivation is invisible. Yet when you spend time with another person, especially a longer stretch, you do find out what motivates that other person. First of all, he or she should have the wish for liberation from samsara; the will to be free. If the teacher doesn't have that motivation toward liberation from samsara, then totally stay away—because how can someone who doesn't have that wish toward liberation guide others in that direction? He or she cannot.

The master should have unbroken samaya. Another point is that when you connect with a vajra teacher, a vajra master, it is a matter of not only being guided toward liberation but also toward complete enlightenment, through receiving reading transmission, empowerments, and the pith instructions of Vajrayana. Unless you have some deep trust, that doesn't become possible. Some devotion is necessary. If you look for a spiritual teacher and you see someone who doesn't actually have that trust in his or her own root guru, you cannot follow such a person either.

Of course, it is wonderful if you could have unshakable or irreversible trust. Whether you have that or not is another matter, but at least you should have some kind of stable mindedness in your trust. The teacher himself should have this stable trust and devotion.

The next thing is the altruistic frame of mind, wanting to help. That should be genuine and authentic, because without that, such a person won't really help others. This benevolent attitude should not be focused inward, in wanting to get something out of it afterwards. The good-heart, altruistic attitude should be concerned only for the welfare of others.

You could encounter this scenario: When you please your teacher, then he wants to help you. If you don't, then he totally wants to kind of throw you away. That is not a sign of having a true, altruistic attitude. It is of no use. When this altruistic attitude is improved or deepened, we call that "compassion." As a matter of fact, a spiritual teacher who just has the altruistic wish and compassion—even though he may not be learned or very special—can actually help others; these two qualities are enough.

Compassion is incredibly important. It is said in the *Bodhicharyavatara* that whoever has this deep compassion, called bodhichitta, will be honored by gods and humans and all other beings as a bodhisattva, an object worthy of respect.

I will tell you a story that happened about fifteen or twenty years ago, when I met a person in France. He told me, "I have trust in all the lamas."

Then I asked, "Who are your lamas?" He replied, "I have three main ones: Karmapa, Dilgo Khyentse Rinpoche, and Kalu Rinpoche."

Next I asked, "What is it that you call trust and faith?"

He said, "They are so special; they are extraordinary, those three."

"Could you tell me a little more about what you mean by that?" I asked.

"They are unlike others," he responded.

I felt that I had to push the question, so I asked one more time, "What do you mean?"

He relaxed a little and shared his heart, saying, "Karmapa is awesome. He has many attendants and his wristwatch is astounding. His shirt is made of brocade, and his skirt is of the most expensive wool. When he walks among other people, he walks like a king. His eyes don't look down on the ground; he just looks up in the air all the time. When I see that, I experience a very extraordinary feeling.

"Lama Kalu Rinpoche is so skinny, very, very skinny. All the time he looks like he is completely exhausted. When he teaches, he is completely perky and present. He's like a man made of skin and bones, but his mind is so strong. So, he is very unusual in that way. Normally, being only skin and bones would hamper a person from being able to teach for so long in one stretch. Yet Kalu Rinpoche is not like that at all; he can teach for a long time.

"Then there is Dilgo Khyentse Rinpoche, who is corpulent, huge. His fingers are long, and his fingernails are very long as well. When he coughs, you can hear it all the way outside the front door. When you look at him, he looks very unusual. Viewed from different directions, all sides of him are huge: big eyes, big nose, big hands, big fingers, big everything. He is also extraordinary." That was that guy's answer; then I broke out laughing. That's my story. I don't know about this recent fashion concerning devotion. Most people are simply in love with their gurus, but that's a different matter.

People say, "I really like that teacher, so-and-so master." Then I say, "Why?" They say, "Because I like him." I say, "That's not so special." There is nothing amazing about that. Therefore, it is of vital importance, first, to check out a teacher, examine the person. Do that ahead of receiving teachings, empowerments, and so forth—because after having received empowerment and teachings, breaking and turning against your teacher becomes very problematic.

Lamrim presents the stages of the path. In the first stages of the path, you need to examine the spiritual friend. Whether the spiritual friend has all the qualities that are described in the text or not, the important questions to ask yourself are these: "Is the spiritual friend able to help me? Can he show me the way to enlightenment? Can he lead me towards enlightenment?" Even though he might not completely have all the qualities, if you find upon examination that he or she has this ability, you can follow him or her.

I have something to add, which is not in the text. Here are a couple of points that I think are important. By listening to recordings, watching videos, and reading books, you are not practicing the Dharma, and you will not get enlightened. You need to rely on a spiritual friend. Having said that, when you receive instruction from your spiritual friend, from your teacher, in order to be able to remember those instructions, you make notations in the text, you have books or you make recordings. If you use them in this way, then that's fine.

I had this question and I asked it to Nyoshul Khen Rinpoche. I really wanted to get an answer on this, so I asked, "Do you receive blessings from listening to teachings that have been recorded?" Khen Rinpoche's answer was very clear. It was: "No." It was a complete no; he did not have the slightest doubt. He was adamant that there are no blessings through recordings. He said great masters made notations on the texts, based on the explanations they received from their teacher. In the same way also, nowadays, you can record the instructions, but those are a way to remember the instruction. If you use them in this way, after having received teachings that's fine.

Repeatedly, I am asked, "Can I receive teachings through the telephone or empowerment via the Internet?" Or when somebody dies and the lama cannot travel immediately, I am asked, "Can we do phowa on the phone?" There is a lot of talk like this.

Here's my opinion on this. If the teacher is teaching on the phone, for example, if he is aware that he teaches on the phone, and then in this way directs his wisdom mind toward the student as he does that, I think that should be okay. The lama needs to direct his wisdom mind toward the student. Likewise, when giving the empowerment, if the master can direct his or her wisdom mind in this way, that's fine. However, when you give the empowerment in this way, such as through the Internet, you won't have all the different levels of symbols and meaning, and correspondence between symbols and meaning. It won't be complete. Nowadays, there are more and more talks, thoughts, and ideas that pop up all the time. At least this is clear: if you don't have a teacher, if you don't follow a teacher, you won't get anywhere by merely picking up books, reading books, and thinking you know teachings that you haven't received.

There are people who come to me and say they used to go to all the teachings before and really make the effort. However, they've come to a point where they've realized that it was actually difficult each time to travel and bring all the conditions together to be able to do this. It was quite challenging. They decided that, if they stayed home reading books and meditating, it was actually more helpful. Actually, that is completely wrong. This is not true at all. What happens is this: Probably, when you spend time at home with your books and things, you have a good time with yourself. It is a nice way to get distracted, basically. Imagine, if you are watching a teaching on TV, it is even more distracting and entertaining. That's the point. You absolutely need a teacher. That's the main point here.

There are so many people who don't have a master these days. You know, there are so many people who have been in the Dharma for like fifteen, twenty, thirty years, and still they are not quite sure who their teacher is. They have many teachers, they know their names, and they say, "I met this and this and that teacher."

Second, what is the way to follow the spiritual teacher? There are three ways to follow a spiritual friend. The best way to follow a master is to practice, offering the service of accomplishment—practicing the meaning of his holy instructions and doing as he commands. The next best way is to serve and attend him to the best of your ability in thought, word, and deed. The least best way is to venerate him and offer all the material things in your possession.

> By means of these three types of pleasing action, regard him as a wish-fulfilling jewel, the medicine that revives one from death, or

> as the heart in your chest. Then follow him persistently, and with boundless devotion and respect.[22]

Dilgo Khyentse Rinpoche said the best was Milarepa. Milarepa received all the instructions from his teacher, Marpa Lotsawa. Then, without anything to eat, or any clothes to wear, he devoted himself totally to practice, spending his time in the mountains. This is what Milarepa did. He received instructions, and with only one thought in mind, he devoted himself to practicing the Dharma. He would not care about anything like food or clothing. He went to the mountains, lived in solitude in caves, and practiced. As a result, he was able to reach the state of enlightenment. Also, he gathered students in very vast numbers, like the stars in the sky or the waters of the ocean. In this way, he established the practice lineage of the Karma Kagyü tradition. That's the best way to follow the teacher, by practicing the instructions, like Milarepa did.

Now, the next best way to follow the teacher is by serving the teacher, working for the teacher. The example for this was Chokyi Thalung, who from the moment he first met his teacher, Phagma Drupa, for more than thirty years, he completely served him wholeheartedly for his entire life. At the moment of death, his realization equaled that of his teacher, Phagma Drupa. It is possible to reach the state of liberation based on serving the teacher.

The third and lowest way is to make offerings of material things or financial offerings. With this, you won't get liberated, but still there is an enormous benefit in doing this. There is an example that Longchenpa mentions in his writing. I don't know if it was in the *Treasure of a Wish-Fulfilling Jewel* or some other treasure. In any case, at some point Longchenpa had signs that he was maybe going to die. There were some negative signs to his life. Seeing that, he offered everything he had to his master Kumaraja, saying, "This is the end of my life. I am going to die, so I am offering all this to you." As a result, the obstacle to his life was eliminated. There is enormous benefit in material offerings as well. This is the oral tradition that is explained at this point in the text, so I also shared that with you.

The *Lamrim* text goes to the next important point:

> The present dark age makes it difficult to find a master endowed with all the qualities mentioned here. Even when finding a master, beings with impure personal perception will see him as having

> faults. Therefore, follow someone who predominantly seems to have good qualities.[23]

This is discussed in a text called *Approaching the Ultimate.*

Due to the age of strife, the masters have mixed qualities and faults. There is no one who is always free of any misdeed.

> The disciple should therefore follow someone who has mostly good qualities and who has been carefully examined.[24]

What that means is, due to the time we are in, the Kali Yuga, it's very hard to find the teachers or masters who have true and complete qualifications, as mentioned here. Not only that, the students or the disciples, because of all their concepts and emotional turmoil, never perceive others as being pure. We always project our own faults onto others, which also makes it difficult. You need to try to find someone who has compassion and who has the ability to show or lead the way somewhat. It's especially important to find someone who has not broken the bond, the samaya with his own lineage of teachers, someone whose samaya is not corrupted. When you find someone who at least has these qualifications, that person is all right to depend on.

When you hear about all these different characteristics that a genuine master should have, like being learned in the six limits and four modes and so forth, and then you set out to find someone you can really depend on, you may travel around the world three or four times, and still not find one. It may seem to us that there aren't any, but that's not true; there are still great masters. The problem could be that you don't have the insight, the wisdom, to perceive who is really a genuine teacher, because of your own attitude or frame of mind. If you were clairvoyant or had psychic powers and scanned the whole world, you probably would find some who were great masters, who may not have their qualities manifest on the outside, but would still be wealthy in spiritual qualities.

For thirteen years, Jamyang Khyentse Wangpo traveled throughout all of Tibet in search of teachers and to receive transmissions. He was also a person of great capacity, of great intelligence. Later in his life, after having received seven hundred volumes of transmissions from many masters—he had one hundred and fifty-five different teachers—that was what he was able to find. Jamyang Khyentse Wangpo had the capability that is called "wisdom perception," so he could see the true qualities of these teachers and also where they came from, their past lives, and so forth. Normal people can't see this.

Also, Dilgo Khyentse, who had four main root gurus, said regarding the more than one hundred and fifty other teachers he found, "There was none of them that didn't have all the qualifications of a true master. They all had." He had more than seventy teachers in the Gelugpa tradition. He had four female teachers as well.

The *Lamrim* presents very briefly how to follow a spiritual friend. Those points are explained at great length throughout the teachings—the sutras and the tantras. Students need to know how to relate to the spiritual friend. The lama is a powerful object toward whom positive and negative actions become multiplied. Extremely powerful objects are the Three Jewels: the Buddha, Dharma, and the Sangha. These three are condensed into the teacher, who is the most precious.

The teacher is very important in all traditions. For example, in Theravada, you consider the preceptor as a father, and the student sees himself as the son, the Buddha said. In Mahayana, you see the teacher as a doctor, a skillful doctor, and yourself as somebody who is sick. Unless you faithfully apply the treatment given by the doctor, your sickness will get worse. You're going to suffer and die. In the Vajrayana, the one who gives the empowerment is seen as inseparable from the mandala, whichever empowerment you receive. The vajra master is known as being inseparable from the main figure in the mandala. With this attitude, you receive the empowerment.

In Dzogchen, you consider the one who bestows these commitments on you as the embodiment of all buddhas. You see the teacher as the Buddha in actuality, not merely as an emanation of the primordial lord, Kuntuzangpo, or as a nirmanakaya or sambhogakaya emanation. You need to see the teacher as the dharmakaya. With that approach, you can receive Dzogchen teachings. That is the essence.

You must follow whatever the teacher says, behave excellently, and have deep devotion. That's the tradition that has been upheld for over twenty-five hundred years, since the Buddha's doctrine was established. The student needs to supplicate from the bottom of his or her heart. Whatever you hear from the lama is like buddhahood placed in the palm of the hand. The speech of the teacher should be held in the core of your heart. This set of instructions to reach the state of complete freedom from all the suffering of samsara, to reach the state of enlightenment, is buddhahood placed in the palm of your hand. If you have buddhahood placed in the palm of your hand, you're rich; you will not stay poor.

It is also said that one moment of remembering your teacher is greater than thinking of one hundred thousand buddhas. When someone like a buddha lives in this world, you need to be able to offer everything and really hold the teacher as supreme, down to the pores on his body. There is no greater merit than to be able to serve and make offerings to such a being.

Sometimes people think that this sort of teacher-student relationship is something that the Tibetans created, but it's not like that. Holding the lama as the most supreme comes from India; it is an Indian tradition. There probably are still Buddhists in India. Also, the Hindus very much have the tradition of a teacher, like the sadhus. The sadhus have teachers whom they consider most precious, the most important thing for them. They will never tell you the name of their teacher, if you ask them. Even if you threaten to kill them, they won't tell you who their teacher is. As in our lineages, they consider them the most sacred. The way that Tibetans relate to their teachers is not quite the same, since in Tibet some teachers are the officials or powerful people, such as ministers.

The message in these teachings is that you need to cultivate a strong sense of devotion and increase that repeatedly. What is the measure of your devotion for the teacher? No matter what happens, no matter what circumstances you find yourself in, you always take support of your teacher. That is your refuge—what you think of in any kind of difficult situation, in this life, in the next, and in the bardo. When you reach that point, you truly see the master as the lord of the mandala. The teacher is the lord, indivisible from the main deity of the mandala, indivisible from all the buddhas of all times and all directions. Really cultivate that strong sense of devotion.

Students' Responsibility[25]

If you are a beginner, be level-headed about examining the teacher and the teachings. I don't have any clairvoyant powers, but still my impression is that most of you in the audience for this teaching are not complete beginners; you are not completely fresh in the Dharma. But if you are beginners, please be really careful about examining a spiritual teacher first, and then forming a link or connection. Be very stable about it.

The words of the Buddha, the instructions, and so forth, are something that is all right to examine closely. The more you look and find out what it actually is, the more trustworthy it becomes; it improves by being examined. On the one hand, if you begin a spiritual practice just because somebody tells you, "It's a good idea. Why don't you try it?" or because one teacher tells you, "You must practice the Dharma," it will not be that stable. On the other hand, it's much better if you are motivated by some weariness, if you are fed up with continuing in samsaric confusion. You want to find a way to be free, so you look for the way that can really be applicable to you. If you follow the teachings of the Buddha, the more you study, the more you examine what the real value is here, what is the worth. You can discover that it is essentially free of all defects and full of great qualities. Through discovering that, it becomes possible to have a very stable or firm sense of trust.

The way to begin is to find out what it means—by studying, learning, receiving teachings, reading books, and so forth. It's also important to examine the teachings, closely scrutinizing what you hear and read by using your own intelligence. Thus, you reflect on it in order to really understand. Whatever you read should be a genuine Dharma book, preferably in the words of the Buddha himself. Otherwise, it should be an authentic teaching by some great master, without any faults.

There is one story I would like to share with you about a geshe from Litang called Jampa Püntsok. He was related to both Jamyang Khyentse and Jamgön Kongtrül as both their teacher and their disciple. He was a Gelugpa. He was an incredibly learned teacher in the Gelugpa lineage, and when he was younger, he had no trust or faith whatsoever in the Nyingma teachings. Not only that, he wrote many denials or objections toward the teachings of Dzogchen. He first studied and then remained a long time in central Tibet at the monasteries of Sera and Drepung. After that, he traveled toward Kham. On his journey, he stopped at Dzogchen Monastery.

He thought to himself, "Let's see if there are some learned Nyingmapa teachers here. Then I will debate with them." He went in and asked, "Who is most learned around here?" One of the monks said, "Matter of fact, nobody here is really learned. But go up to Champa, to the upper hermitage. There are a few learned people up there. Try." When he went up, there was one khenpo from Dzogchen Monastery called Khenpo Dorje, one of the root gurus of Jamyang Khyentse. The geshe said, "Let's have a philosophical dispute." But Khenpo Dorje replied, "It's good you have studied in this way, but I have no time for this. I may die at any time. I don't have the leisure to spend on debating."

There is nothing the geshe could do about it. That evening he had to spend the night at the hermitage. At the hermitage, many of the khenpo's disciples were staying in shelters made from shrubs underneath the trees, with one person under each tree, dividing the night into parts. The first part of the night they would spend sitting in samadhi; the second, the medium part of the night, they would spend lying down and taking rest. When he stayed there and looked around, he also sat during the first part of the evening. He thought to himself, "These are actually nice practitioners around here. It's a shame they have wrong view." He thought, "Yeah, they all have wrong views, but maybe I should find out exactly what kind of wrong view they have."

In the morning, he went back to Khenpo Dorje, and he asked, "Please lend me the text you use, the one you consider the most precious, the most profound. Let me read it." Khenpo said, "All right." He took out his handbag and gave him one book. The geshe himself was a really good practitioner, a good monk, and also a renowned teacher. He went and sat by a tree, leaned up against it, and opened the book. He saw it was *Yizhin Dzö, The Wish-Fulfilling Treasury.* When he read through it the first time, he saw that there were not that many mistakes in it.

However, when he read it again, he couldn't find a single fault. He read it a third time, trying really hard to find some fault, something that he could object to, but he was totally at a loss. He couldn't find any fault. He thought to himself, "I have been 100 percent wrong. I want to receive this teaching. I have to."

Then he said to the Dzogchen Khenpo, "Please give me this teaching." But the khenpo said, "You have to receive empowerment first. You probably have a connection with Jamyang Khyentse at Dzongsar Monastery. Why don't you go there first, to receive empowerment, and then come back, and I will explain it to you."

When the geshe came to Dzongsar Gompa, Jamyang Khyentse was not giving any Nyingma empowerment; as a matter of fact, he was giving a Gelugpa transmission for the *Guhyasamaja Tantra*. He was wearing a yellow hat, giving the *Guhyasamaja* empowerment. At the end of the empowerment, he started explaining the tantra of *Guhyasamaja* from the beginning and down through the book. Then the geshe thought to himself, "The khenpo there at the hermitage played a trick on me. This is not a Nyingma teacher. He is Gelugpa, a fantastic Gelugpa master. How learned he is. How wonderful."

Then Jamyang Khyentse told him at the end, "Come back tomorrow. I'll give you another teaching." When he came back the next morning, the shrine master was already standing at the door with the vase ready to pour water as the preparation of empowerment. The geshe found out it was a Guru Rinpoche empowerment, but he didn't know what it was. At the same time, he had a really strong kind of wind in the heart, like chest pain, an anxiety attack, which he had already had for a long time. However, just by receiving that empowerment, this nervousness totally disappeared, and it never came back. He was totally cured.

At the end of the empowerment, Jamyang Khyentse told him, "Best for you is to remain Gelugpa for the rest of your life, but you can read any text you want. You can also read Nyingma scriptures. According to our lineage of Nyingmapa, we regard something called the Three Roots as really important: lama, yidam, and dakini, these three. If you want to receive those in detail, there are thousands of empowerments. But if you want it all in short, in brief, all three can be condensed into the guru principle. All gurus are included within Guru Rinpoche, which is the empowerment I gave you. Now you can go wherever you want." Later, Litang Geshe became Nyingma. There was a painting of this Litang Geshe on the wall of Dilgo Khyentse's monastery in Boudhanath in Nepal. He is wearing a yellow hat.

At some point then, Jamyang Khyentse told Litang Geshe, "I want to receive from you the explanation of *Prajnaparamita, The Ornament of*

Realization, The Abhidharma, Abhisamayalankara. In Jamyang Khyentse's private room, Litang Geshe gave the explanation of *Prajnaparamita, The Ornament of Realization.* Jamgön Kongtrül and Mipham Rinpoche were also present there. Since he was so learned, he could explain both the root text and the commentary, all from his memory.

Just on the title, *Prajnaparamita,* "transcendent knowledge," he spent an entire day, from morning to evening, explaining that word. Jamyang Khyentse was really impressed, and from that time on he called him Geshe Manjushri, Manjushri Geshe.

Later on in his life, the geshe got a sickness on his tongue. It split open and lots of pus and blood came out. He wrote letters to Jamyang Khyentse and also to Jamgön Kongtrül explaining his state of health. Dilgo Khyentse later read those letters, and in one of those letters, the geshe said, "I am really sick. My tongue has split open. Blood and pus are pouring forth, but I am delighted. Why? Because the negative karma created by defaming or criticizing the Nyingma teachings when I was young seems to be purified in this very lifetime, so I am very happy."

There are teachings that do not diminish in worth, the more you examine them. Furthermore, if you are really diligent and really learned, the more you look, the more you scrutinize, the deeper a value you discover. But we are speaking about genuine teachings here, not any and every Dharma book. I am not saying that all Dharma books, or all books that have the name "Dharma" written on them, are authentic and perfect.

First, start by reading and gaining more information, and if you feel more trust, like this is something you want to really know about and apply in your own life, slowly connect with some good teachers, genuine masters, receive instructions, and carry them out as they are being explained.

Tibetans don't think twice. They just have spontaneous faith in teachers, and they don't question anything. However, among ordinary Tibetans, there are very few that have the faith that results from knowing the reasons. That's why the Chinese called it "blind faith" or "stupid faith," which is actually how most Tibetans are.

If there are beginners among you, please go about it in a steady, intelligent way. Be intelligent about it. Yet most of you have already made up your minds. You have found teachers and received teachings and empowerments. After connecting with a teacher, cultivate devotion and pure perception

If you have already received empowerments and teachings that correspond to the different levels of tantras, there is no opportunity left to start questioning or examining your teachers. As a matter of fact, if you have received so many empowerments that your head is flat (laughter) and so many teachings that your ears are scorched (laughter), and then you think, "Now I'd better find out if those teachers are really genuine," it's really too late.

Now the task, instead, is to train as much as you can, if possible, in having devotion and pure perception. Someone who has no faith, no pure perception, appreciation, or devotion, does not really have the path for making progress.

On any and every level of Buddhist teachings, from Theravada up to Dzogchen, the bottom line is that you must respect the one from whom you receive teachings. You can't disparage that person. Some living masters are predicted as being incarnated sublime beings, who are like Manjushri, Vajrapani, and Avalokiteshvara in person. When incarnated great beings appear, it's not that they become of a lesser quality. The incarnation is an improvement, actually. Sometimes I said directly to Dzongsar Khyentse Rinpoche, "How amazing that you are both an emanation of Manjushri and King Trisong Deütsen in one person!" Right now, on the face of this earth and below this sky, I have faith in no one more than Dzongsar Khyentse's incarnation.

But honestly, if someone speaks like that, or thinks like that, it requires an apology. One should apologize for that. We have all kinds of thoughts, we have impressions, and so forth, but those are all impermanent, unstable. Pure perception, pure appreciation, however, is something that should be developed further. When hearing that one should have pure perception and devotion to great masters, it's actually not in order to manipulate people, and to use them in some way. That's not the purpose.

Since it is really important to follow a teacher, if you haven't connected with one yet, be sure to check that person first. However, if you have already connected, that's it. Also, before accepting a student, a teacher should check that person out, examining carefully. That's one thing. Disciples can check themselves anytime, to see whether all the qualities are present or not. Feel free to do that, anytime. If they are not complete, then make them complete. That's also all right. The teachers are also allowed to check at any time, to see whether they have the qualifications or not. Like me, I can scrutinize myself at any time, asking, "Am I really qualified to be a teacher or not?" That's fine to do that.

In short, the students should check their own qualifications, individually. However, after connecting with a teacher and receiving the instructions, the disciple should go and stay in a quiet place. There is a great benefit in that. There are descriptions of the ten or twenty benefits of doing so and, conversely, the defects of not doing so. It's very good to go to a quiet place, in retreat; but, when staying in a quiet place, you should also practice. Otherwise, it's just like being a deer in the mountain, or a bird—it's no use.

Characteristics of the Qualified Student[26]

The root text of the *Lamrim Yeshe Nyingpo* describes the characteristics of the qualified student, specifying:

> The disciple who has faith, renunciation, and compassion, and who has sharp faculties, intelligence, and discipline.[27]

As previously mentioned, the question is this: to what kind of disciple should a qualified master give the instructions? As the *Lamrim* states:

> Impart the teachings to one who has faith, diligence, and discipline. *The Guhyagarbha Tantra* instructs: Teach the worthy one of excellent character. Give to the one who can surrender his body and possessions.[28]

Jamgön Kongtrül Rinpoche elucidates these points in the following enumerated way:

> To possess the roots of all the virtuous qualities of admiring, longing, and trusting faith; to have the attitude of renouncing samsaric existence by realizing samsara to be like a fiery pit or a prison; to be endowed with the compassion of delighting in benefiting others, because of perceiving sentient beings as one's own parents; to have the sharp faculty of correctly understanding the meaning merely by hearing it, due to the awakening of one's potential through former training; to have the great intelligence of being able to accommodate without doubt the view and conduct of the extensive Mahayana and the profound Secret Mantra; to possess the courageous discipline to engage in any practice without

> feeling intimidated or discouraged—since these six virtues embody all good qualities, a qualified master should accept a disciple endowed with them.[29]

Jamdrak Rinpoche explains how this should be, saying:

> A worthy recipient is someone who respects his master with great faith; takes delight in dharma practice with great diligence; has sharp mental faculties, with great intelligence; and is able to keep the secrecy of the samayas. The teaching should be given to a person whose temper is steady, like the flow of a river; whose character is precise, like spiritual practice; whose intentions are excellent, like gold; whose mind is stable, like a mountain; and who is able to surrender his body and possessions to the dharma and his master.[30]

I think nowadays, as was said, masters probably do not have all the qualities that are described in the text. However, for the students, I'm sure that this is the opposite—students have all those qualities! (laughter) Nevertheless, please check for yourself to see whether they are all complete or not.

When you do, see if you have the first characteristic, faith. There are three kinds of faith that are mentioned: admiring or inspired faith, longing faith, and trusting or confident faith. Actually, there are four kinds of faith. The fourth is irreversible faith, but here it mentions only three. Basically, the point is that you need to be able to identify if you have them or not.

If we had a khenpo around, he could give a really detailed, clear presentation of these four kinds of devotion. But if you asked that same khenpo, whether he had thought about those four types of faith individually, he would most likely say no, as khenpos usually do not think in this way. If you also asked the students of these khenpos, "Which one of these kinds of faith do you possess?" they get blocked and cannot reply.

Inspired faith would be feeling something like, "Wow, he's such a great person." Longing faith is thinking, "He's very important to me because I want to free myself from the cycle of existence of samsara. I want to reach liberation, and to do that the teachings and a teacher are indispensable."

The third type, confident faith, is described in the teachings of the sutras and tantras. It says that you need a teacher in order to reach the state of enlightenment. Without the teacher, you cannot achieve this. You need to follow a lama with the qualities just mentioned and have trust. This is not something you merely say with your mouth; you need confidence in this from within the depth of your mind. The fourth type of faith is irreversible faith. With confident faith, sometimes you have it, sometimes you do not; mind is not stable, so you get doubts. However, irreversible faith is unchanging, all the time. Irreversible faith cannot be affected by any circumstances. If you have that kind of faith, and the teacher comes in and kills a hundred people, you still have the same faith; it doesn't change. Within these four different faiths, the one that you need is irreversible faith, confidence that is unalterable.

The inspired and longing faiths are not that useful. The first one, inspired faith, is a little bit like when you're in love with somebody. Personally, I have absolutely no idea what kind of faith I have for my teacher. I must have one type of those, but I'm not sure which one it is. Is it that I love my teacher, or I'm kind of inspired by him, or is it confidence? I'm not sure.

As for irreversible faith, when the teacher gets slightly upset with you, you get sad. That didn't happen so much to me, as my teachers were not upset with me too often. But it did happen a few times, and each time was the same: something happened, and I immediately got sad. Don't lose faith the moment the teacher is tough with you. Therefore, you need to identify what kind of faith you have. Mostly, the case with the lamas nowadays is more in the mode of "I love you" kind of faith.

The second characteristic of a qualified student is *that he or she has renunciation.* A student really needs to have the understanding that samsara is like a fiery pit or like a prison, a terrible place, or like an island with cannibals. You need to see the faults of samsara. If you do not, you don't need a lama. Now, take myself as an example again. I do have a little sense that samsara has faults, but it's not very strong. Now, if you see faults in samsara, you will have diligence to practice day and night to become free of samsara. Not having this diligence is a sign that you do not see the faults in samsara.

I've never been in prison, but prison is probably not really pleasant; once you have spent a single day there, you want to escape. That is the example for samsara, comparing samsara to a prison, though samsara is even worse than a prison. If you spent a few years in prison, it would feel like a lifetime, and you would want to break out. But you don't have that feeling when you think of samsara. You have been in samsara from time without beginning, circling in samsara from top to bottom, and you still don't try to get out of it.

The third characteristic that you need is compassion—seeing all beings as your parents and being *endowed with the compassion of delighting in benefiting others*. Now, compassion is something extremely hard to cultivate. This type of compassion is for all sentient beings, in infinite number. I have pretty good compassion for myself, but when it comes to others, this is a bit more problematic. This compassion for all sentient beings is a compassion that naturally arises, unfabricated. It's not something fake; it is natural compassion. Following the path to liberation is not merely for yourself; it is for the sake of all sentient beings, infinite in number, as vast as space. You can say that with your mouth, but if you look carefully in the depth of your mind, it is challenging.

The fourth characteristic is *to have the sharp faculty of correctly understanding the meaning merely by hearing it, due to the awakening of one's potential through former training*. We are the types who have trained quite well in the three poisons, and if we think about this, we have to say that it is so. I really do not know what to do about this: there are so few who trained previously on the path of Dharma. I don't know what I did in the past, but I don't have any of those qualities that come from previous training.

The fifth is to have a mind that is open enough to accommodate the teachings of the Mahayana and Vajrayana: *to have the great intelligence of being able to accommodate without doubt the view and conduct of the extensive Mahayana and the profound Secret Mantra*. That is also difficult, trying to be open to appreciate the Vajrayana teachings. For myself, the appreciation I have for the Vajrayana teachings is more like a pale reflection of the actual Vajrayana teachings. To fully accommodate the Vajrayana teachings as they are found in the *Guhyagarbha Tantra* is extremely unfathomable. The sixth characteristic is *to possess the courageous discipline to engage in any practice without feeling intimidated or discouraged*.

Each of you needs to check, individually, to see which of these characteristics you have. If you are lacking any, attempt to obtain them. That is the key point of what is being taught here. If you do have them, that is ok, rejoice; if not, endeavor to get them. Do not merely give up. I am sure you have never checked this out before. These are the six condensed characteristics of a qualified student. Texts like the *Treasury of Precious Qualities* go into much greater detail about this.

Some students go to a lama and say, "Well, I'm coming to you as a teacher because I don't have those qualities, and I hope that you can help me gain them. If I had all those qualities, why would I come to you?" If all these qualities are complete, then the student is authentic, qualified. It does not mean that if you do not have all of these attributes, you cannot be a student.

There is an endnote by Jokyab Rinpoche to further clarify these points. It says:

> Padmasambhava, the precious master of Uddiyana, has taught in detail on the necessity of having faith, diligence, and discriminating knowledge, and how one is not a suitable recipient for the Secret Mantra when lacking faith.

The traditional example given is the milk of a lioness. If you gather milk from a lioness, you need to put the milk in a golden vessel. If you put it in any other vessel, it will get spoiled. Likewise, a student without faith, diligence, and discriminating knowledge is wasting the teacher's time, and the teachings will be spoiled.

Just previously, when I spoke about the qualities of a genuine student, when I said that you students had most of these qualities, not all of them, you laughed. That makes me think maybe you did not understand what I meant, so I will explain again.

Now the teachings have spread to the West, where Dharma teachings were not present before, and this is due to the kindness of the teachers. Thanks to the kindness of the teachers, their compassion, their aspiration prayers, and the blessings of the Buddha, the teachings have come to the West and North. They did not come through waging war. However, since the teachings have arrived, the people who actually devote themselves to them are extremely few. For those people who have that genuine interest in the teachings and are students of the Dharma, their qualities are described in brief in the *Lamrim Yeshe Nyingpo* with six points, as I stated.

I said that those qualities are mostly complete within the students—and I said *most* of those qualities, I didn't say *all* of those qualities. When you laughed, as I said before, I decided to reclarify. I know my own good qualities and I think it is important that everyone recognizes the qualities that she or he has. Later in the text, under the preliminaries, there is discussion about the eighteen freedoms and favors, which are the eight freedoms and the ten favorable conditions. Within the favorable conditions, there are the five favorable conditions from you and five favorable conditions from others.[31] These five favorable conditions from you are, for the most part, complete within you.

I spoke about the three types of faith: inspired faith, longing faith, and confident faith. These are necessary. As it is said, to be able to readily embark on the virtuous activities that lead to liberation, you first need to have faith. If a Tibetan master wants to gather students, he cannot conquer the students, like the Chinese who took over Tibet did. People go to the teachers only because of their faith; that is the only way that a master can gather students. Amongst the three types of faith, this is the lowest, but it is still very good to have that type of faith. If you look in the world, most people nowadays don't have respect for any faith or for religious traditions.

To have longing faith is even better than having inspired faith. This longing faith is thinking that the lama and Dharma can really bring you something special. You think, "I can receive teachings from a lama that bring happiness, peace, and liberation." Thinking like that is very good. Nobody goes to a lama thinking that they will get money and goods. Confident faith is best. I think that Westerners have confident faith in the beginning. Then, somewhere along the way, they tend to lose it—not everyone, but some. The point is that if you have any of those three types of faiths, this is very good.

I am not sure that Western people see samsara as an ocean of suffering, but they do know that it is not a very satisfying place. They understand that they can get peace of mind from the Dharma, not from samsara. In Tibet, from a very young age, children are taken to study the Dharma and to receive long life empowerments. It is a tradition, a way of life. They also become monks, mostly because their parents put them in monasteries. However, I am not sure that many Tibetans have thought about renouncing samsara and its suffering. For Westerners, once their education is finished, each one thinks about samsara and then they go from worldy life to the Dharma. This is really special.

Westerners begin in the samsaric life and train in it. Then they start to see the faults of samsara. I do not know whether they have renunciation or not, but they see samsara as not a very happy, gratifying place. Some can see that worldly work never ends; some see that worldly work has no benefit. After thinking about this, they can determine the qualities of samsara as well as its faults. Then they come to the Dharma.

In some Eastern countries, individuals use lamas, teachers, and the Dharma to be more successful in business. They have these habitual tendencies from the past. However, I see the situation with Westerners as quite special. I do not know whether you all see samsara as this unbearable fire pit, but you have the sense that you want to be free from samsara.

The third quality is compassion, and there are so many different kinds of compassion. If you look at the texts, such as the *Introduction to the Middle Way,* you encounter many different categories and types of compassion described there. I don't know whether you have vast compassion that is directed toward all sentient beings without partiality. However, at least it's obvious that you have a more limited compassion that would be directed toward your parents, relatives, or people that are close to you. You are definitely not the type of people who want to kill anyone you see. This is probably because you've been born in countries where the Judeo-Christian teachings have been present for a very long time. Now, I think that acting for the benefit of others is a bit more difficult. Nowadays, you receive teachings on this from many lamas, so you have probably developed a sense of wanting to help others. At least, you know the worldly way of helping others. That is definitely something you have.

The next quality is *the awakening of one's potential through former training*. I have absolutely no doubt that this is the case for all of you. Why is this so? If you look at the Western countries, where you were born, the number of people practicing the Dharma is very small. Investigating this from different levels, you realize that there is no government encouraging you to practice. Your parents do not either, and your friends are not leading you to the Dharma at all. The fact that you came to the Dharma teachings from these situations is the sign that there must have been past habitual tendencies and aspirations that have awakened. As you know well, most people in your countries think that people who practice the Dharma are crazy. The fact that you push hard to practice the Dharma, to use Dharma language, is because you have great merit, hundreds of thousands of kalpas of merit. Whenever a qualified master teaches Mahayana and Vajrayana, you have a genuine interest in those teachings. It's not like you are not interested at all; you really have that strong interest.

For these reasons, as I have just explained, you have most of the qualities of authentic students. Among these, the awakening of your potential based on accumulations in past lives is definitely there.

Removing Obstacles

Lamey Tukdrub Barchey Künsel is the most profound terma of the universal monarchs, Chokgyur Dechen Lingpa and Jamyang Khyentse Wangpo. There are many different sections of this teaching: the main part and the secondary teachings associated with this cycle. As it is said, "First you need to hear the history in order to bring about confidence in the teachings. Next you receive empowerment in order to ripen your mindstream. Then you receive the instructions and follow them in order to achieve liberation." In accordance with this quotation, I will first tell a little bit about the history of these teachings, in order for everyone to gain confidence and trust in their authenticity. In the land of the Aryas, in India, there were no dissimilarities in terms of the different sets of teachings. When the teachings were later brought to Tibet, distinctions arose between the Nyingma, the old school, and the Sarma, the new school. The *Tukdrub Barchey Künse*l is part of the Nyingma teachings.

Within the Nyingma tradition, as I previously said, there are three sets of teachings: the long lineage of the oral instructions of the Kama, the short lineage of the profound Terma, and the extremely short lineage of Pure Visions. *Tukdrub Barchey Künsel* belongs to the profound teachings of Terma. There are different kinds of termas: earth treasures, mind treasures, treasures revealed through remembrance, and treasures revealed through a rediscovered terma. This is an earth terma, which Chokgyur Lingpa discovered as a yellow scroll in Da-Nying Khala Rong-Go, when he was twenty-five-years old. Jamyang Khyentse Wangpo also revealed these teachings as a mind terma, called *Tukdrub Deshek Dupa,* which he considered to be almost the same in terms of both words and meaning as the earth terma of Tukdrub Barchey Künsel; so he then decided to bring those two termas together.

These teachings originally came about as follows: The precious master Padmasambhava was residing at Samye in Central Tibet, invited by Dharma King Trisong Deütsen. One day, in the turquoise-covered chamber, one of the temples, Padmasambhava sat with nine of his closest disciples: the king; his three sons (the three princes); the consort appointed by the vajra command, the dakini Yeshe Tsogyal; the great master Vairochana, whose realization was equal to that of Padmasambhava himself; the monk Namkhai Nyingpo; and the Ngakpas Dorje Dudjom and Nubchen Sangye Yeshe. Together, they supplicated him many times, offered a mandala, and made other offerings. Wholeheartedly and earnestly, they asked these questions: "When there are hindrances and obstacles for enlightenment, at this time and in future times, what are the methods to dispel these obstacles? When the hindrances are cleared, how does one reach attainment? What are the ways for that to happen?" The Precious Master replied:

> Right now, at present and in future generations, there will be countless varieties of obstacles for enlightenment and attainment on the path. The one single method that suffices for clearing away all obstacles and hindrances is to call upon your guru—from the core of your heart. That itself will remove every type of obstacle. Once hindrances are cleared away, attainment is reached, right at that moment.

In short, it's exceedingly important to supplicate your guru.

This could be one of the most important sentences Padmasambhava has said. It is found in the first volume of *Barchey Künsel* and in the text called *Sheldam Nyingjang*, the essence manual of all instructions. It says to call upon the guru, your personal guru, who shows the path to enlightenment. Your personal guru may have every virtue equal to all buddhas of the three times; still, in terms of kindness, your personal guru is kinder than all other buddhas. Due to the power of incredible aspirations and merit made by a buddha in the past, another buddha manifests, awakening to true and complete enlightenment and teaching the 84,000 sections of the Dharma. In our aeon, the Buddha Shakyamuni has done so, but we did not have the fortune to meet him and receive his teachings.

For us, our individual root guru is the person who shows what to adopt, what to avoid, and how to follow a true path. Having a root guru is the same as a blind person getting an eye operation and then being able to see. Therefore, the person who shows you the path in an authentic way, the master who teaches the Dharma, is your personal root guru, your primary teacher. That kindness has no equal. To appreciate that with respect and trust from the core of your heart, from the marrow of your bones, is exactly what is needed. Without that trust and devotion, the plant of progress in the Dharma is, you can say, rotten from the root.

These days, many teachers give teachings, empowerments, and advice. It's fine to have many teachers, and it shows earnestness and sincerity in finding and understanding the Dharma. However, you need to have one particular person who opens up and clarifies the path, saying *that* is the way to go. You need to have a personal teacher and to know who that is. This is not a simple matter. It takes a lot of combined merit and noble wishes from many, many lifetimes to be able to connect with one person and have that trust and devotion. You shouldn't think it's easy.

When you look at the life stories of past masters, often you see that after having done a lot of practice, yidam practice for example, he or she may have had a vision of the wisdom deity, who makes a prediction that such-and-such person is their root guru. Meeting such a person transforms your experience completely, and that is one of the sure signs of having found the personal root guru.

For example, in the Nyingma tradition, Prahevajra's root guru was Vajrasattva, and Manjushrimitra's root guru was Prahevajra, and so forth. Each of these had very clear indications pointing to his or her primary master. So this is how we have one after the other in an unbroken lineage. In the Kagyü lineage, we have lists of masters: Vajradhara, Tilopa, Naropa, Marpa, Milarepa, and so forth. We can count them, one after the other; they are called the Golden Rosary of the Kagyü Masters. When you read their biographies, you will understand. For example, Naropa was already a great, learned master, a pandita, when he had a vision of a dakini who told him he must meet Tilopa, in order to attain the supreme siddhi of Mahamudra. Naropa set out to find him, and after finding Tilopa, he was forced to undergo many very difficult trials. At the end, he attained realization of the supreme accomplishment of Mahamudra. In all of these biographies, you see that the Kagyü lineage masters found one outstanding person who was their unique, personal master. Read their biographies, think about them, and gain some understanding of this point.

According to the tantras, there are four different kinds of gurus: the guru from whom you receive empowerment, the guru who explains the meaning of the tantras, the guru who gives oral transmission, and so forth. These are counted in different ways, according to the degree or profundity of kindness, whether it's a triple, double, or singular kindness. But the root guru who introduces you to the view of Mahamudra or Dzogchen, bringing you face-to-face with your mind's nature—not only pointing out the state of pure knowing, but also infusing your being completely with the blessings to realize and recognize the true state of Mahamudra or Dzogchen—that is called the extraordinary root guru. That kindness is inconceivably great. When someone who is completely caught within the web of emotions, ignorance, and karma is shown, in one instant, the awakened state of all buddhas, which can halt and end samsara, how can there be any greater kindness given? If you have stayed in a dark dungeon for countless aeons, and then a person comes and switches on the light, dispelling all the darkness in a single moment, how amazing! In essence, you are brought face-to-face with your own nature, the dharmakaya nature of all buddhas. What greater kindness could there possibly be? If you have a root guru like that, great! If you don't, make sure to get one, because without such a guru, there is no way to be enlightened.

According to the sutras, the guru is a spiritual friend or guide, who shows us what to do and what not to do, so we can progress. But according to the Mantrayana or Vajrayana, empowerment is the entrance door to practicing the tantras. Of the four empowerments, the most important is the fourth, which empowers you so the play of pure knowing ripens. Without having a guru to point this out, so you can recognize this basic nature, there is no way to practice Vajrayana.

Here in this text, Padmasambhava says:

> When a person wants to practice the Dharma in an authentic and true way, he or she needs to follow a guru. When following a guru, trust, real trust from the core of one's heart, from the marrow of one's bones, is of utmost importance; otherwise, the root of Dharma practice has rotted.

What does it mean for a root to be rotten? It means something is wrong, like when the seed of a flower or plant becomes spoiled, preventing growth. No petals, leaves, or plant will come out of it. The Three Precious Ones are present as the root guru, so without a root guru something really important is missing. Moreover, the guru is the root of blessings, so without a guru and devotion to a guru, there will be no blessings and no inspiration. Whether you have trust or not depends upon your mind; but without having a true object of trust, a person you have properly identified and in whom you place your trust, there is absolutely no way to attain enlightenment.

The lama is the root of blessings, the yidam is the root of accomplishments, and the dakinis and dharma protectors are the roots of activities. Those are the Three Roots. Actually, the Three Roots are all gathered into the lama. The title of this practice refers to the lama, indicating that this is a practice to accomplish the lama. If you are able to merge your mind with the wisdom mind of the lama, then you are accomplishing the lama, Guru Rinpoche. If you are actually able to accomplish the indivisibility of your own mind with the wisdom mind of the lama, then you are accomplishing Guru Rinpoche. If not, you are not accomplishing the lama.

If you have already found a genuine master, then Padmasambhava's advice to supplicate one's guru becomes relevant. The precious master Padmasambhava appeared in Tibet and taught his primary twenty-five disciples. He empowered them to appear at various intervals in the future, manifesting, for example, as the one hundred major treasure-revealers. But understand that all of them are indivisible from Padmasambhava; they are the magical web, the play of his wisdom mind, without exception.

Padmasambhava is Buddha, and Buddha is dharmakaya. Dharmakaya permeates, or is present as, the nature of mind of every single being in a constant, spontaneously present, and all-pervasive way. Thus, firmly resolve that your personal root guru is indivisible from the Precious Master Padmasambhava. Your personal root guru is none other than the dharmkaya of all buddhas. Having understood this, call upon Padmasambhava from the core of your heart with complete surrender. He says there is no deeper advice than supplication. This is the intent of all sutras and tantras. You can supplicate in many ways, but the condensed essence of all supplication is calling upon your root guru. To clear away all hindrances and gain every accomplishment, there is one supreme method, which is calling upon your root guru. Padmasambhava has personally said there is no deeper advice than that.

There are many obstacles and blockages as well as methods to overcome them. All mistaken experiences are a hindrance, but once you understand that every thought-state is your own display, there is no hindrance whatsoever. If you don't understand this, there are many obstacles. For a person who wants to practice the Dharma in an authentic way, it is possible to diagnose exactly what's wrong—the outer hindrances, the imbalances of the four elements, the imbalances in this illusory body and in the subtle channels and energies, and the hindrances created by fixating on duality and having deluded thinking. Just being overcome by obstacles and leaving it like that is absolutely not all right. You need to identify exactly what's wrong, and Padmasambhava, who is omniscient, made categories for all the obstacles and hindrances.

Now, let's get back to the rest of the history of this cycle, the *Tukdrub Barchey Künsel.* After listening to Guru Rinpoche's advice for overcoming obstacles, heartfelt supplication to the guru, his three main students, King Trisong Deütsen, Yeshe Tsogyal, and Prince Murub Tseypo, reflected on his words. They came to realize Avalokiteshvara is the main deity associated with Tibet and Guru Rinpoche is the chief lama associated karmically with Tibet. As for themselves, they had no other refuge, no other lama than Guru Rinpoche. They asked him to give an actual means of accomplishment, a way to be able to really eliminate obstacles. Guru Rinpoche agreed. Placing his left hand on the head of Yeshe Tsogyal, his right hand on the head of King Trisong Deütsen, and his forehead on the forehead of Prince Murub Tseypo, he brought forth from the vast expanse of his dharmakaya wisdom mind the prayer called *Sampa Lhündrub.*

Then they told Guru Rinpoche this was an extraordinary prayer that all his students would recite, but they still requested him to give an actual sadhana, an application, to eliminate obstacles. Guru Rinpoche agreed, and he manifested the *Tukdrub Barchey Künsel* mandala. Padmasambhava is the main deity, as the nirmanakaya Nangsi Zilnön. Above him is the sambhogakaya Avalokiteshvara, and above him is the dharmakaya Amitabha or Amitayus, together with the twelve manifestations of Guru Rinpoche, the four gatekeepers, and the dakas and dakinis in union. Guru Rinpoche displayed the mandala and gave this teaching, complete with the root tantra as well as the sadhanas and the different texts for accomplishing the activities through this teaching.

Later these teachings were transmitted to his disciples, who practiced them and, in this way, removed all obstacles and attained accomplishment. Yeshe Tsogyal wrote down the teachings. Twelve years after Guru Rinpoche left Tibet, she hid this terma in the cave of Da-Nying Khala Rong-Go, according to Guru Rinpoche's prophecy. King Trisong Deütsen's middle son, Murub Tseypo, made very deep and noble wishes, which, combined with Guru Rinpoche's blessings, enabled him to appear as Chokgyur Dechen Lingpa and reveal this terma. He kept this terma secret for eight years, just practicing it himself. At the same time, King Trisong Deütsen incarnated as the great master Jamyang Khyentse Wangpo. These two together brought forth this terma treasure of incredible blessing and swift results, known as *Lamey Tukdrub Barchey Künsel.* With the help of Jamgön Kongtrül, an incarnation of the translator Vairochana, these teachings were spread throughout Tibet and are now present up to this day.

Lamey Tukdrub Barchey Künsel is the guru's heart practice that clears away all hindrances, thus actualizing the siddhis. To combine everything in essence and clear hindrances and obstacles, supplicate the root guru. Outer hindrances, caused by the eight or sixteen types of threats, can be removed by calling upon the root guru. All the hindrances inside the subtle channels and energies, which result from mistaken use of the structured channels, the moving energies, and the blissful essences, can be cleared away by calling upon one's root guru. Defilements can also be cleansed by supplicating your root guru. On a secret level, deluded thinking, the multitude of different thoughts that well up, can be purified as well by calling upon your root guru.

This is a short explanation that hits the point. In order to apply this deep method, you need to be a person of higher capacity, someone who has identified and has trust in a root guru—not just lip service, platitudes, or other superficial forms of trust, but a deep willingness from the core of your heart to see the root guru as the Buddha in person. Having this trust, you are able to feel complete devotion and surrender, seeing whatever the guru does as perfect and whatever he or she says as excellent. If you are that kind of disciple, able to call upon the root guru out of deep yearning and devotion, with or without words, from the basic seed of your mind, completely surrendering to the root guru from the core of your being—that is enough. But if you aren't, and you need more of a detailed way of going about removing obstacles, then you should supplicate the four additional deities in this cycle—Arya Tara, Achala, Mewa Tsekpa, and Dorje Bechön—to clear away outer, inner, secret, and innermost obstacles. For each of these deities, there is an empowerment, a sadhana, pith instructions on how to practice, activities to carry out, and so forth—many details.

Questions & Answers

Student: What does it actually mean to see the lama as the dharmakaya? How do we do it?

OT Rinpoche: This is not an easy question to answer. It is said in all the teachings that you need to see the teacher as the Buddha. In terms of qualities, you need to see the teacher as having the same qualities as the Buddha. But in terms of kindness, you need to see the lama as superior to all the buddhas. However, for the person seeing this, it is very difficult to do so.

Even though it's difficult, it is possible. If you are someone who has had the nature of mind pointed out and you recognize this naked essence, then you see that all expressions, all thoughts, are nothing other than the display of the dharmakaya of the buddhas. The methods for seeing the nature of mind and perceiving everything as the dharamakaya display of the buddhas have been clearly elucidated in the snowy land of Tibet by the writings of the Omniscient Longchenpa. These are extremely precious.

Based on these Dzogchen instructions and your practicing them, you see everything that arises—all appearances, all thoughts—as only the display of the dharmakaya. Then the lama is not separate from that; you will see the lama in that way. Through the teacher's great love and compassion and through the profundity of these instructions, supplicating the lama, to mingle your mind with his, becomes the method to see the teacher as the Buddha.

Nyoshul Khen Rinpoche gave key pith instructions on the method of being able to see the lama as the Buddha. He said that praying to the lama is one thing, but immediately upon remembering the lama, unfabricated devotion develops. The one who is thinking of the lama should look at the nature of his or her mind, remain in rigpa, and be free. This is the loving compassion of the teacher, and you will receive the blessings of the teacher.

It is not like water and milk mixing; do not think that your mind and the lama's mind are different. It is like water mixing with water. If you do not see it that way, you will not receive the blessings. In short, see the teacher as being the same as the Buddha. See your mind as being the same as the Buddha's; then that is all right.

Overview of the *Lamey Tukdrub Barchey Künsel*

When listening to teachings, studying, and practicing, even if you are a seasoned practitioner, you should do so in order to bring all sentient beings to the state of true and complete enlightenment. Please keep that resolve in your mind as you read this.

Moreover, if you are studying Vajrayana, then you should not look at things in an ordinary way. Instead, you should see everything that appears and exists as all-encompassing purity. In other words, do not see the teacher as an ordinary human being, but as the dharmakaya buddha, Vajradhara, Guru Rinpoche, or any other buddha. Likewise, you, the student, should not think of yourself as merely being comprised of the five aggregates, the five elements, sense organs, and so on, but rather as having the divine nature of deities.

That's the traditional opening remark that a lama is supposed to make at the start of a sadhana teaching. At the beginning of *The Way of the Bodhisattva,* Shantideva states that he doesn't have any special virtues and is not very eloquent or poetic, so he has written in a frank, straightforward way. Here I will try to emulate his model. I have no pretense of composing great poetry or astounding you with my eloquence, but I will try to explain what I know. Don't expect to be shocked or overwhelmed either. Also, some masters may be able to liberate the students' mindstreams merely with the sound of their voices and the profundity of their instructions on development and completion stages. I doubt there is anyone like this alive anymore.

I came here for the purpose of teaching, but if the teaching is just like a lecture and there is no follow up with practice afterward, then, while you cannot say it's completely pointless, it's like going to the movies. You drive over there, pay for a ticket, watch the movie for a couple of hours, and then you go home. It was fun. Also, a lot of people these days go for the show of it, to see what the lama's going to talk about, what he or she is like. Then they drive home, and that was it. It is like going to last weekend's Reggae festival close by, where about twelve thousand people got together to be entertained. Now I am going to try and make sure there's something valuable coming out of this. So when you listen, and also when it gets recorded and written down and somebody else sees it, there should be some benefit coming out of that.

I have been asked to begin with development and completion stages. It is pretty easy to explain, but the main point is to become practiced, to grow used to the meaning. It is best if you can combine development and completion stages together in one sadhana. All the tantras and scriptures, headed by the *Guhyagarbha Tantra,* explain Vajrayana in terms of development and completion stages.

In our tradition, the scripture *Light of Wisdom*[32] (*Lamrim Yeshe Nyingpo*) explains the development stage in great detail. Also, Jigme Lingpa's *Staircase to Akanishtha Buddhafield* and a text by Paltrül Rinpoche are both exquisite. We have many teachings on the development stage, but unless you link the teachings with a sadhana, they become disconnected from your practice; it seems like practice is one thing and the teachings are totally different. Therefore, you need to unite the teachings with the sadhana practice. Once you understand how to combine all the vital aspects of the sadhana into a very simple form, you can apply the same model to any sadhana you might practice. Here I will connect the instructions with the sadhana of Padmasambhava known as *The Concise Daily Practice of Tukdrub Barchey Künsel.*

According to the terma tradition of Chokgyur Lingpa and Jamyang Khyentse, there are four levels of heart-practice or guru sadhanas: the outer is *Barchey Künsel,* the inner is *Sampa Lhündrub,* the secret is *Tsokye Nyingtig,* and the innermost secret is Dorje Draktsal. According to Chokgyur Lingpa's personal tradition, the primary or root practice is the *Gongpa Kündü, Embodiment of All Realization,* while the two subsidiary practices are *Barchey Künsel* and *Sampa Lhündrub.* The root text of the *Barchey Künsel* is a scripture called *Sheldam Nyingjang, The Essence Manual of All Oral Instructions.* The *Barchey Künsel* cycle's structure is like the analogy of a precious vase.

Most termas explain that the qualities, virtues, and effects of their practice are great, but as explained in this terma, the benefits of practicing the *Barchey Künsel* are incredible. In the terma text, Padmasambhava states that anyone who hears or practices the teachings of *Tukdrub Barchey Künsel* will immediately be free of any misfortune and will avoid rebirth in the lower realms. At the end of the terma text, he says:

> Wherever the *Barchey Künsel* is kept will be indivisible from the highest buddha realm known as Vajra Akanishtha, and the dakas and dakinis will swarm about, like gathering cloud banks. If that is not true, then I, Padmasambhava, will have lied to future generations.

After Chokgyur Lingpa revealed the *Barchey Künsel* terma, he practiced it in secret for eight years, as I mentioned earlier. During this period, he wrote part of it down but did not pass it on to anyone, including the main holders of this terma lineage. After having realized the teaching, he first offered it to Jamyang Khyentse Wangpo, who was the destined holder of this lineage. A prediction about decoding the dakini script said the mother and child would meet together and establish the teachings. Only Jamyang Khyentse Wangpo was able to see all the writing that manifested from the yellow parchment. The "mother" refers to the yellow parchment script, and the "child" refers to what Chokgyur Lingpa had written down. Jamyang Khyentse Wangpo saw both the mother and child script. What they decoded is the "grandchild." It was said that the mother and child should then be allowed to disappear; therefore, they were eliminated. Jamgön Kongtrül was then given the teachings. Due to these three practicing and propagating the *Barchey Künsel,* it became so widely spread that almost all masters had received the empowerments and practiced it.

From the original parchment, various root texts appeared, including the *Nyingjang, Yangjang, Yujang,* and *Güjang*. The *Yangjang* describes what and how the tertön himself should practice. The *Nyingjang* is the *Sheldam Nyingjang,* the large volume we have today. Apparently, there was also a *Yujang,* which means a "turquoise manual," and a *Güjang,* a "manual of necessities," but they seem to have been lost.

Today, we have the short instruction written down by Chokgyur Lingpa. As the years pass, personal instructions evaporate; they disappear. Chokgyur Lingpa's son, Wangchok Dorje, also received some personal instructions, but he died young and took those teachings with him. Nonetheless, though Chokgyur Lingpa was quite young when he revealed the *Barchey Künsel,* he did succeed in making it extremely complete. Many important points, subsidiary aspects, and so forth were written down, and the stream of its practice is still vibrant.

Fortunately, the lineage for *Tukdrub Barchey Künsel* is still alive and active; we should not let it die, but keep it vibrant through practice. Just having texts lying around is not that useful; they need to be put into practice. This particular text is being practiced here in Western countries, as compared to other places. My commentary is backed up in writing by the extensive version of the sadhana; by the commentaries of Chokgyur Lingpa, Jamyang Khyentse, and Kongtrül; and so forth. It brings all of that together, although I still haven't seen one commentary that puts it all together into one.

Misinterpretations can lead to doubts, so it is important to clarify the correct visualization for the development stage and make this available, not only for the present but also for the future. In this way, a lot of questions come up, and if correct teachings are given, recorded, and written down, then there is something for the future; otherwise, they just vanish. Once the master dies, the knowledge is gone, like that. It is the same with a lot of other teachings. Unless the teachings are kept, they vanish with the master. These days, we only have the essence manual; we don't have the quintessence manual. It and another important manual have both disappeared.

For development stage, the visualization of the deity is one of the more important points. When I explain, I will start with the dharmakaya's basic space of suchness, which is the samadhi of suchness, and the other samadhis. Therefore, this commentary is based on what can be definitively known from the extensive version of the sadhana, known as *Trinley Gyepa,* and from the commentaries by Chokgyur Lingpa, Jamyang Khyentse, and Jamgön Kongtrül. What we know today is about this much. (*Rinpoche gestures.*) Even if we were to run around and try to dig up things, we wouldn't find any more than what exists today. If you want to make up lies, you could, but what is straightforward and truthful is about this much. (*Rinpoche gestures.*) I will not make anything up and have only included what can be authenticated in the existing sources.

Commentary on Padmasambhava's *Concise Manual for Daily Practice According to Lamey Tukdrub Barchey Künsel, The Guru's Heart Practice, Dispeller of All Obstacles*

The sadhana of Guru Rinpoche from *Tukdrub Barchey Künsel* exists in four versions of varying length—the very extensive; the medium length; the essential, which is *Trinley Nyingpo;* and the concise version for daily practice, the *Gyüngyi Köljang. Trinley Nyingpo* means *Essence of Activity.* Just as the essential part of milk is contained in butter, the essential blessing of the elaborate, extensive form of the sadhana, *Trinley Gyepa,* is condensed in the *Trinley Nyingpo.*

Previously, when explaining the title, I used the image of the vase with ornaments, such as lid, latticework, and the like. There are four sets of teachings connected to *Tukdrub Barchey Künsel.* Among these, this is a practice for a yogi who wants a concise way to practice on a daily basis. Yidam practice is a yoga that you never part from. In other words, you always practice it on a daily basis. Therefore, it better be short, condensed, concise, and all-inclusive.

༔ནམོ་གུ་རུ༔

The yogin of true simplicity,༔
When practicing this essential daily yoga,༔
Should gather all the necessary articles in solitude,༔
To be a suitable vessel for meditation.༔

Then, with one-pointed concentration, he should ༔
Enter the meaning of deity, mantra, and wisdom. ༔

Simplicity here means not having many elaborations in this context. It refers to someone who either does not like a lot of details or cannot get it together to do a very detailed practice. Simplicity can also refer to the key points of the development and completion stages combined into a simple form. *Yogin* means the practitioner, who is practicing in that way.

Daily yoga indicates that you should practice this sadhana once every twenty-four hours. As the twenty-four hour period is continually replicated, by extension, it becomes a month, a year, and, ultimately, the rest of your life. That is the type of practice this should be. It is called essential because the *Tukdrub Barchey Künsel's* entire body of teachings is condensed into this single text, just as milk can be condensed into butter.

In solitude means a place that is not disturbed by human beings during the day or ghosts at night. There are no thieves or bandits. Go to a blessed place, where great masters of the past have resided; the best is a place that Padmasambhava has blessed as a site of accomplishment. It could be a meditation hut, a cabin or straw hut, a cave, or a house. However, it should be out of the sun and rain, so that the elements do not disturb you and prevent you from practicing. Also, food is the main article to bring along when practicing. In other words, the human body needs to be replenished regularly, in order to stay alive. So, it is important to bring enough along when doing retreat. Also, you will need practice articles, such as a vajra and bell, amrita, rakta, and torma, feast articles, and so forth. All of these are necessary to make your space suitable for practice. All these are subsidiary circumstances, but you should still gather them completely, or as much as you can.

One-pointed concentration means that you are making up your mind to practice in a situation where you don't have to be concerned by anything else. Nothing else preoccupies your mind, so you are able to practice one-pointedly and *enter the meaning of deity, mantra, and wisdom.* The *deity* is Padmasambhava, the *mantra* is the Vajra Guru mantra, and *wisdom* refers to the enlightened mind of Padmasambhava. You train in all three of these.

NAMO ༔
I and all beings equal to the sky ༔
Take refuge in the ones who are the supreme refuge. ༔

The first two lines are for taking refuge. If you don't take refuge, you are not counted as a Buddhist, so this is an indispensable part of practice, which you should always include. It's important to acquaint yourself with the following points and be clear about them. You should know exactly: who the objects of refuge are; who is taking refuge and what they are supposed to be like; how you take refuge; the duration of refuge, which is from this moment until you attain enlightenment; as well as the benefits of taking refuge and the shortcomings of not taking refuge. You should also understand the three statements: having taken refuge in the Buddha, do not pay homage or bow to mundane divinities or gods; having taken refuge in the Dharma, do not hurt sentient beings; and having taken refuge in the noble Sangha, do not associate with extremists. These three statements are pretty easy to comprehend, but the implications can be understood in various ways.

There are different styles of paying homage: ultimate homage means acknowledging the view, symbolic homage denotes respectful gestures, and so forth. When you consider the meaning of these, and compare that with having taken refuge in the Buddha, whereby you do not pay homage to mundane or non-Buddhist deities, then all of a sudden it seems that a lot of people could actually be considered non-Buddhists. The way I see it is that if, in your heart, you regard some other object or entity as being superior to the Buddha, it means you have stepped outside of the Buddhist ranks.

When you think about not hurting sentient beings, you realize it is extremely difficult. It's easier to not hurt someone's physical body; however, it is extremely difficult to avoid hurting their mind, simply because it is very hard to be in full control of your own mind. Guarding your mind is not that simple. You need to be very alert to this, because it is easy to be a Buddhist in the morning and an ordinary person in the afternoon or a Buddha at the beginning of a session and an ordinary person by the end of the session. This is why all the masters say that good motivation is important.

The third statement—having taken refuge in the noble Sangha, do not associate with extremists or non-Buddhists—doesn't only mean sadhu babas with dreadlocks. In Tibet, the non-Buddhist extremists did not come in person, but there was still something that resembled them. Paltrül Rinpoche stated this quite clearly, but these days it is probably even worse than that. There are probably thousands of sadhu babas with dreadlocks.

When you chant the lines for refuge, you should chant them very nicely, because without the refuge precepts, there is really no way to progress. The good thing is that as you go along, you can continually improve and take the refuge precepts again and again, by chanting these lines. You take refuge at all times and in all situations but, in particular, you renew the refuge vows at the beginning of every sadhana practice and in every session.

Here, taking refuge is not just for you but also to benefit other beings. In order to benefit beings, you must make up your mind to do so. That is the bodhisattva resolve, and these are the next two lines:

> Developing the bodhichitta of aspiration and application,༔
> I will accomplish the level of the Trikaya Guru.༔

Without the aspiring and applied resolve of bodhichitta, there is no basis for attaining enlightenment. Isn't it true that the two aspects of the Vajrayana path—development stage and completion stage—are applied for the sake of attaining enlightenment? However, without bodhichitta, this is not possible. There is amazing benefit due to developing bodhichitta, as is stated in Shantideva's *Way of the Bodhisattva:*

> All the buddhas who have contemplated it for many aeons
> Have seen it to be beneficial;
> For by it, the countless numbers of beings
> Will quickly attain the supreme state of bliss.

The root terma for the *Concise Daily Practice* does not have refuge and bodhichitta itself, so Chokgyur Lingpa copied these four lines from the *Trinley Nyingpo* and inserted them here. He did this for a very profound reason.

> Hung༔
> From the space of emptiness, all-illuminating wisdom,༔
> The seed-samadhi hrih emanates light༔
> And all appearance and existence is the realm of Padmajala.༔
> Amidst this wonderfully decorated inconceivable mandala.༔

The first sentence includes the first two samadhis: the samadhi of suchness and the samadhi of illumination. The first sentence means that the state of unconditioned suchness, the primordial purity that pervades all of samsara and nirvana, is endowed with a spontaneously present, luminous wisdom. To apply this personally, the ideal is to mingle your state of mind with the dharmakaya of all buddhas. To do this, we simply drop our visualization and totally relax into the state of awareness, or emptiness, naturally, without following after any thoughts of the past, present, or future. For a short while, simply let be in naturalness. If you have already had the state of rigpa pointed out to you by a master, and you have recognized it, then this is the occasion to remain in the state of composure, sustaining the continuity of rigpa, which is a wakefulness that defies thoughts, words, and descriptions. But if you have not had the pointing out instruction, then you should do the following: Focus on your faculty of sight, the eye consciousness, and simply direct your gaze into the openness of space before you. Let your tongue remain suspended in your mouth, not touching the upper palate or gums. Remain totally disengaged, uninvolved in either recollecting the past or planning the future. Just allow the present moment to be, like a drawing on water. Then, for a short while, you will experience some openness, a naked state of being open and awake, and that's it. However, if you are not able to just let be, then at least think that all phenomena in samsara and nirvana, whatever appears and exists, are, by nature, emptiness. This emptiness is not a blank void state; it is endowed with luminous wakefulness. This concept, of course, may not be dharmakaya, but if one does not know how to recognize the natural face of dharmakaya, then one must at least use thought to loosen one's dualistic concepts.

The second samadhi, the samadhi of illumination is a compassion that is nonconceptual and undirected, embracing all those who fail to understand their basic nature of suchness. It is the natural expression of the dharmakaya of all buddhas, which is the sambhogakaya. So, to practice this, let the awakened state of the first samadhi manifest as a magical compassion for all sentient beings who fail to recognize this intrinsic wakefulness.

The second line refers to the seed samadhi HRIH, and so all three samadhis are included. All beings without exception are already the dharmakaya of all buddhas. Their basic nature of suchness is the sugata-essence, but failing to realize that, they continuously stray into the deluded ways of experiencing. That is the reason for compassion. Since only a buddha, the awakened state, is completely free of delusion, and everyone else, you could say, is submerged in a deluded way of experiencing, there is reason for compassion. This delusion causes our present experience of samsara to emerge. As compassion manifests from the state of emptiness, sambhogakaya appears from dharmakaya. The unity of the two, the indivisibility of emptiness and compassion, takes the form of the seed syllable, which is the third samadhi. That syllable, HRIH, corresponds to nirmanakaya. Whether it is in the shape of the Indian or Tibetan syllable, the HRIH we visualize is indivisible from our own minds. The syllable radiates brilliant rays of light, symbolizing that our buddha nature is naturally endowed with inconceivable great qualities.

In the vast space of emptiness, sambhogakaya's illumination takes the form of a white HRIH. In other words, imagine that in the middle of the vastness of space, a brilliant white HRIH emits light in all directions. This is the samadhi of the seed syllable, which corresponds to nirmanakaya.

In short, out of the dharmakaya space of suchness, compassion manifests, fulfilling activity that assures the welfare of all sentient beings. These three samadhis are incredibly profound. In the pure aspect, they correspond to the dharmakaya, sambhogakaya, and nirmanakaya of all buddhas. On the impure level, they purify any habitual tendencies related to birth. All Mahayoga sadhanas include training in these three samadhis. This could all be explained in great detail, but it is important to know how to apply it in a practical way, by means of the pith instructions of a master. According to Mahayoga, unless you are able to apply the teachings, there is no framework for the sadhana. On the other hand, if you do not know all the finer details, but do practice these three basic principles, then at least the framework for sadhana has unfolded. This is an extremely vital point.

All the followers of the Nyingma tradition regard the Glorious Copper-Colored Mountain buddhafield as inconceivably wonderful. The other schools laud the great virtues of the other buddhafields of the five buddha families, such as Sukhavati; however, for the Nyingma, it is the Palace of Lotus Light on the continent of Chamara. You could say that our headquarters are on the Glorious Copper-Colored Mountain. When the great masters are emanated to incarnate in this world, they come from the Glorious Copper-Colored Mountain. When they die, they return there. During their visions of revelations, they go to the Glorious Copper-Colored Mountain to receive the transmission and then come back to this world. When they receive messages from Padmasambhava, the messengers come from the Glorious Copper-Colored Mountain to deliver them. All the threads, all the connections are gathered in one place, which is the Glorious Copper-Colored Mountain buddhafield. So you could say that it is the power spot of this [the Nyingma] world. The Glorious Continent of Chamara can only be perceived in a pure state of mind.

All appearance and existence is the realm of Padmajala,༔

The Lotus Net is where the Glorious Copper-Colored Mountain is. I am not personally sure what it looks like, but I do know from Chokgyur Lingpa's descriptions of his own visits there, which are included in his biography, and also Jigme Lingpa's *Aspiration for Rebirth in the Glorious Copper-Colored Mountain,* as well as the chronicles of many other Nyingma masters. There are many sources and descriptions.

What does an ordinary person like you or me imagine at this point? We imagine something that is just amazing—amazing scenery, amazing decorations, and so forth—utterly splendid. *Wonderfully* means what is not usually witnessed in this world, something beyond or extraordinary. This is like the usual descriptions of pure lands, where, for example, all material substance is actually made of jewel light—the mountains, meadows, houses, and mansions are made of jewels and shine with various colored light. According to the four directions, they have different colors, such as white, yellow, red, blue, and green. In the main mansion, which is in the center, a jewel throne sits upon a lotus topped with sun and moon discs. You then visualize that the seed-syllabe HRIH comes down and lands on the throne. This HRIH is actually your own mind, which now turns into the form of Padmasambhava. This is all described in the following verses:

Upon a jewel throne, lotus, sun, and moon,༔
The syllable HRIH transforms and in an instant, I become
Mahaguru Orgyen Tötreng Tsal,༔
The glorious subjugator of appearance and existence, white-red
with a peaceful-wrathful expression.༔
My right hand raises a five-spoked vajra into the sky༔
And my left holds in equanimity the skull cup with life vase.༔
In the crook of my left arm, the secret consort is embraced in the
concealed form of a khatvanga.༔
I wear the lotus crown, secret dress, gown, dharma robes, and
brocade cloak.༔
With two feet in the playful royal posture, I am majestically poised
in a sphere of rainbow light.༔

Above my head sits the sambhogakaya, mighty Avalokiteshvara༔
And the lord of the family, Amitayus.༔
Above, below, and in all directions are the twelve manifestations,༔

> And an ocean of the Three Roots and dharma protectors gathers like cloud banks.ༀ

Avalokiteshvara is in the form of the white Tamer of Beings, with four arms as described in the *Trinley Nyingpo.* The lord of the family for both Padmasambhava and Avalokiteshvara is Amitayus, who is red in color, with one face, two arms, and hands in the gesture of equanimity, holding a life vase with the nectar of immortality.

The visualizations for the *Trinley Nyingpo,* the twelve manifestations, each have very specific locations. The first four are in the cardinal directions, and so forth. Here the locations are not specified and the manifestations are more like a multitude, like a crowd in a marketplace. This doesn't just include the twelve manifestations starting with Gyalwey Dungzin and ending with Dechen Gyalpo, but also many other gurus, yidam deities, dakas, dakinis, bodhisattvas, Dharma protectors of the male, female, and neuter classes, and so forth. Hundreds of thousands of them are gathered in all directions, above and below. They are everywhere, filling space, like countless cloud banks extending in all directions. Tertöns compare this to opening a bag of sesame seeds; in other words, there are a lot, almost inexhaustible in number. *Cloud banks* are like seemingly endless cloud formations you sometimes see in the sky, stretching beyond the horizon in all directions. Of course, these are metaphors.

> This is the primordial, spontaneously present indivisibility of samaya being and wisdom being.ༀ

In other words, it is not necessary to make the invocation, sealing and empowering at this point. In my commentary on *Trinley Nyingpo,* I mentioned that when you make the invocation for the wisdom deity to dissolve indivisibly into the samaya being, you should not have the notion that something superior is coming to be inserted into something inferior or that they stay separate as a higher and lower quality. Rather, primordially, since the very beginning, they are spontaneously present, meaning that they are automatically already indivisible. That is what is meant here.

In this sadhana, you visualize the main deities as follows: Padmasambhava, with Avalokiteshvara above his head, and Amitayus above him. All the other deities are just trusted to be there in an unspecified multitude. This is in accordance with the tantras. This is analogous to when a king arrives: his retinue and emissaries arrive with him; they do not need to be invited separately. Since Padmasambhava's retinue is the display of his original wakefulness, the aspects of his retinue are already present.

If you happen to be a person of the highest capacity, who is capable of visualizing the entire mandala with all the details clear and distinct, you are certainly allowed to visualize in this way. Please understand that development stage and visualization are completely free and open. It is not like one thing is allowed and another not, or one thing is appropriate while another is totally inappropriate. No one is saying that if you picture something it will be in conflict with another aspect of the visualization, or if you visualize too many things, they start crowding one another because there is not enough room. Please do not hold such narrow-minded concepts.

At Neten Gompa back in Kham, one wall had a painting of Padmasambhava that Karmey Khenpo had personally commissioned and supervised. People used this as the support for their visualization to begin with, and here we can sit in front of a great thangka and do the practice. Look at the thangka exactly as described in *Light of Wisdom,* Vol. II, and your visualization will definitely improve. If you try to jump directly to the stage of being adept from the beginning, rather than climbing the staircase step by step, with only a few key words guiding your visualization, it will be very hard to successfully bring the image to mind. First succeed in visualizing just one simple form of a deity, like Padmasambhava or Vajrasattva; afterwards, it suddenly becomes quite easy to visualize any other deity.

There are some key techniques used when visualizing, and you should use them. In this case, where the three chief figures are Padmasambhava, Avalokiteshvara, and Amitayus, set aside the two above and just focus on the main figure, Padmasambhava. Once you begin to stabilize this—not necessarily a perfect image with complete detail or continuous vividness, but a somewhat decent visualization of yourself as the form of Padmasambhava—immediately, you can start to visualize the other two deities. At that time, it will feel much easier. This does not mean the others are not necessary at the beginning, but rather than seeing all the details, simply imagine that they are there.

Once you become quite good at visualizing the three main figures, you can expand to the twelve manifestations. There is a saying that nothing is difficult once you get used to it. If it were impossible, then Padmasambhava would definitely not have taught it. The *Light of Wisdom* and these practices were meant for people in the future. If Padmasambhava knew that they would not be able to do such practices, it wouldn't have made any sense to pass on these teachings.

The three aspects of visualization are vivid presence, stable pride, and pure symbolism. Without these three, there is no real development stage. Compared to vivid presence and distinct features, stable pride is more important. You may be able to picture something clearly in your mind, but unless you are confident that the ultimate nature is the deity itself in this form, you won't have trust. Without trust, your visualization will never be stable; it will be just like watching a movie. Whatever you visualize—regardless of all the different features—you should have the confidence or assurance of knowing this is the form of the real deity, which is something true. In other words, you are acknowledging what you really are, namely, the divine nature of the deity. That is how to have stable pride. In this way, stable pride can be very firm and very profound.

Recollection of the pure symbolism deals with thinking of the virtues and qualities of the deity. The deity's qualities are not material, physical, or tangible, but rather a play of the mind, a play of emptiness.

> Light rays emanate from the hrih in the heart center of the lord of the family.ཿ
> Gathering all the life nectar of samsara and nirvana, they dissolve into me.ཿ

This is the red syllable HRIH in the heart center of Amitayus, and it is surrounded by the mantra OM AMARANI JIVANTAYE SOHA. The rays of light that emanate from the mantra in all directions gather back all the essences of samsara and nirvana, which then overflow and dissolve into you.

> By the compassionate, miraculous manifestation of the Noble Tamer of Beings,ཿ
> The six kinds of beings' sufferings and their causes are purified.ཿ

This refers to the four-armed Avalokiteshvara, in whose heart center the white HRIH, surrounded by the six-syllable mantra OM MANI PADME HUNG HRIH, radiates light into all six realms of samsara. This light purifies the karma, obscurations, suffering, causes of suffering, and six types of negative emotions of all sentient beings. Through this, all beings turn into the form of Avalokiteshvara.

> In the heart center of myself as the guru embodying all familiesཿ
> Is a golden vajra with the letter HRIH in the center,ཿ

Encircled by the mantra chain emanating rays of light.༔
They make offerings to the noble ones and accomplish the benefits of beings.༔
The outer vessel is the Akanishtha realm of all-encompassing purity.༔
The inner contents are the mudra deities of appearance and existence as manifest ground.༔
Resounding sounds are mantras, and thoughts are the space of luminosity.༔
The activities of the four common karmas are naturally fulfilled,༔
And the supreme level in the vajra continuity of unchanging great bliss,༔
The Immortal Trikaya, is attained.༔

The guru embodying all families means that even though Padmasambhava is an emanation of Buddha Amitabha, which is the lotus family of magnetizing activity, he is also the single figure that incorporates all buddha families, just like the very identity of Vajrasattva—as well as being the guru principle. In this way, everything is embodied in a single figure.

The golden vajra with the letter HRIH is encircled by the mantra OM AH HUNG VAJRA GURU PADMA SIDDHI HUNG. Their light rays radiate and absorb, making offerings and benefiting beings. Again the light radiates, transforming the outer vessel of the world into the Akanishtha realm and *the inner contents are the mudra deities of appearance and existence as manifest ground*. Sounds are mantras and thoughts are luminosity. When that is the case, it is the supreme accomplishment. The common accomplishment is the fulfillment of the four activities, which occur automatically.

The vajra continuity of unchanging great bliss refers to the state of unchanging samadhi. Once you have firmly planted the stake of unchanging samadhi, then, the visualization of deity, mantra, and concentration are no longer that necessary. It is as if you take hold of the moon in the sky, whereby you have automatically grasped all its reflections in countless ponds of water. In the same way, once you capture the stake of unchanging samadhi, all the aspects of practice—all the visualizations, the radiating and reabsorbing of light, and so on—are subsumed within the expanse of that dimension. By practicing in this way, you attain the level of the Immortal Trikaya.

OM AH HUNG VAJRA GURU PADMA SIDDHI HUNG༔

The three syllables are the three kayas, inseparable. The three syllables are OM AH HUNG. VAJRA GURU is the family lord, the name of the lord who encompasses all the families. In this particular case of the mandala of Tukdrub Barchey Künsel, PADMA is manifest as the mandala circle of the lotus family. PADMA specifically refers to this. SIDDHI HUNG invokes the siddhis. The siddhis are the accomplishments. This was an explanation of the VAJRA GURU mantra.

This vajra mantra—where approach, accomplishment, and activities are condensed into one—༔
Fulfills all the activities.༔

In other words, the recitations for the approach, accomplishment, and enactment of activities are all carried out and accomplished by chanting a single mantra. It is said that the meaning of the twelve aspects of dependent origination are contained in the twelve syllables of the Vajra Guru mantra. It is also said to bring liberation through seeing, hearing, touching, and remembering. In the termas of Karma Lingpa, there is a text that explains the benefits of the Vajra Guru mantra. To sum up the virtues of the Vajra Guru mantra, the *varja mantra . . . fulfills all the activities.*

I have personally met many people who have said they use this Vajra Guru mantra for different purposes, even quite mundane ones. For example, some people recite the mantra, blow on a handful of sand, and then throw it on a field to protect the crops from insects. When chanting and throwing it at a water source, it will rain; or used in another way, it will stop the rain. I have met many people who have claimed to have success in these sorts of things. When Dilgo Khyentse Rinpoche would blow on people for specific purposes, such as curing them of illnesses, the mantra he chanted first was the Vajra Guru mantra. It must be true that it fulfills all activities, so chant the Vajra Guru mantra. However, I haven't actually seen these sorts of things supported in writing.

Adeu Rinpoche told me that Samten Gyatso used it as his main practice. At the end of whatever practice he did, he would chant this mantra to conclude his session. For the main mantras in the morning, he would chant OM AMARANI JIVANTAYE SVAHA. In the middle of the day, he would chant OM MANI PADME HUNG HRIH. In the evening, he would chant OM AH HUNG PEMA SIDDHI HUNG. In other words, his main life practice was actually this text. This is actually very interesting, because as you see Avalokiteshvara and Amitayus present above Padmasambhava's crown, the rays of light and what they accomplish synchronize exactly with the description here, even though this text only mentions the Vajra Guru mantra. The other two may be there in a hidden way, who knows? Maybe he received some kind of personal advice through the lineage—in any case, it is very neat.

> In the end of the session supplicate the guru,༔
> Who embodies all the families, and mingle your mind with his.༔

When you are about to finish a session, make another prayer to Guru Rinpoche and then mingle your minds into one. There are many supplications to Padmasambhava, such as the *Barchey Lamsel, Clearing the Hindrances to the Path; the Sampa Lhündrub,* the Spontaneous Fulfillment of Wishes; the Seven Line prayer, and the *Dusum Sangye*. The one that appears the most appropriate at this point is the Dusum Sangye, so chant it a couple of times.

His Holiness Dudjom Rinpoche wrote an explanation of the Dusum Sangye supplication.[33] I have asked some of my own teachers about the meaning of this chant. The first sentence includes the *Barchey Künsel. The buddhas of the three times* are those of the past, present, and future. They are all included in or embodied by Guru Rinpoche, who is the source of all siddhis and the dispeller of all obstacles. *The Lord of Siddhis* refers to Guru Dewa Chenpo, who is the central figure of the *Sampa Lhündrub* mandala. The thirteen aspects of the guru surround him. The third sentence *Dispeller of all obstacles, wrathful tamer of Mara* refers to the secret sadhana level, which is for the wrathful Guru Dorje Draktsal. In this way, the outer cycle of *Barchey Künsel,* the inner cycle of *Sampa Lhündrub,* and the innermost cycle of *Dorje Draktsal* are all included in this chant. The next three lines, *I supplicate you: bestow your blessings; pacify the outer, inner, and secret obstacles; and spontaneously fulfill all wishes,* are pretty easy to understand. However, please note that when making this supplication, you are actually supplicating all the deities of all three mandalas in one sweep.

After Chokgyur Lingpa revealed this six-line supplication, the local guardian of Tibet, Nyinchen Tongla, spread it all over Tibet. Within one month, people all over the country knew this chant. It was said that a man wearing a white chuba would teach it to everyone, even the kids. There are almost no Tibetans who don't know how to chant it. Even the

Gelugpas at Sera, Drepung, and Ganden chant it, even though they may not know whose terma it is. It is called the Vajra Supplication in Six Lines. Chokgyur Lingpa also provided an extraordinary melody to accompany this chant.

Supplicating does not just mean chanting it with your voice, but with your mind and heart as well. Of course, there is some benefit when singing a song, but the benefit is limited. When chanting with complete surrender and trust, the effect is unfailing.

Mingle your mind with his presumes that you know how to meditate; otherwise, it is not for real. I have often been asked, "How do I mingle my mind with the guru's mind? Isn't it enough to just give him a hug" In fact, there is only one way to mingle your minds into one—through the practice of meditation.

It seems that these days the guru-disciple relationship is like a marriage. This is a new style, and I don't know if such an approach actually brings about a mingling of minds or not. However, the reality is that mingling the minds into one requires that you practice meditation. When you understand that the guru's mind is emptiness and you acknowledge the emptiness of your own mind, then it becomes possible for your minds to mingle. You are not only uniting with your guru's mind, but also with all the buddhas of the three times, all the infinite number of yidam deities, and so forth—all their minds are already mingled. So, you could say that at the same time, the power of their realized awakened state becomes intermingled with your own as well.

There are only two methods for mingling the minds into one: trust and devotion. Teachings are the inroad, but reading teachings only takes you part of the way. You can try all kinds of other tricks, and people do, but they won't get you all the way, unless you mingle your minds. Whether you sit up or lie down or whatever, all these are just physical gimmicks. Some try to breathe very slowly and gently, some hold their breath, and some close their eyes—all in an effort to get there; but to be honest, I am not so sure any of that helps. However, trust does make a difference, because once you have established firm trust, there will be room for devotion, and through devotion, there will be space for the meditative state. You could say that the expression of devotion makes room for the meditative state. That was about mingling the minds into one.

> Then seal by dedicating the gathering of virtue and make aspirations.༔

In other words, you dedicate the goodness created by taking refuge, doing the visualization, chanting the mantra, supplicating, mingling the minds, and so on, and then you make aspirations. Dedication is like the example of throwing a drop of water into the ocean. As long as the ocean has not dried up, some of that drop will remain there. You should dedicate the merit in the same way as all the awakened ones, until all beings are liberated. Then that merit will not be exhausted. This is how it is taught.

When something is sealed up or given a seal, there is nothing more to see. In the same way, you share the merit; you give it all away. I have met some Tibetans who get a little scared at this point and say, "I can't give away *all* the merit, because I need some of it myself!"

Here comes a story about two old ladies, the mother of the Lama Chömgyur and her friend, who was the grandmother of my mother's main attendant. Shortly before she died, I went to see her and to do phowa. You have to arrive a little before, so you can do phowa as they die. This old lady was having a conversation with Lama Chömgyur's mother, and she was expressing deep regret that she never had the chance to do pilgrimage to the three main stupas in the Kathmandu valley. Lama Chömgyur's mother said, "I have been to these three places many many times, I will give you some of the merit I received by going there. I will give you the merit from one circumambulation of each place." The old lady was very happy and exclaimed, "Oh, there is nothing greater that you could give me!" A few days after her friend passed away, Lama Chömgyur asked his mother, "Why didn't you just give her the merit of all your circumambulations?" She replied, "No, no, no I couldn't—I need to save some of that merit for myself, for I am also going to die at some point!"

Dedicating the merit and sealing with that is very important.

> Ho ༔
> By the power of accomplishing the mandala of the vidyadhara guru,༔
> May I and all the infinite sentient beings without exception ༔
> Spontaneously accomplish the four kinds of activities ༔
> And be liberated into the luminous space of dharmakaya.༔

That was the apsiration. Next comes the verse of auspiciousness followed by some advice from Padmasambhava.

May the blessing of the root and lineage gurus enter my heart.ༀ
May the yidams and dakinis accompany me like a shadow follows the body.ༀ
May the dharma protectors and guardians clear away all obstacles.ༀ
May there be the auspiciousness of attaining the supreme and common siddhis.ༀ

*By supplicating constantly with devotion to the root guru inseparable*ༀ
*From the great master Padma,*ༀ
*All obstacles will be cleared and the accomplishments attained.*ༀ

*Samaya, seal, seal, seal.*ༀ

There is a point to this. Padmasambhava is considered something incredibly special, but he appeared far back in time and is no longer with us. In contrast, the personal guru, who gives empowerments and instructions, is considered to be of a lower rank. Perhaps he has received some of Padmasambhava's blessings, and maybe Padmasambhava sent him; he is at least a helper. Thinking like that is a mistake. The tertön at some point in the past was a disciple of Padmasambhava and received the empowerments, instructions, and blessings. Therefore, he considers Padmasambhava as his root guru. In some of the songs of Chokgyur Lingpa, he says, "As the sun rises, I remember my guru Padma, and when the sun sets over the Five-Peaked Mountain in China, I remember my guru Vimilamitra." He considers both to be his gurus. When someone like that makes such a supplication, he or she immediately has a vision of that root guru. Ones like you and me think they have received empowerment and instructions from their personal root guru, not Padmasambhava. But what you should think is that your personal root guru is like the play of the wisdom mind of Padmasambhava, and in this way is totally indivisible from Padmasambhava. That is how you should regard your root guru.

It is also a fact that if someone is emanated from Padmasambhava, or appears through Padmasambhava's blessings, then, in actuality, that person is not separate from Padmasambhava. He or she is indivisible from Padmasambhava. In this way, there is no difference in quality, for better or worse. The fact that we don't see someone in the same style as Padmasambhava's life story is only due to our own impure perception. Even if it is true that someone is the emanation of Padmasambhava, that doesn't necessarily mean we can see it. It could be that the guru himself doesn't see it.

I asked Tulku Urgyen Rinpoche about this once. There is a certain kind of emanation that is like a primordial emanation, which emerges from the compassionate capacity. It comes from above and is already pure from the beginning. However, since such an emanation has appeared into a setting of delusion, we may not know who this emanation is. We discover this at the moment their body is released at the time of death, when the emanation merges back with the source, and it becomes obvious. It is said that when you hold a crystal up in a beam of sunlight, the rays of color manifest, and you see the colors as being over there even though the crystal is here. That is where they are seen, but the moment the crystal is moved from the light, the colors appear to be reabsorbed by the crystal and are no longer visible. Therefore, though someone may be an emanation, it does not mean that they are aware of it themselves. Tulku Urgyen himself clarified this from many masters, especially Shechen Kongtrül.

For us, it is perfectly all right to imagine or trust that our personal guru is an emanation or manifestation of Padmasambhava and indivisible from him. Also the great master Adzom Drukpa said that these days a lot of followers of the Nyingma tradition regard Padmasambhava as being so special. They make a lot of supplications and prayers, but they fail to understand that Padmasambhava and their own root guru are indivisible; thus, they minimize their benefit. Therefore, supplicate *constantly with devotion to the root guru inseparable from the great master Padma.*

Right now, we are still in a time when we can meet masters who can give empowerments and instructions, but there will be a time when this is not possible. Both Padmasambhava and Gampopa have said that in the future, when there is no longer any direct link between empowerment and teaching, if someone supplicates with a sincere heart to either of these masters, they will still come to bless them and accept them as disciples. Of course, when possible, it is better if you have someone from whom you can receive empowerments and instructions. Even if it is not possible to connect with anyone, you can still make supplication and receive benefit. When you do so, all obstacles in this lifetime will be cleared away; for the future, the supreme and common accomplishments will be attained as well. It is also said in the *Sheldam Nyingjang* scripture that when hindrances are removed, siddhis are attained automatically.

Samaya is the seal for the pledge and *seal, seal, seal* are the seals for body, speech, and mind.

> *This is the perfect essence of the profound Dharma treasures of the incarnated great treasure revealer Chokgyur Dechen Lingpa.*

Incarnated means that he is an emanation of Prince Damdzin, who was accepted as the direct disciple of Padmasambhava.

There is a difference between a *great treasure revealer* and a minor treasure revealer. When a tertön has the three primary termas known as *la, dzog,* and *tuk*—for Guru Sadhana, Great Perfection, and Avalokiteshvara respectively— he is called a major tertön. *Chokgyur* means supreme, most eminent. It is said that Chokgyur Lingpa is the most eminent, most supreme among the 108 major tertöns who have already appeared. Though he is one tertön, he had three names: Chokgyur Lingpa, Dechen Lingpa, and Shikpo Lingpa. Dilgo Khyentse Rinpoche wrote a text in which he compares these three names with the meaning of the ground, path, and fruition of the Great Perfection. Among the many profound treasures that he revealed, this is *the perfect essence,* meaning the most important part.

Though this does not appear in the version you have, in some of the versions of this scripture, there is a short note by Chokgyur Lingpa added here which says, "I added the refuge and bodhichitta at the beginning, and the dedication and auspiciousness at the end in order to make it complete." When there is a note like this from the tertön himself, it is special. When a tertön does something like that, it is based on the command of Padmasambhava and then carried out by the tertön.

I heard the story that Chokgyur Lingpa wrote down the terma for the *Tukdrub Barchey Künsel* first. Then years later, he met Jamyang Khyentse and they wrote it down together from the dakini script on the yellow parchment. When they compared it to what Chokgyur Lingpa had already written down, there were some things that were not very clearly written. Jamyang Khyentse pointed to them and asked, "What does that mean?" Chokgyur Lingpa replied, "It wasn't that clear." Then Jamyang Khyentse Wangpo gave him a slap in the face. Even if there was just one word wrong, it was cleared up when they were together. That was how they gained complete trust in one another.

Questions & Answers

STUDENT: I have a question about the post-meditation practice. I have heard the saying that Tibetans have a hundred yidams but don't accomplish any, so just have one and accomplish it. But I am personally not willing to give up my other practices and I have more than one yidam. So I would like to know how to practice the post-meditation in this case.

OT RINPOCHE: There is talk like that. Think about it, all right; you have several yidams, and you probably prefer one even just a little more than the others, so it is fine to use that one during the post-meditation. If your physical being is that of the deity, your voice sounds the mantra, and all states of mind are original wakefulness, there is no breaking of samaya. Also, there is a saying that all conquerors are identical in the single expanse of original wakefulness.

You are also allowed to transform a peaceful deity into its wrathful form; for example, imagine Avalokiteshvara and then, in an instant, become Hayagriva. It is also perfectly fine while practicing Vajrasattva to instantaneously transform into Vajrakilaya or Vajrapani. The reverse is also true; you may visualize a wrathful deity like Vajrakilaya. However, a wrathful deity is not actually angry; it is totally peaceful at heart, so Vajrakilaya can change into Vajrasattva without a problem. As a matter of fact, it is all allowed. It is all free and open. It is like when you get angry in a completely ordinary way. You do not have to stay angry forever; you can change moods.

There is a certain style of combining all aspects of deities and masters into a single figure. Those who practice the *Tukdrub* can simply use Padmasambhava as their yidam for any occasion. The Nyingmapas speak of Padmasambhava as being pretty inconceivable, in that he is the single figure encompassing all buddha families, while being present in all buddhafields simultaneously. As the central figure of the eight heruka mandalas, he continually emanates and absorbs countless mandalas of peaceful and wrathful deities through every pore of his body.

If you are practicing Dzogchen, then you don't have to imagine anything, right? Very simply, sit there with a gaping mouth. For Westerners, Dzogchen practice is very convenient. You don't have to sit in the full vajra posture; you can sit like a dog or squat like a rishi or lie down like an elephant. It's very cozy. For Tibetans, this is extremely difficult. For Tibetans, even sitting in a chair for any length of time is actually quite uncomfortable.

STUDENT: Could you please explain these lines [four lines from the invocation for recitation of mantra] from the *Trinley Nyingpo?*

> HUNG HRIH!༔
> In the essence mandala of bodhichitta,༔
> Gathering of deities reveling in wisdom magic,༔
> Without departing, remember your vajra samaya༔
> And bestow blessings, empowerments, and siddhis!༔

OT RINPOCHE: The word *nyingpo,* or "essence," has the same meaning as in buddha nature and in *Lamrim Yeshe Nyingpo.* It means the "root," the most basic, most essential part of all phenomena and all teachings.

The way to understand this sentence is by realizing it has to do with Dzogchen. The very basis for everything, every incident of phenomena, is primordial purity. Whatever occurs, including compassion, is the natural expression of primordial purity. In other words, the entire mandala is manifested out of compassion, in a magical way. All the forms of deities—the central figure, the surrounding figures, all of them—are the play of the primordially pure awakened state of Padmasambhava's mind.

Even before anything ever manifested, the state of primordial purity had been innately endowed with spontaneously present qualities, which appear through the eight gates, or modes, of spontaneous presence. That is how everything unfolds in both samsara and nirvana—without a creator. In other words, this mandala of mind does not come from anywhere else. This verse here refers to the pure aspect, which is the essence mandala of bodhichitta. Where it says *Gathering of deities reveling in wisdom magic,* the word *reveling* means that something comes into play—in other words, something becomes visible from the unmanifest, in the form of the mandala. *Mandala* refers to the setting of the central figure and surrounding deities, which is a magical form. Thus, it looks like the whole mandala and all the deities are there but, in fact, there is no concrete thing; it is like magic. When we call upon them, the words *without departing* mean, "do keep your oath; don't let it slip." From the perspective of primordial purity and spontaneous presence, nothing needs to be invoked in order to be present; it is already like that. Also, no one is separate from this setting. However, from the perspective of ordinary thinking, we have to ask for something in order to get it. Therefore, it is necessary to make the request, "Please, without departing, remember your vajra samaya." *Vajra* here means "indestructible;" it is firm and unfailing. If someone makes a vajra samaya, they will always keep it and never break their vow. At the end of the verse it says, *Then bestow blessings, empowerments, and siddhis.* In other words, that is the real accomplishment, so please give it.

These four lines are actually also found in the extensive and medium versions of the sadhana as well, in the section known as "receiving the siddhis." In the *Trinley Nyingpo,* however, they are found in the invocation for the recitation of mantra.

According to Genden Chophel, the word *mandala* was first used for the mahashvara's lingam. In Tibetan, it is translated as *kyilkhor* and is used quite a lot. *Kyil* means "center" and *khor* means "encircling," which refers to the surrounding retinue. Then it can be explained as "the support and the supported" and in many other ways. It was translated from Sanskrit into Tibetan. Now, in English, how should it be translated? If you only use the literal meaning, it may be somewhat awkward, but I don't know how it is going to end up.

The word *nyingpo* also has various connotations. The simplest connotation is "essential liquid." Sometimes it means "the basic, the principal," like the mother. Also, the word *bodhichitta* has many connotations.

First, here, *the essence mandala of bodhichitta* refers to the Dzogchen connotation. You should look upward, not just downward, taking the lowest common denominator. Since you are already practicing the Mahayoga setting, then when you come across something like this, you should look upward toward the Atiyoga perspective and not downward to a Mahayoga interpretation.

In short, to make one categorical interpretation of a root text is not simple, because you can pull it in any direction. It is a very flexible piece of literature. For example, we chant the Seven Line supplication in both Tibetan and English, but, honestly, if you read Mipham Rinpoche's explanation of those seven lines, you can almost no longer understand what they mean, as there are so many levels. On one level, the country of Oddiyana refers to your heart chakra, but sometimes it indicates your eyes. The northwest is not necessarily the geographical location, as it can be the northwest side of the heart chakra.

When something is terma-treasure literature—I am not going to say that every single tertön is authentic—but let's say, the wording in revelations from authentic tertöns is extraordinary. These days it seems like a lot of people just put the terma symbol at the end of the lines, so it becomes a terma. In the northeastern region of Kham, these days, there are many people who have twenty or thirty volumes of so-called terma teachings—but real terma texts are extraordinary. Even someone like me is impressed, and I am not easily impressed.

Someone like Jamyang Khyentse Wangpo could discern whether a text was genuine, authentic terma writing or not, simply by looking at a single sentence. He was someone who could clearly and distinctly see the words and meaning of every single terma from the past up until that time, including every single terma from the south of Nepal to Amdo in the northeast, without a single exception. He could see not only those revealed in the past but also those still concealed in the ground, yet to be revealed. He saw all past termas as well as all future ones in completeness. Spending a couple months in a row in his meditative state, he could see all of them. Later on, they sort of slipped from sight, but even though he couldn't see them completely all the time, he could still focus on any he wanted to. He told this to Jamgön Kongtrül. Once you attain the seventh bhumi and up, it is probably like that. People like us must first look, then think, and then speak. I must first think about what I have read before I understand something. Although, I do get a feeling for whether something is authentic or merely looks real.

The Practice of the Single Form of Vajrakilaya

According to the Teaching of Sangtik Nyingpo

Sangtik Nyingpo is actually the destined terma belonging to Jamgön Kongtrül; however, Chokgyur Lingpa helped him out. Chokgyur Lingpa revealed the *Trilogy of the Secret Heart Essence* and then handed it over to him. Jamgön Kongtrül, himself, revealed what is called the *Three Yidams,* the three cycles of the guru of *Sangtik* and the three cycles of the dakini of *Sangtik.*

According to the Dharma tradition of Chokgyur Lingpa, before enjoining any Dharma protector to carry out the activities, you need to visualize yourself in the form of the yidam deity.

There are three aspects to explaining Vajrakilaya, Dorje Phurba: how to visualize the deity's form, the body aspect; how to recite the mantra, the speech aspect; and how to rest in the samadhi of thatness, the mind aspect. In a separate text,[34] Karmey Khenpo explains these in great detail from the Chokling Tersar. Karmey Khenpo says he wrote this text according to the personal instructions and advice of Chokgyur Lingpa, as well as from his own experience of teaching it several times to the congregation of monks, who practice it daily in his own monastery.

Chokgyur Lingpa had three types of Phurba termas: The Mahayoga one for tantra is the *Zabdun Phurba,* from the Sevenfold Profundity; the Anuyoga one for statements is the *Lungluk Phurba;* and the Atiyoga one for instructions (men-ngag) is this one, the *Sangtik, The Secret Essence Phurba.*

The *men-ngag* style means you simply visualize Dorje Phurba as a single figure, yourself as the yidam deity. The surrounding deities are the ten wrathful ones with their consorts, another ten with their consorts, and the gatekeepers. All of these together as one are called the men-ngag style. Otherwise, generally speaking, altogether there are seventy-five deities in the Phurba mandala.

The Nyingma tradition has two sections: tantra and sadhana. This belongs to the sadhana section, among which are the *Drupa Kagye,* or *Eight Heruka sadhanas: Manjushri Body, Lotus Speech, Vishuddha Mind, Amrita Qualities,* and *Kilaya Activity*. This belongs to the *Kilaya Activity* sadhana.

For the most part, the siddhas of both India and Tibet attained complete accomplishment by means of Kilaya practice. The exposition connected to the empowerment for this practice explains this. The peaceful forms are Vajrasattva, Vajrapani, and Vajravidarana. The wrathful forms are Vajrapani (also); another form of the Vajrabhira, according to the new schools; and Vajrakilaya. These different deities actually have the same identity. They just look different, but their essence is the same.

When Padmasambhava was practicing Yangdak Heruka in the Asura Cave at Yangleshö and was about to attain the supreme siddhi of Mahamudra, the maras created many obstacles. To dispel these, he unfolded the mandala of Vajrakilaya and attained supreme accomplishment. Later, he bound all the spirits under oath in Tibet, also by means of Vajrakilaya.

The great pandita Vimalamitra was also an accomplished master of Kilaya practice. At one point, when there was a major obstacle, he raised and pointed his phurba, reversing the flow of the Ganges River. Later, when Padmasambhava opened the mandala and gave the transmission, instructions, and so forth to his close disciples in Tibet, Yeshe Tsogyal received that specific transmission, and with Vajrakilaya as her main yidam, she attained the accomplishments. At one point, by simply pointing her phurba, she made a crow fall to the ground.

Jamyang Khyentse Wangpo personally performed about fifty-five different types of Kilaya practice. His disciple Shechen Gyaltsab Pema Namgyal was also a master of Kilaya practice. And his disciple the omniscient Tashi Paljor, Dilgo Khyentse Rinpoche, also received the Kilaya practice from the Chöwang tradition, which he used as his extraordinary personal yidam. He also performed the full recitation according to seven different Kilaya traditions, including *Zabdun Phurba, Nyanglu Phurba,* and *Nyen-gyu Phurba.*

These have been a few remarks on generating certainty by means of explaining the historical background, which is a requisite topic when giving teachings in the Kilaya tradition.

The many authoritative scriptures include original tantras like the *Bum Nag, The Black One Hundred Thousand,* and the *Bumtig*. Sakya Pandita also made expositions on Kilaya transmission, and Jamgön Kongtrül's vast commentary on it is included in *Gyude Kundu, The Collection of Sadhana Practices,* and so forth. So the Kilaya scriptures form a vast array.

In the Nyingma tradition, itself, nearly every single tertön has revealed at least one Phurba terma, and some have revealed many. Among contemporary tertöns, Dudjom Rinpoche has two phurba practices, *Namchak Putrii* and the *Rekpong,* and Dilgo Khyentse Rinpoche has one called the *Nyakluk Phurba,* which is extremely detailed. But here we are studying the *Sangtik Phurba* of Chokgyur Lingpa.

What we have here is called the *Practice of the Single Form of Vajrakumara (tib. Dorje Shonnu),* according to the teachings of *Sangtik Nyingpo. Vajrakumara* is just one of many in the vast teaching cycle of the *Sangtik Nyingpo.* There could be many ways to practice each, such as extensive or condensed; but this is the single form, called the single mudra.

Next comes the homage:

Namo Vajrakumaraya༔

The first few lines are:

For this activity practice of the
Great Glorious Vajrakumara, condensed to the essence.༔

Thus, this practice is a concise form of the great Glorious Vajrakumara. Here, I am not going to go through the practice word-by-word, because that would take several days, and Karmey Khenpo has already written an excellent, detailed explanation, which you are welcome to read and study. Also, it is not appropriate to just explain some of the words and leave others out. For instance, a lot could be said about just the term great *Glorious Vajrakumara (palchen Dorje Shonnu),* but I am not going to do that.

Visualize all the objects of refuge before you.༔

In the sky before you, visualize the objects of refuge, including Vajrakumara, all the gurus, yidams, dakinis, and all the Dharma protectors of this lineage. Imagine them as vividly present in the sky before you. In front of them, you take refuge, together with all other sentient beings as infinite in number as the sky is vast. With a respectful gesture, join palms in front of your heart; with a respectful voice, chant the lines of refuge; and with a respectful mind, entrust yourself to the meaning of taking refuge. As a daily practice, you would chant these four lines of refuge three times, but if you are doing it at the beginning of enjoining the protectors, then you only chant them once.

> Gurus and Three Jewels,༔
> Herukas and dakinis,༔
> In all of you, the ocean of objects of refuge,༔
> I take refuge until enlightenment.༔

The next four lines are for the bodhichitta resolve:

> For the sake of all sentient beings,༔
> I intend to attain complete buddhahood.༔
> In order to tame the maras, who create obstacles,༔
> I will attain the level of the great Glorious One.

The Drukpa Kagyü monasteries that chant the *Sangtik Phurba* have a particular style in which they chant refuge and bodhichitta three times each and then accompany the verses for the main visualization with a drum beat. In our tradition at Tsikey and Neten gompas, we simply chant the whole thing straight through from the beginning, without any repetitions or drums. However, since refuge and bodhichitta are indispensable at the beginning of any sadhana, they are repeated again and again.

Now the main part begins:

> Vajra-wrath cuts through aggression.༔
> The great, blazing blue color༔
> Manifests as a drop in the center of space.༔
> By light rays of HUNG radiating in the ten directions,༔
> Appearance and existence are the realm of Kilaya.༔

Amidst the space of the dark blue E,༔
Upon the great rock, lotus, sun, and Mahadeva,༔
From the transformation of the letter HUNG,༔
A dark blue vajra appears, marked with HUNG.༔

By dazzling rays of light blazing forth༔
From the vajra state of dharmadhatu,༔
The overwhelming, blazing Wrathful One appears.༔

Among the three samadhis, the first sentence, *Vajra-wrath cuts through aggression,* pertains to the samadhi of suchness. It refers to emptiness, but in a wrathful way. So what can cut through aggression, really? There is nothing other than compassion. So you could say that compassion is the real weapon against anger.

The great, blazing blue color[35] represents the second samadhi. It is the unity of emptiness and compassion, manifest *as a drop in the center of space,* which is the seed-syllable HUNG, the third samadhi. Karmey Khenpo provides a very complex commentary on this; but in short, that is the meaning.

Here, *vajra* refers to emptiness, because emptiness is endowed with the seven vajra qualities: uncuttable, indestructible, firm, solid, true, undefeatable, and unimpeded by anything whatsoever. Emptiness is, therefore, said to be like a vajra. The only weapon that can subjugate and destroy aggression or hatred is compassion. So that is the meaning of *the great, blazing blue color.* This compassion that cuts through anger is inseparable from emptiness and manifests *as a drop in the center of space,* with the syllable HUNG. In this way, the three samadhis of suchness, illumination, and the seed syllable are complete.

The first two sentences actually appear with the same wording in most Kilaya practices, including the Kilaya from the oral tradition in the Sakya lineage. They can even be found in Sakya Pandita's Tibetan translation of the Indian Kilaya tantra. Jamgön Kongtrül's explanation of these two sentences is easier to understand, but I have used Karmey Khenpo's, since he was a personal disciple of Chokgyur Lingpa.

The HUNG appears in the middle of space just like a rainbow, a sun, or a moon in the center of the sky, and it radiates light in the ten directions. This light transforms whatever it touches into the buddhafield of Vajrakilaya. Vajrakilaya's buddhafield is a bit different in that it has a wrathful palace, a charnel ground, and wrathful ornaments and decorations. This means that all appearances, whatever is perceived, are the forms of Vajrakilaya; all sounds are the natural sounding of the Vajrakilaya mantra; and every state of mind is the all-pervasive, awakened state of Vajrakilaya. Even though the sadhana does not refer to the palace, Karmey Khenpo makes special mention of it. In the center of the palace is a dark blue Tibetan letter E, which refers to a triangular shape, like a platform.

What does the wrathful palace look like? Its walls are made of fresh, old, and new skeleton heads. It has water monster ornaments and human skin banners. Its crown ornament at the top of the palace is Rudra's heart, and so forth. Every wrathful deity is standing on a huge boulder, like a stone mountain.

Vajrakilaya is standing *upon the great rock, lotus, sun, and Mahadeva,* which is actually comprised of two figures, one male lying face down and one female lying face up.

According to the explanations of the wrathful mandala, hung doesn't just float down and land in the center of the palace; rather, it strikes like a flash of lightning. Instead of immediately transforming into the deity, it first assumes the form of a dark blue vajra marked with the letter hung, which shines in all directions with dazzling rays of light that make offerings of all types to all the buddhas. The rays gather back the blessings of body, speech, and mind—and especially those of activities—which dissolve into the vajra. The vajra then transforms into Vajrakilaya.

> He is dark blue, with three faces and six arms.༔
> His right face is white, his left one is red, and his central one is blue.༔
> His nine eyes fiercely glare in the ten directions.༔
> With open mouth and rolling tongue, he bares his fangs,༔
> Roaring the great sound ARALLI.༔
> His beard and eyebrows blaze like fire.༔

It is said that one face is awe-inspiring, another is laughing, and the other is roaring. Each face has three eyes, altogether nine that glare in the ten directions. His mouth is gaping and his tongue is rolled back, baring his fangs. In some of the Kilaya texts, it is said that one of the faces is clenching its teeth, but here all the mouths are open. You can see the rolled-up tongue and all four fangs. There are many explanations of the symbolism. For example, the three faces illustrate the transformation of the three poisonous emotions, and the twelve fangs represent the reversal of the twelve links of independent origination. The tongue that is rolled back roars with the sound of ARALLI, or joyful laughter. His moustache and goatee are aflame.

> His hair streams upward, marked༔
> In the middle with a half-vajra,༔
> With Guru Akshobhya in its center.༔

It is said that 21,000 hairs stream upward. You should visualize the half-vajra in the center of the hair, tying it up. The vajra is hollow in the middle, and the guru in the form of dark blue Akshobhya sits there, naked except for bone ornaments.

> His first right hand holds a nine-pronged vajra;༔
> His middle one aims a five-pronged vajra in the ten directions.༔
> His first left hand holds a mound of fire;༔
> The middle one holds a trident khatvanga.༔
> His last hands roll the sumeru kilaya.༔

The purpose of the nine prongs is to establish the realization of the nine bhumis, while the five prongs are for eliminating the five poisons. The nine-pronged vajra is turned upward, while the five-pronged (vajra) moves around in the ten directions. Of his other hands, one holds a mass of fire like a heap. Another hand holds a trident khatvanga. The mound of fire heap has five points of flames to consume the five poisons, while the three points on the khatvanga are to pierce the three poisons. His main two arms are in front of his heart, where he holds a phurba dagger the size of Mount Sumeru. Since this dagger is known as a sumeru kilaya, some thangka painters depict the top of the handle in the shape of Mount Sumeru, but as Dilgo Khyentse personally told me, that is a big mistake. However, some lamas mistakenly assume such is the case. The Kilaya tantras also state that this means the dagger is as large as Mount Sumeru.

There are three main Kilaya mandalas: The root mandala is yourself in the form of Vajrakilaya; the wrathful mandala is the ten wrathful deities, which surround you; and the substance mandala is the kilaya dagger you hold in your hands.

With vajra-jewel wings outspread,༔

The right wing is made of vajras and the left wing is made of jewels. They are fully spread out. I have seen some thangkas in which the wings have the vajras and jewels only at the very tips. However, that is incorrect. The entire wing is made from vajras and jewels, with the very top having feathers like a bird.

He wears an elephant and human skin above,༔
And a tiger skin as a skirt.༔
Wearing the threefold head garland,༔
His head is adorned with five dry skulls,༔
Each with jeweled points.༔

Ornamented with wreaths of five classes of snakes,༔
He is smeared with blood, fat, and ashes ༔
And wears the six bone ornaments and so forth;༔
Thus, the tenfold glorious attire is complete on his body.༔
His four legs are poised in the dancing posture.༔

His upper garments are made from elephant and human skins, and his skirt is made from a tiger skin. He has three belts of decapitated heads wrapped around his torso like a bandolier. One is made of fresh heads, one of old rotting heads, and the other is made of skulls.

Together with the other ornaments, he wears the ten glorious ornaments of a heruka. These are made from the various things he acquired after subjugating Rudra. There are variations to this list, such as the eightfold charnel ground attire, to which are added the wings and the mass of fire, but I recommend following Karmey Khenpo's version.

He is standing with one leg stretched out slightly in front of the other. This is somewhat like a standing version of the seated playful royal posture.

On his lap is the consort of union,༔
The dark blue, blazing Diptachakra.༔
Her right hand, with a blue lotus, embraces the lord,༔
And her left proffers a skull cup of blood.༔
She is endowed with the expressions of a fully bloomed maiden.༔
She wears the five mudra ornaments.༔

> Her left leg, bent, embraces the waist of the lord,༔
> And with her right leg extended, they are joined in great bliss.༔

His consort, Diptachakra, is on his lap. She is dark blue and blazes. Her right hand embraces him while holding a blue lotus. In some versions, she is holding a khatvanga instead. The *Zabdun Phurba* doesn't mention it in the visualization, but the praises say she is holding one. *She is endowed with expressions of a fully bloomed maiden.* In other words, she has full breasts and a fully developed secret place. She is almost bare except for the five mudra ornaments, which are five different types of bone jewelry. Her bent left leg embraces Vajrakilaya around the waist. She stands with the right leg extended, and they are joined in great bliss. It isn't mentioned here explicitly, but actually she also has a leopard skin skirt.

> At the top of his head are OM HUNG TRAM HRIH AH,༔
> Possessing the nature of the five wisdoms.༔
> The three places, marked with OM AH HUNG,༔
> Are blessed as body, speech, and mind.༔

At the top of his head are the syllables OM HUNG TRAM HRIH AH, which are inside small skulls. Potentially complicating the visualization, a jewel point is on the top of his head and something with the wrathful deity is below that, which refers to his possessing the nature of the five wisdoms, symbolized by the lines, *His head is adorned with five dry skulls, Each with jeweled points.*༔

He is also marked in his three places with the syllables for body, speech, and mind: OM AH HUNG. This means you can visualize the three forms of deities in a more elaborate style, the three emblems in a medium-level visualization, and the three syllables in a condensed version. In this way, he is blessed with body, speech, and mind.

> From the letter HUNG at the secret place of the lord,༔
> A vajra appears, marked with HUNG in its center.༔
> From the letter BAM in the secret space of the consort,༔
> A sun appears, marked with ANG in her lotus.༔
> They sport in the space of great bliss.༔

In the center of the male figure's secret place is the syllable HUNG. The female deity has the BAM syllable. At the tip, meaning inside, is the AM

(ANG) syllable. According to Karmey Khenpo, the HUNG and the AM are touching. In this way, *They sport in the space of great bliss.*༔

> His body hairs are half-vajras,༔
> And he wears an armor of crossed-vajras.༔
> Kilaya tsa-tsas shoot out like stars.༔

Every single hair on Vajrakilaya's body is a half-vajra, and each of these also sends out sparks in all directions, just like shooting stars. Most wrathful deities have armor that's interwoven and sends out tiny Vajrakilaya figures, like shooting stars.

> In his heart center, amidst a dome of light,༔
> Upon a seat of lotus, sun, and moon,༔
> Is the wisdom-being, Vajrasattva.༔
> White and luminous, holding a vajra and bell,༔
> He embraces Atopa, who is holding a knife and skull.༔
>
> He is seated cross-legged, and within his life-sphere,༔
> Upon a jewel octagon, sun, and moon,༔
> Is a blue vajra with a deep blue HUNG,༔
> Resting upon a sun in its center,༔
> Around which are the self-resounding nine syllables.༔
> Immense light rays radiate from them,༔
> Making pleasing offerings to the body, speech, and mind༔
> Of all the victorious ones of the ten directions.༔

Up to this point, we've been talking about the development stage of the body aspect. Now we come to what is inside his heart center; it's like a dome of blue light. In Tibet, we didn't have any blue tents, but they are quite common here in the West. This one has eight sides, so it's an octahedron. Inside of this is a lotus flower with sun and moon discs upon it. On this sits Vajrakilaya's wisdom-being, Vajrasattva. Luminous and white, he holds a vajra and bell and embraces Atopa, who holds a knife and skull. This is the typical depiction of Vajrasattva in union with his consort. Vajrasattva is sitting cross-legged; his consort is not sitting in full cross-legged position.

Within Vajrasattva's life-sphere (inside his heart center) is a jewel octagon, which has a tip on the top and bottom and eight facets. Inside of that are sun and moon discs, on which a blue five-pronged vajra rests. In the center of the vajra is a sun disc, on which stands a deep blue HUNG. This is surrounded by the syllables of the mantra OM BENZA KILI KILAYA HUNG PHAT, each resounding on its own (not the long mantra). The vajra is the same size as the first segment of your thumb, about one inch. The sun disc is the size of a pea split in half. The HUNG letter on top of the half split-pea sun disc is the same size as a grain of barley. The nine syllables OM BENZA KILI KILAYA HUNG PHAT are as fine as if they were written with a single hair. Each syllable resounds with its individual sound. The immeasurable light rays emitted by the syllables shine in all directions, making offerings that are pleasing to the body, speech, and mind of all the buddhas in the ten directions.

> All the blessings of the body, speech, and mind ༔
> Are invited as white OM, red AH, and blue HUNG,༔
> In an immeasurable amount.༔
> As they dissolve into my three places,༔
> I obtain the empowerments, blessings, and siddhis.༔

All the blessings of the buddhas' body, speech, and mind come back in innumerable forms of OM, AH, and HUNG in the three colors. They dissolve into your three places of heart, throat, and forehead. We imagine that they dissolve into the white OM, red AH, and blue HUNG at our three places. In this way we absorb and are blessed with all the empowerments, blessings, and siddhis of the buddhas' body, speech, and mind.

> The sugatas and gurus are pleased;༔
> Breaches with dharma brothers and sisters are mended;༔
> Grudges of dakinis and dharmapalas are cleared;༔
> All the drekpas are brought to action;༔
> Maras and samaya-breakers are reduced to dust;༔
> And all the obscurations of beings' three gates are purified.༔

Again the light radiates out, making offerings to all the sugatas and masters. Again rays of light stream out, touching all your Dharma brothers and sisters and purifying their broken samaya vows. Your Dharma brothers and sisters are those with whom you have received empowerments, explanations of tantras, and so forth. This mends any breaches of samaya with them. Again rays of light stream out, clearing any debts or grudges with the dakinis and Dharma protectors. This means any samaya breaches that are held by the dakinis and Dharma protectors are cleared. Again rays of light stream out, making the eight classes of drekpas get into line and carry out the activities. Again rays of light radiate out, eliminating all the mara demons and samaya violators. In other words, when the light rays touch the maras and samaya violators, they scatter and disappear, just like blowing on a heap of dust. By radiating to all the sentient beings in the three realms of samsara, the rays purify and totally remove their obscurations, negative karma, and deluded way of perceiving.

> All sights are the form of deities,ༀ
> All sounds are the sound of mantra,ༀ
> And thoughts are visualized as the display of wisdom.ༀ

> *The essence of your mind should be regarded*ༀ
> *As Vajrakumara himself.*ༀ

> OM VAJRA KILI KILAYA SARVA BIGHANEN BAM HUNG PHATༀ

Thus recite.

You chant the eighteen-syllable mantra written here. Sometimes three mantras are mentioned: a nine-syllable mantra for approach; the above eighteen syllables for accomplishment; and another, called the *Marayama,* for enacting activities. There is also another in which the approach, accomplishment, and activities are all combined into one. To have all of them complete is quite difficult, in that it is difficult to find a terma text that has all the mantras together in one. I'm not sure why this is. Perhaps some instructions are kept secret for some reason. In any case, it is rare to find all of them in one text. Even the extensive *Zabdun Phurba, The Kilaya of the Sevenfold Profundity,* does not have an in-depth visualization of the simple recitation practice, despite being quite detailed when it comes to the lower activities.

For the meaning of the eighteen-syllable mantra, you should rely on Karmey Khenpo's explanation. Whatever the case, this was the guidance in the speech aspect of recitation. Most importantly, you should regard the essence of your mind as Vajrakumara himself. That is the meditation state itself, though I do not really know anything about it and so I am not going to try to explain.

Offer torma in the session breaks.༔
Visualize the glorious torma༔
To be the deity and receive the empowerments.༔
Begin by offering the flower.༔

Offering the flower actually means performing a mandala offering. Later in the text, there is a torma offering. According to the Tersar, after having done the mantra recitation in daily practice, you immediately make the torma offering and then proceed to the self-initiation. Self-initiation is only done in retreat or similar circumstances, not otherwise.

Guru Glorious Heruka,༔
Vajrakumara, lord and consort,༔
Please bestow the blessings upon me༔
And grant the supreme empowerment of body, speech, and mind.༔

Thus supplicate and visualize yourself as the deity.༔

From the three places of the deity, the torma,༔
Three rays of white, red, and blue light stream out.༔
As they dissolve into my three places,༔
All the obscurations of the three gates are purified,༔
And the empowerments of body, speech, and mind are obtained.༔

The torma is made in a particular shape, according to the tradition. But when relating to the torma, you should regard it as Vajrakilaya with consort, surrounded by the ten wrathful ones with their consorts, the twenty tratap and the four gatekeepers and the twenty-one supreme sons, all in completeness. The torma is regarded as the four notions. In this case, it is the notion of being the deity. Visualize that at the three places of the torma, which represents the deities, rays of white, red, and blue light radiate. When the light dissolves into your three places, *All the obscurations of the three gates are purified*. This refers to your body, speech, and mind and to obtaining the empowerments of body, speech, and mind.

According to the empowerment explanation, when receiving the white rays of light, you imagine that Vajrakilaya emits countless small bodily forms of the wrathful deities, which enter into your own forehead (you being in the form of Vajrakilaya as well), purifying all obscurations and negative karma committed with bodily actions in the past. By doing so, you receive the blessings and empowerments and siddhis of Vajrakilaya's body. When receiving the red light from Vajrakilaya through the throat center, again countless tiny forms of Vajrakilaya enter your body, purifying the negative karmic actions committed with your voice and cleansing all the obscurations of your voice, such as muteness, stuttering, hesitant speech, and feeble voice. At the same time, you receive the siddhi for Vajrakilaya's speech. Receiving the blue ray of light from Vajrakilaya's mind into your own heart center purifies all negative karma produced on a mental level throughout countless lifetimes until now, all obscurations, and so forth—as well as fainting, insanity, and other mental disorders. Thus, you obtain the siddhi of Vajrakilaya's mind.

Then you imagine that all of the deities represented by the torma—Vajrakilaya and all the surrounding deities—dissolve down into you, as Vajrakilaya, through the crown of your head. When conferring the empowerment of the self-initiation, there is a chant in which you call upon each master of the lineage for his blessings, accomplishments, and so forth. All of them in totality become indivisible from your own stream of being.

The chant for this is as follows:

HUNG༔
The torma vessel is the blazing space of the dark blue triangle.༔
The torma essence is the great Glorious Heruka.༔
Bhagavan Vajrakumara, king of the wrathful,༔
With supreme consort, Tara Diptachakra,༔
Mara tamers, ten dancing wrathful ones and consorts,༔
Supreme sons and all gatekeepers and protectors,༔

Open the gate of your powerful samaya now,༔
And bestow upon my body the majestic, supreme body empowerment.༔
Clear away physical sickness, negative forces, evil deeds, and obscurations.༔
Make me accomplished in the rainbow body vajra form.༔

Bestow upon my speech the supreme empowerment of Brahma's voice.༔
Clear away speech obscurations, stuttering, and muteness.༔
Please grant the siddhi of the power of wrathful mantras.༔

Bestow upon my mind the supreme mind empowerment of simplicity.ꔷ
Pacify mental obscurations, insanity, strokes, and illness,ꔷ

And grant the siddhi of the mind of great bliss.ꔷ
Moreover, avert sorcery and evil spells,ꔷ
Annihilate viciousness and ill-will,ꔷ
And increase life, merit, splendor, and wealth.ꔷ

*At the end of the mantra, attach this:*ꔷ

Kaya vaka chitta sarva siddhi phala abhikhentsa hohꔷ

*Thus receive the empowerment.*ꔷ

Now you come to the torma offering. In the first section, you consecrate the torma by turning it into nectar.

*For the torma offering, say:*ꔷ

Ram yam kham burns, scatters, and washes away the torma.ꔷ
From the state of emptiness, upon wind, fire, and a skull-stand,ꔷ
A vast and extensive skull cup manifests from bhrum.ꔷ
Inside it, the five meats appear from go ku da ha na,ꔷ

And the five nectars flow from bi mu ma ra shu.ꔷ
The lid is a sun and moon marked with a vajra.ꔷ
By the joining of fire and wind, the nectar melts and boils.ꔷ
The steam gathers all the essences of samsara and nirvana.ꔷ

They become the forms of the five families of lords and consorts, united in great bliss.ꔷ
Together with the lid, they melt into bodhichitta.ꔷ
Samaya and wisdom mingle indivisibly as nectar.ꔷ
An offering cloud of desirable objects fills the sky.ꔷ
Om ah hung hohꔷ

*Raising the right hand and pointing the left,*ꔷ
*Consecrate with the mudra of joined thumb and finger.*ꔷ

Here, while reciting RAM YAM KHAM, visualize that the vajra flames, wind, and torrent purify the torma by burning, scattering, and washing it away. Then, visualize that from the state of emptiness, a skull vessel resting on a stand appears. The skull cup is as vast as space, and beneath it are wind and fire. Inside of it, the five meats appear from the five syllables GO KU DA HA NA and the five nectars arise from BI MU MA RA SHU. These fill the skull cup, on top of which is a lid made of a sun and moon with a vajra handle. The wind fans the flames, heating the contents of the skull cup until they begin to boil and steam rises up. This steam gathers and summons all the essential nectars from all samsaric and nirvanic states, which then become the five male and five female buddhas, who are joined in union. The bodhichitta streams that emerge from the five male and female buddhas also dissolve into the big melting pot. At the end, in the state of great bliss, they dissolve into the nectar of bodhichitta together with the lid made of sun, moon, and vajra. In this way, the samaya being and the wisdom being are indivisibly mingled into nectar, which emits infinite cloudbanks of desirable objects and sense pleasures that fill the sky. While visualizing this, chant om ah hung hoh three times with a particular mudra and then perform the garuda mudra, according to the Chokling tradition. *Raising* and *pointing* actually refer to the same gesture that you do with both hands. Mindrolling style is immediately one mudra (garuda).

This is like preparing a meal before throwing a party. Now that the torma offering is ready, you invite the guests to join you.

HUNG ༔
From the palace of dharmadhatu, ༔
Bhagavan Vajrakumara, ༔
With your retinue of protectors and pledge-holders, ༔
Please bestow the empowerments and siddhis, ༔

In order that I may accomplish the Kilaya of existence. ༔
Wrathful Wisdom, please come. ༔
Wrathful Wisdom, having now arrived, ༔
Manifest the signs and marks ༔
And bestow the accomplishment of Kilaya. ༔
VAJRA SAMA DZAH ༔

This is quite easy to understand. From yourself as the great Glorious Vajrakilaya, rays of light stream into all directions, as you request

Vajrakilaya to manifest from the palace of dharmadhatu, together with his retinue of protectors and pledge-holders, who are mainly the twelve types that carry out the activities of Vajrakilaya. You ask them to approach and bestow empowerments and siddhis. You perform another mudra, and if you have musical instruments, you should play them now.

At this point, you should imagine that all the guests of the seventy-five-fold mandala of Vajrakilaya are present in the sky before you.

> Hung ༔
> This sacred and supreme offering ༔
> Radiates the light rays of the five wisdoms, ༔
> Fully adorned with the five desirable objects. ༔
> As your heart-samaya, accept these as you please. ༔

> Om shri vajra kumara dharma pala saparivara ༔
> Pushpe dhupe aloke gandhe naividya shabda praticchaye svaha ༔
> Maha pancha amrita kharam khahi ༔
> Maha rakta kharam khahi ༔
> Om vajra kili kilaya saparivara idam baling grihanantu ༔
> Mama sarva siddhi mem prayaccha ༔
> Om vajra kili kilaya dharma pala saparivara ༔
> Idam balingta kha kha khahi khahi ༔

These are the words for the offerings. This mantra incorporates the traditional offerings—from flowers to music in the second line—and then has one line each for amrita, rakta, and the main torma offering. We imagine that all the deities enjoy the torma nectar we have consecrated. As a ray of light extends from their tongues to the nectar, they absorb this essential liquid just like we drink soda (with a straw). At the same time, you perform the mudra and snap your fingers, first for the wisdom beings and then for the surrounding retinue.

Kha kha khahi khahi means "please have, please have."

After they have received the torma offering, you offer praise:

> Hung ༔
> Skillfully acting for the sake of beings, ༔
> Through love and compassion you tame whoever needs help ༔
> And perfect the activities of the buddhas. ༔

To all Kilaya Activity deities, I prostrate and offer praise.༔

Having offered the torma and uttered praise, you call upon the guests, in this case asking them to carry out specific activities.

Hung༔
From the uncontrived space of suchness beyond constructs,༔
Manifests the blazing form of spontaneously present great bliss,༔
Bhagavan great Glorious Vajrakumara,༔
With the supreme consort, Tara Diptachakra.༔
All knowledge-holders of Vajrakilaya,༔
The ten wrathful ones, lords and consorts, hosts of devourers and slayers,༔
Twenty-one supreme sons, four female wrathful gatekeepers,༔
Hosts of shvanas, sovereigns, bhumipatis, and great beings,༔
Together with the ocean of Kilaya protectors and pledge-holders,༔

This verse comprises those to whom your request is directed. You call them by name. Next you make your request:

Manifest here in form, from invisible space.༔
Accept the samaya substances of outer, inner, and secret offerings,༔
And the offerings of amrita, rakta, and torma.༔
For all of us, masters and disciples, patrons and recipients, together with our retinues,༔
Protect our three gates as well as our riches;༔
Bestow the siddhis of body, speech, and mind;༔
Pacify all illnesses, negative forces, and obstacles;༔
Increase our life spans, merit, glory, and riches;༔
Magnetize the three realms and the three existences;༔
Perform the activity of reducing animosity and obstructing forces to dust.༔
Turn away all black magic and evil spells,༔
And make auspicious goodness manifest.༔

Thus entreat.༔

First you ask them to receive the offerings and then you request their activities. *All of us, masters and disciples, patrons and recipients,* means all your benefactors and so forth together with their followers and retinues. Protect our three gates refers to body, speech, and mind as well as our riches and belongings. The remaining list of petitions includes all four types of activities.

Dissolve the wisdom beings into yourself. ༔
Let the loka beings leave to their own places. ༔

After this, you dissolve the wisdom beings, who are present in the sky before you, into yourself and ask their retinue of mundane divinities to return to their own places.

Next, the verses state the results of doing this practice:

Through this, all obstacles will be pacified ༔
And all wishes will be fulfilled. ༔
Therefore, exert yourself in this. ༔
This profound oral instruction ༔
Is concealed for the sake of future times. ༔
May it meet with the person of right karma. ༔

Having such virtues, therefore exert yourself in this practice.

This profound oral instruction ༔ *is concealed for the sake of future disciples.* ༔ Guru Padmasambhava said this. *The person of right karma* refers to the tertön, in this case Chokgyur Lingpa.

Samaya gya gya ༔

When you do this in the solka style of practice, first do the supplication to the lineage masters written by Wangchuk Dorje. Next do the main sadhana, beginning with refuge and bodhichitta and then the visualization. For the recitation, you chant the mantra one hundred times. Then skip the self-initiation and go straight to the torma offering, after which you do the requests. If you have petitions for the Dharma protectors, you do them next.

According to Tulku Urgyen's tradition, when you do extensive petitions to the Dharma protectors, you use the *Sungma Chitor*. We (Neten Gon) use the *Damchen Chitor.* These texts have their own offerings and praises and dedication at the end. But if you just do the Lama Yidam and

Tseringma chants to the Dharma protectors, then you should conclude using what is found at the end of the feast text, which includes the offerings and praises, dissolution and re-emergence, dedication, and verses of auspiciousness, and so forth. This is not found in the *Sangtik Phurba* itself, but in another text entitled the *Lungluk Phurba.* Jamgön Kongtrül inserted it here, so that is the tradition.

If you do the *Sungma Chitor,* it has its own conclusion at the end, including the verse of auspiciousness. So you don't need to bring it in from elsewhere.

Question & Answers

Student: How do we organize the feast?

OT Rinpoche: It is okay to combine the feast text with the terma root text. Jamgön Kongtrül himself said so. There is also an arrangement for this Phurba text put together by Wangchuk Dorje. You can choose either one to use with the feast text. I myself prefer Wangchuk Dorje's when performing the feast. However, when not performing the tsok, just use the terma root text itself. When making a feast offering, you need the various offerings, such as the gektor and different things that can be done all together in Wangchuk Dorje's text. If you use the terma root text itself, then you don't have to prepare a torma; you can use a biscuit or something like that. In the monastery, as part of the daily rituals, the monks use the terma root text at the time of enjoining the protectors to do their activity.

When Chokgyur Lingpa was alive, at first he would just use the *Kunchok Chidu* terma as the framework for the offerings to the Dharma protector. But on the second of his four trips to the Derge area, he revealed this terma up at Tsadra Rinchen Drak, and from then on he used it instead. He asked Jamyang Khyentse how to do the solka for the Dharma protectors and he was told to use the Mindrolling style of the *Damchen Chitor,* while adding in some of the protectors for the Tersar. Chokgyur Lingpa then asked Jamgön Kongtrül to write something for that. So there is the Six-Armed Mahakala, *Lekye Shinje, Tseringma, Lutsen Barwa Pundon,* the Seven Brothers, and *Shona*. Altogether, they comprise the *Damchen Chitor,* the General Torma for the Vow-Holders, written by Jamgön Kongtrül. The Mindrolling style only contains nine. This is how *Damchen Chitor* was created. Some years after Chokgyur Lingpa passed away, Karmey Khenpo wrote the *Sungma Chitor.* He first wrote an extensive one called the *Ngodrub Gyatso,* Ocean of Siddhi, which combines all the protectors of the Chokling Tersar. Then I heard he got a scolding from Jamgön Kongtrül, who thought some of the protectors were a bit too tough to just be passed around like that, so it was inappropriate. So he made an abbreviated form, which is known as the *Sungma Chitor*, the General Torma for the Guardians. Mindrolling style has both an extensive and an abbreviated version as well, the abbreviated being the *Damchen Chitor*. So for the Chokling tradition, we have the extensive Ocean of Siddhi and the abbreviated General Torma for the Protectors. This is how the tradition slowly took form.

In the beginning, Chokgyur Lingpa was just by himself. But when he reached the age of twenty-eight or twenty-nine, his fame spread. Even before that, when he went up to see Jamgön Kongtrül for the first time at Tsadra Rinchen Drak, he was known as Kyater; he dressed as a simple monk and was alone. He did, however, already have a good reputation for doing pujas that were beneficial. Nonetheless, the word spread that when inviting Kyater to perform a puja at one's house, it wasn't necessary to send a horse, as people would have done when inviting more celebrated lamas. So, in his early days, Chokgyur Lingpa would just walk.

From the age of twenty-eight until he died in his forties, his fame continued to spread. At the time of his death, he had large monasteries with congregations of monks and so forth.

At the beginning, he was a Drukpa Kagyü monk, and his main practice was *Konchok Chidu*. After discovering the *Sangtik Phurba*, he used it, because before making an offering to the Dharma protectors, you need to do a yidam practice. Since then, the tradition for using the *Sangtik Phurba* for that has been unbroken.

When Chokgyur Lingpa performed his first drubchen, there were only twelve participants, including himself and some lamas and monks. During his short life, he performed more than fifty drubchens. If you include the shorter *drubchö* and other extensive rituals, he probably performed more than one hundred. He didn't have only one monastery either but three: Kela, Neten, and Karma Gon. Now there are more than one hundred associated monasteries, but not in the past.

The concluding verses here, which Tulku Urgyen Rinpoche suggested, come from the end of the feast offering. But before that, just after finishing the torma offering and making the request, you go back and repeat the offering and praises once more. Then you chant the end of the feast offering. But if you do extensive chants to the Dharma protectors, such as the General Torma Offering to the Protectors, then you don't need to chant those concluding verses, for they are included. However, if you are doing the abbreviated chants to the Dharma protectors, then you must include these concluding verses.

Student: When chanting the lines at the beginning for the three samadhis, should we visualize a blue sphere becoming the letter hung?

OT Rinpoche: Actually, the hung is the blue sphere, as it glows with light in the shape of a sphere. In his commentary, Karmey Khenpo gives a detailed explanation of the meaning of the color and so forth. He shows off his erudition and scholarship. I wondered why he did that, but it likely came from his habit of standing up and giving a lecture to a large congregation of monks, when it was necessary to show off a bit. It's often like that; when something is a bit difficult to understand, then a learned person will stir up a lot of quotations from various sources, in order to clarify certain points. If it were easy to understand, you couldn't take people for a ride like that. Unless you say something to clarify those three sentences at the beginning, *Vajra-wrath* . . . , they are not so easy to understand. If it had a form with face and arms, then it would be more tangible and easier to understand. Later, in Tibet, I saw another version of this text by Karmey Khenpo, in which he hadn't added this stuff. So there are different handwritten notes in existence.

At the end of the year, at Ka-Nying Shedrub Ling monastery, they perform the Gutor ceremonies, where they throw big tormas as a sort of exorcism. This is done twice, first as Dorje Phurba and then as Dorje Shonnu. However, in Tibet, I once found a small note by Chokgyur Lingpa, which stated that Dorje Phurba doesn't need to throw anything. Since Shonnu is already his wrathful manifestation, the deity himself doesn't need to carry anything out personally, which is quite an interesting concept. It is quite appropriate, but nobody seems to follow this advice, so there is no tradition to do it that way.

Student: What color is the jewel octagon?

OT Rinpoche: The jewel octagon is a different color than the deep blue dome of light. The jewel is translated as a lapis, but I am not sure that is actually the case. It is said that it has a slightly greenish hue to it. Whatever the case, the samadhi being is very tiny, and in the pith instructions in the Kilaya tradition, the samadhi being is very vital. In the tradition based on the *Zabdun Phurba,* which is more detailed, it states that outside the octagon is another tiny, tiny deity, who is Hayagriva standing on a god; he is like a body guard.

Student: Does the dome of light have eight sides like the eight-sided jewel?

OT Rinpoche: The dome definitely has eight sides as well. Back in Tibet where I grew up, the tents had lots of different tethers extending in all directions, but this kind of tent or dome doesn't have any ropes; it stands up by itself. In those days, if anybody described a tent without ropes, nobody would understand what they were talking about or be able to picture it in their minds.

Commentary on *Essence of the Two Accumulations*

Personally, I am very fond of this Tara cycle, *Zabtik Drolchok.* Among the seven lines of transmission that Chokgyur Lingpa was endowed with, this one comes through mind treasure (*gong ter*). This Tara practice includes outer, inner, secret, and innermost sadhanas, and it is connected to a specific empowerment, known as a "permission blessing" or "entrustment," written by Jamgön Kongtrül, called *The Mandala Ritual, The Essence of the Two Accumulations.* This Tara sadhana is very widespread and is practiced by almost all the Nyingma traditions. Most Sakyas and Kagyüs also practice it, although they do not know who wrote it, as the colophon is not included with the text. The colophon did not come until after the inner sadhana, which followed this outer one, so you might say its "tail" accidentally got cut off.

This terma is endowed with incredible blessings. The present Dzongsar Khyentse told me that he considers the *Zabtik Tara* practice as the most profound of all Chokgyur Lingpa's termas. In Bhutan, he personally sponsors it to be done annually, one hundred thousand times.

The text opens with *NAMO guru Arya Tareye,* which means, "Homage to the guru, Jetsün Noble Tara."

> Honoring Tara, mother to the guides
> And their offspring of the three times,
> Who has wonderful resolve and activity,
> Here I shall explain the practice according to Kriya and Charya.

The guides are the buddhas of the three times and their offspring are the bodhisattvas. Tara's tenacity is immense. Buddha Shakyamuni vowed to awaken to enlightenment in the age when people's life span had degenerated to one hundred years. His resolve is considered superior to that of other buddhas. Buddha Shakyamuni himself, when teaching a sutra and a tantra on Tara, said that among all the other buddhas, Manjushri and Tara are the two who have exceedingly great resolve. Tara is like an emanation of the mother of all the buddhas of the three times. She carries out all their activities, dispelling the obstacles created through the eight or sixteen types of fear. Most significantly, she vowed to emanate in female form until all of samsara is emptied. When anyone supplicates Tara, her response is swift. The activities resulting from her aspiration are extraordinary, and there is ample evidence of this, right up to the present day.

Both Buddhists and non-Buddhists alike honor the divinity Jetsün Tara. There are quite a few traditions for her sadhana practice, not only in the sutras but also in the tantras, in which each of the four levels of tantra, from Kriya to Anuttara, has its own distinct way of practicing Tara. Here, Jamgön Kongtrül states that he will explain this in accordance with the Kriya and Charya tantras:

> Since this Profound Essence is a condensation of every quintessential profundity, it is not required to resort to much elaboration. Nevertheless, there are two degrees of detail: one slightly elaborate and the other as a daily practice.
>
> For the first, in front of a painting or statue of Jetsün Tara, or whatever image of the Three Jewels you can acquire, on a clean surface, arrange the two waters, the general offerings, the round white torma, cleansing water, the offering mandala, grain for tossing, and other articles.

Some people say that, together with the seven general offerings, four mandala plates are also required, each with twenty-one heaps, but I personally do not find this necessary. It was probably necessary for some more elaborate Tara sadhanas, but it is not required here. It also does not mean that you meditate on the twenty-one Taras in four different places. Of course, you can put a mandala plate on the shrine, but the mandala is composed of what you have to offer. If you have a mandala plate on hand, it is good to use it, but if you do not it is also fine.

If you can, keep the conduct of bathing and cleanliness. If unable, at least perform the practice before you have consumed any meat or alcohol, such as in the morning.

If possible, it is good to maintain the behavior regarding cleanliness, as recommended by Kriya yoga. In the old days, these would have been very difficult for Tibetans to apply, but these days, especially in the West, it is much easier. Everyone washes their hands and face at least once a day. However, if you cannot maintain this, then you must at least do the practice before consuming any meat or alcohol. Most probably, this means doing it in the morning. As many people eat eggs for breakfast, it is important to note that they are considered to be meat as well and so are prohibited. Dilgo Khyentse Rinpoche said that this particular version is according to Kriya yoga; however, the basic intent is according to Anuttara yoga. Therefore, if you are completely unable to maintain these rules, unavoidably, then it is fine. This means that eating eggs or meat or even having a glass of beer is no excuse for not doing the practice.

The above are the recommended guidelines providing the best conditions for practice. What is necessary, however, is having stable renunciation of samsara, cultivating the attitude of bodhichitta, and taking refuge. If you do not already have the attitude of renunciation and bodhichitta, form them in your mind and assume them now.

With the attitude of bodhichitta and renunciation of samsara, for refuge and the resolve, imagine that:

In the sky before me, Noble Tara is present in person.

In the next verse, the first two lines are for refuge and the last two are for bodhichitta.

Namo
In the Noble Lady, embodiment of all Precious Ones,
I and all beings take refuge.
I form the resolve, aspiring to enlightenment,
And I will enter the profound path.

Next, gather the two accumulations by reciting the Seven Branches.

To gather the accumulations, say:

> To the Noble Jetsün Tara
> And to all the conquerors and their offspring,
> Who reside in the ten directions and three times,
> Sincerely and delightedly, I pay homage.
>
> With flowers and incense, lamps and perfume,
> With food, music, and the like,
> Materially present and mentally created, I make offerings;
> May they be accepted by the Noble Lady's assemblage.
>
> From beginningless time until today,
> For the ten non-virtues and the five without interval,
> I apologize for each and every evil deed committed,
> While influenced by disturbed states of mind.
>
> I rejoice in all the merit and goodness
> Created throughout the three times
> By the shravakas, pratyekabuddhas, and bodhisattvas,
> By ordinary beings, and all others.
>
> In accordance with the capabilities
> And individual aspirations of sentient beings,
> I ask you to turn the wheel of dharma
> Of the general, greater, and lesser vehicles.
>
> Until samsara has been emptied,
> Do not pass into nirvana, but out of compassion,
> Please consider every being,
> Sinking into the ocean of suffering.
>
> May whatever merit I have gathered
> Become a cause for enlightenment,
> And may I, in the near future,
> Be a splendid guide for sentient beings.

These verses come from the sutra. While reciting them, contemplate the meaning of each aspect, from homage down to the dedication of merit.

Having uttered this, next consecrate the offerings:

> Om vajra amrita kundali hana hana hung phat
> Om svabhava shuddha sarva dharma svabhava shuddho ham

The first mantra is for purifying the belief that phenomena are solid and concrete, and the second is for realizing the empty nature of everything.

Next you imagine your environment is a pure land.

> Here, in the Realm of the Lotus Array,
> With perfect shapes and boundless decorations,
> There are offerings surpassing thought,
> Divine articles created from samadhi.

The Realm of the Lotus Array is another name for the Turquoise Petaled Buddhafield, which is the pure land permeated with the compassionate capacity of Arya Tara. You should imagine that it surpasses all imagination. As a matter of fact, all the scenery, adornments, and so forth are not human-made nor are they materially manifest anywhere. They are all conjured forth through samadhi. This goes for the offerings as well, which you have set up on the shrine. Imagine that they multiply into an inconceivable number.

> Om benza argham ah hung
> Om benza padyam ah hung
> Om benza pushpe ah hung
> Om benza dhupe ah hung
> Om benza aloke ah hung
> Om benza gendhe ah hung
> Om benza naividya ah hung
> Om benza shapda ah hung

> Om vajra argham ah hung, Om vajra padyam ah hung, Om vajra pushpe ah hung, Om vajra dhupe ah hung, Om vajra aloke ah hung, Om vajra gendhe ah hung, Om vajra naividya ah hung, Om vajra shapda ah hung, Om vajra sapharana kham

These are the mantras for each of the offerings, while the following mantra makes the offering inexhaustible:

Om benza sapa rana kham

Following that, begin with honoring and making offerings to the Precious Ones in general. The masters as well as conquerors and their offspring of the ten directions and four times are all in the sky before you, benza samadza.

The ten directions are the four cardinal ones, the four intermediate ones, and the spaces above and below. According to the *Gyutrül* or *Mayajala* intent, the four times are the past, present, and future as well as the inconceivable time. According to the lower vehicles, first you make the request and then you make the actual invitation, so now comes the invitation:

Protectors of all sentient beings without exception,
Deity who defeats the endless hordes of maras,
Since you are fully omniscient,
Blessed One and your retinue, please approach this place.
Padma kamalaye satvam

Padma kamalaye satvam is the request for them to remain; it means, please remain seated on these lotus thrones. After having asked them to approach and remain, you present them with the Seven Branch offering, which comes from the *Songchen Mönlam, The Aspiration for Noble Conduct.*

However many sugatas, the lions of men, there are
In the worlds of the ten directions and the three times,
To all of them without a single exception,
I pay homage with delighted body, speech, and mind.

Through the power of this aspiration for excellent conduct,
I vividly visualize all the jinas in my mind,
And bowing with as many bodies as there are atoms in the world,
I fully prostrate to all the victorious ones.

On each particle are seated as many buddhas
As there are particles, each amidst their offspring;

I imagine all of dharmadhatu, without remainder,
As being completely filled with jinas.

As endless oceans of veneration to them all,
With infinite sounds in an oceanic range of melodies,
I fully express all of the victors' virtues
And praise all of the sugatas.

With beautiful flowers and glorious garlands,
Cymbals and the most refined perfumes,
The best lamps and exquisite incense,
I make offerings to all the victorious ones.

With the best garments and delightful fragrance,
A heap of massage powder equal to Mount Sumeru,
The finest of all noble and exquisite arrangements,
I make offerings to all the victorious ones.

I imagine that all these unexcelled and extensive offerings
Are for all the victorious ones.
By the power of faith in this excellent conduct,
I pay homage and make offerings to all the jinas.

Whatever misdeeds, caused by the power of desire, anger, and delusion,
That I have committed
With my body, speech, and mind,
I apologize for each and every one of them.

In all the jinas and their buddha offspring in the ten directions,
In all the pratyekabuddhas and those at the levels of learning and non-learning,
And in the merit of each sentient being,
In all of these, I fully rejoice.

All these lamps illuminating the worlds in the ten directions
Gradually attained enlightenment, the unexcelled buddhahood.
I beseech all of these protectors
To turn the wheel of the unexcelled teachings.

To those who intend to display passing beyond sorrow
For the benefit and happiness of all beings,
With joined palms, I make the request
That you remain for as many aeons as there are atoms in the world.
By prostrating, making offerings, apologizing,
Rejoicing, beseeching, and petitioning,
I dedicate what little virtue I have accumulated
Toward enlightenment.

To get an explanation of these verses, you should ask someone who has studied these in class. There is an excellent commentary on the *Songchen Mönlam* by Minling Lochen. You can also find this aspiration in Shantideva's *Way of the Bodhisattva*. Of all the Buddhist chants, this one is perhaps the most elegant. For now, just remember that these verses cover the Seven Branches.

Having completed the general Seven Branches for gathering the accumulations, you now make the specific offering of the mandala:

OM AH HUNG ༔
I and all the infinite beings ༔
Offer our bodies, luxuries, and all our virtue,༔
The four continents, Mount Sumeru, the sun and moon,༔
As well as the inconceivable riches of gods and men.༔
This vast offering cloud of Samantabhadra,༔
Unceasingly displayed,༔
I offer continuously and with veneration ༔
To the rare and sublime Three Jewels and Three Roots,༔
As well as to the ocean of dharma protectors and wealth gods.༔
With the accumulation of merit totally perfected,༔
May the illumination of wisdom spread.༔
OM GURU DHEVA DAKINI SARVA RATNA MANDALA PUJA MEGHA AH HUNG ༔

With that, present the mandala offering.

This is the long version of the mandala offering, as it is found in the ngöndro for *Tukdrub Barchey Künsel*. After making the mandala offering, you ask for what you want, saying the following:

NAMO༔
Buddha, Dharma, and Sangha,༔
Guru, Yidam, and Dakini,༔
Dharma guardians, wealth gods, and treasure lords,༔
From the single identity of wisdom,༔
The unobstructed nature can appear as anything at all,༔
With the capacity for wondrous enlightened activities,༔
Sources of refuge and protectors of all beings.༔

To all you sovereigns of wisdom and compassion,༔
I pay homage and take heartfelt refuge in you.༔
I present my body and wealth as offerings.༔
With your compassion, please always protect༔
Me and the countless other sentient beings.༔
Pacify illness and evil influences.༔
Increase our life span and merits.༔
Grant your blessings that everything we wish for༔
Be accomplished in harmony with the dharma.༔

With that, request the desired aims.

This is an extract from the *Tukdrub's Sheldam Nyingjang, The Essence Manual of All Oral Instructions.*

Having completed the general homage and offerings to the Three Jewels, now begin the actual Tara practice.

Next, recite three times the specific offering to the Noble Lady and the tantras of praise:

Perfected in an instant of recollection,༔
I am vividly present in the form of the Noble Lady.༔

With the first thought of Tara, you immediately and instantaneously visualize yourself in the green form of Tara. You should study and memorize the various details for how to visualize her.

Upon the moon in my heart center,༔
Boundless rays of light from the green TAM radiate,༔

Inviting the twenty-one emanations of the Noble Lady ༔
And billowing clouds of an ocean of Precious Ones ༔
To appear in the sky before me. ༔

The twenty-one emanations are explained in the Tara tantra. In the *Tukdrub* and *Zabtik,* the emblems they hold are slightly different from the tantras, and there are some slight variations in color, but they are the same twenty-one emanations, with Green Tara in the middle surrounded by her twenty emanations. They emanate billowing clouds of an ocean of the Three Jewels. Now having made the request, you make a formal invitation:

TAM ༔
From the nonarising space of luminous dharmakaya, ༔
In the unobstructed wisdom form of the Noble Lady, ༔
Manifest as the Magical Net to influence whoever may be in need. ༔
Please approach, ARYA TARE JAH! ༔

Just as Dilgo Khyentse Rinpoche said, those words are not from the Kriya tantra level.

With the next four lines, you request her to remain.

Because you have love for me and all sentient beings ༔
And possess such miraculous powers, ༔
For as long as I may honor you, ༔
Blessed One please remain! ༔
PADMA KAMALAYA SATVAM ༔

The next lines are for making offerings together with a mantra.

Lavishly filling the realm of phenomena ༔
With an offering cloud of Samantabhadra, ༔
Actually present and mentally created, ༔
I make offerings to the victorious sugatas and their offspring! ༔

OM ARYA TARE SAPARIVARA MANDALE BHYA ARGHAM PADYAM PUSHPE DHUPE ALOKE GANDHE NAIVIDYA SHAPDA PANCHA KAMAGUNA PRATICCHA SVAHA ༔

With that, make the general invocation and offering.

Next comes the mandala offering.

> OM AH HUNG ༔
> Three realms and worlds, the beings and their splendor,༔
> My body, wealth, and all my goodness ༔
> I give to you who have compassion.༔
> Accept them and bestow your blessings.༔
> OM SARVA TATHAGATA RATNA MANDALA PUJA HOH ༔

With that, present the specific mandala offering.

Those who want to do a more elaborate version of this sadhana often perform the mandala offering twenty-one or one hundred times, but doing it once or three times is fine. Among the offerings here, you should give special attention to the mandala offering.

Then chant twice the Homage in Twenty-One Verses from the Tantra of the King of Praises.

The Nyingma version of the Twenty-One Praises has an extra four-line verse, which is a summary of the root mantra; without this last verse, it would lack the necessary number of verses. The last line itself says, "This praise, rooted in mantras, has twenty-one sets of homages." The new schools (Sarma) skip this last line and immediately start over from the beginning. It is said that the blessings are multiplied if this line is included, but I am not sure why that is.

This praise is composed of tantric verses, which I do not feel qualified to explain. Once I asked Dilgo Khyentse Rinpoche to explain the reference to the "seven worlds," mentioned in one of the verses. He replied that according to the commentary on the Twenty-One Praises by Jonang Jetsün, usually the nagas are included in the animal realm, but if they are counted separately, then it makes seven worlds. I then got hold of this commentary but found it to be very complicated. You might say I understood what he was talking about, but I did not really understand what he was saying. Tantric verses like this require at least one hundred explanations; tantric verses are not easy to understand.

Anyway, having repeated these twenty-one verses twice, you then repeat the mandala offering one more time. This time, however, you visualize that Tara's right hand, which was in the gesture of supreme giving, now assumes the gesture of bestowing protection.

Having made the offerings and presented the mandala as above, then say:

Her right hand, in the mudra of supreme giving,༔
Turns into the gesture of giving refuge,༔
Which covers me and all those to be protected,༔
Assuring us of relief from all threats.༔

Since you yourself are in the form of Tara, you imagine anyone who seeks protection comes under Tara's right hand, including you, in your normal form. Some people then think that Tara has a very big hand, but simply imagine that those who need protection most are directly beneath, while all the others are gathered around.

While imagining this, chant the Homage in Twenty-One Verses three more times. Once more make the offerings and present the mandala.

Then say:

A stream of nectar flows from her body,༔
Entering me and those to be protected༔
Through the crown of the head, completely filling our bodies,༔
So that we receive all of her blessings, without exception.༔

While imagining this, chant the Homage in Twenty-One Verses seven times followed by the benefits.

With true devotion to this goddess,
Whichever wise person chants this,
At dusk or rising at dawn,
Bringing it to mind, is granted total courage.

It pacifies every misdeed,
Overcomes every road to the lower realms,
And one soon receives empowerment

From seven million conquerors.
In this life, one achieves superior qualities,
And ultimately, one reaches the state of the Buddhas.

By remembering this, even dreadful poisons,
Locally found or from elsewhere,
Which are ingested or imbibed,
Are completely expelled.

Harm from evil, affliction from plague or venom,
It fully eliminates all such miseries,
For other sentient beings too.
When chanting it twice, thrice, or seven times,

Those who want offspring will get children.
Those who want wealth will be prosperous.
One's every wish will be fulfilled,
Obstacles will vanish, and every problem will be overcome.

Then you offer a torma if you have one.

For the torma, sanctify and purify with the following mantras:

Om vajra amrita kundali hana hana hung phat ༔
Om svabhava shuddha sarva dharma svabhava shuddho ham ༔

In the state of emptiness, from the syllable om appears ༔
The supreme and vast jewel vessel, within which ༔
The torma arising from the three syllables ༔
Turns into unconditioned wisdom nectar. ༔
Om ah hung ༔ [*three times*]

For the chief figure, say this offering three times:

Om arya tare saparivara idam balingta khakha khahi khahi

For the guests, say this offering three times:

OM AKARO MUKHAM SARVA DHARMANAM ADYENUPEN NATOTA OM AH HUNG PHAT SVAHA

First, you sanctify and purify the torma with the mantras, recite the lines, and then consecrate the torma by repeating OM AH HUNG three times. Then, as you have a front visualization of Tara, imagine that she ingests the nectar of the torma through a "straw of light" coming from her tongue, as you repeat OM ARYA TARE SAPARIVARA IDAM BALINGTA KHAKHA KHAHI KHAHI three times. The other mantra starting with OM AKARO . . . is also repeated three times; it is for the twenty other emanations and all the surrounding deities of the Three Roots to accept the torma.

Then, with the next four lines, you request the siddhis.

OM ༔
With your great wisdom, consider ༔
This sublime torma of offering;༔
Accept it as great bliss ༔
And bestow all siddhis without exception.༔

With that, request the desired aims. Then, make the following offering:

OM ARYA TARE SAPARIWARA BENZA ARGHAM PADYAM PUSHPE DHUPE ALOKE GANDHE NAIVIDYA SHAPDA PRATICCHAYE SVAHA

This is followed by two verses of praise.

OM ༔
You appeared from the face of Lokeshvara,༔
In the lotus family of Amitabha,༔
Mistress of activity of all the buddhas,༔
Noble Tara, I honor and praise you.༔

To everyone worthy of praise,༔
With bodies as numerous as the dust motes in the world,༔
With deep respect and fervent devotion,༔
I will always honor and offer praise.༔

The first line refers to the fact that the lord of the world, Avalokiteshvara, made three attempts to liberate all sentient beings in the billionfold universe. Each time, however, some remained. Seeing this, out of his great compassion, tears began to stream down his cheeks, from which Arya Tara first appeared.

Having offered that praise, join your palms and say:

Sublime and Noble Lady, with your circle,
Lovingly regard me with compassion, free of thought.
Bless me so the aims of all my prayers,
Without obstacles, can be fulfilled.

May the Buddha's teachings spread and flourish!
May its holders live in harmony and good health!
May obstacles that threaten them subside!
May their activities of teaching and practice prosper!

May sickness and famine, fighting and strife, all recede!
May spiritual richness increase even further!
May the spiritual rulers' kingdoms expand!
May every country near and far have harmony!

Protect us from the sixteen threats and untimely death,
From menacing dreams and sinister omens,
From the miseries of samsara's lower realms;
From every peril, now and always!

Increase our life, merit, capacity, experience, and realization!
May harmful notions not intrude!
May the twofold awakened mind arise, free of effort!
May our aims be fulfilled in accordance with the dharma!
From now until supreme enlightenment,
Like a mother protects her only child,
Always guard us with your kindness!
Let us be indivisible from you!

This is very nice poetry, and it's easy to understand.

With this extraordinary supplication for your desired aims, invoke the oath:

Next comes making supplication and invoking the heart promise. When you invoke the heart promise of a deity, it doesn't mean there is any need to do so, because the buddhas do not necessarily act for the sake of beings just because they are asked to. Their activity completely transcends such things. But sentient beings from their side have the idea that if they do not ask for something, it will not be given. So they must make a request, as we do now.

After that, imagine that the form of Tara visualized in front dissolves.

The front visualization melts into light and dissolves into me.༔
With the blessings to be indivisible,༔
I turn into the form of Noble Tara,༔
Visible and yet insubstantial.༔

And then comes the recitation of the mantra.

While you keep in mind the vivid presence and pride of being the Noble Lady yourself, recite the ten-syllable mantra as many times as you can and follow that with the Hundred Syllable mantra.

OM TARE TUTTARE TURE SOHA

At this point, you do not need to visualize the mantra itself circling the seed syllable in the heart center. Just keep the vivid presence of being the deity, while reciting the mantra.

Then for mending any shortcomings, recite the Hundred Syllable mantra.

The next four lines comprise the request for forgiveness.

For incompleteness and failure to provide,
For whatever I could not do,
And for whatever mistakes I have made,
I must ask your forgiveness.

You would only say the next four lines if you didn't have a shrine object—which would be almost unbelievable. Therefore, you should skip the next four lines.

Om
Remain inseparable from this image
For as long as samsara exists,
Fully bestow upon me everything sublime,
Including good health, longevity, and mastery.
Om supra tishtha vajraye svaha

Since this is for the lower tantras, there is no specific consecration of the shrine object. Consecration belongs to the higher tantras. On the other hand, if you make the consecration request, it is perfectly fine.

Here is what's important at this point:

As the deity is indivisible from my own mind,༔
I settle within the original state of dharmadhatu.༔

In other words, let your mind be in the natural state—whatever it is that you call the natural state—and just sustain that.

With that, make the dedication and aspiration.

Through this virtue, may I quickly
Accomplish the state of Noble Tara.
May I bring each and every being,
Without exception, to that same state.

Next chant the lines for auspiciousness:

Like the wish-fulfilling jewel and the vase of bounty,
Unimpeded, every wish you do fulfill.
Noble Tara, conquerors, and offspring,
Bestow the auspiciousness of being forever nurtured by your compassion.

With that, utter verses of auspiciousness and toss flowers.

Then for a short daily version, it says:

Second, when performing the daily practice, it is excellent if you can arrange a shrine for the Noble Lady. If you cannot, it will suffice to visualize it mentally. Lay out the mandala and the offerings as mentioned above, and perform the refuge, bodhichitta, and consecration of offerings, beginning with dun-gyi namkar, "In the sky before me" and so forth.

Since it is not necessary to make the general offering to the Precious Ones, continue the chant from Rang-nyi keychig drendzog su Jetsün and so forth. Do the offering, mandala, and praises three times, and with the third, chant the Homage in Twenty-One Verses together with the benefits. At the end, if you prefer, you can do the request for desired aims, beginning with Jestün pagma khordang chey and so forth. If not, it is also all right.

Then chant Dunkye ozhu and so forth. Apologize for mistakes, as above. The request to depart is not necessary. Then complete it with the dedication of merit and the utterance of auspiciousness, chanting Lhadang rangsem and so forth.

Basically, there are only two short things left out of the daily practice: the general homage and offering to the Three Jewels. Then at the end, the longer request for the fulfillment of wishes can also be omitted. The third point is that if you have a shrine object, fine; but if you don't, that's fine as well. But these days it is impossible to find anyone who does not have a shrine object, because people are making countless photos and posters, so it's impossible not to have one. But if by all means you do not want to have one, you are not required to.

There is a lineage prayer that people add at the beginning. It is said that Jamyang Khyentse Rinpoche wrote it, but when I look at it, I am not so sure. Perhaps it is true, but since it praises him to the skies, he probably didn't write it. However, it is possible that someone else at a later date added those lines. Whatever the case, the main seats for Chokgyur Lingpa, such as Neten and Tsikey, where the woodblocks for the Chokling Tersar lineages were carved, did not include this lineage supplication in the Tersar printing. Tulku Pema Wangyal was the one who found it.

Dakinis[36]

In the Indian languages, the word *dakini* connotes someone who is not quite human, not an ordinary girl or woman. The image it conveys is a little scary: a blood-drinker with fangs, red hair, long nails, and so forth, who can perform a few miracles now and then. In India, generally speaking, there are quite a few of them, especially in the twenty-four sacred places and valleys, and particularly in Dhumathala, which is the most eminent among all the sacred places. This is, shall we say, the capital of the dakinis. There is a place in Pakistan, which seems to be the present-day region of Uddiyana, where a lot of women have facial hair resembling a mustache. They are naturally somewhat fierce and have certain tricks, or miracles, they can play, just by their nature. So the word generally refers to some kind of witch.

Dakini is translated into Tibetan as *khandro,* which doesn't have exactly the same meaning. The Tibetan connotation of *khandro* is "great gals," but in India if you call somebody a dakini, they will scratch your face and get angry, as it implies somebody who eats flesh, drinks blood, and casts spells. Most of the witches in Uddiyana could fly through the air. That's why they're called "sky-farers" or khandros, but I hear that these days only a few remain.

There are various types of dakinis, such as wisdom dakinis, karma dakinis, charnel ground dakinis, and something called "flesh-eating" dakinis. The wisdom dakini, according to the Sarma schools, is Vajravarahi, Dorje Phagmo. According to the Nyingma school, she is Samantabhadri, and so forth. The other primary wisdom dakinis according to the Nyingma traditions are the eight consorts of the eight great herukas and the five consorts of the five male buddhas. Among the five buddha families, the five male buddhas represent the *upaya* aspect, skillful means, while the five female buddhas represent insight, the *prajñā* aspect.

There's also a dakini that is not necessarily a wisdom dakini or a flesh-eating dakini; she is known as the Queen of Dharmadhatu, Ekajati. Also, there are five classes of karma dakinis, corresponding to the five aspects: pacifying, increasing, magnetizing, subjugating, and one for the supreme activity. The charnel ground dakinis are the eight sisters and so forth.

Those are the main ones, the chiefs of the one hundred thousand different types. In short, every woman is a dakini. They're more intelligent than men and more sharp-minded. Nevertheless, they seem to think more; in other words, they have more plans, but more worries too.

Each of the main dakinis has a sadhana practice. *The Padma Khandro* practice belongs to the cycle of the Lotus Family of Speech, *Pema Sung,* which has many inconceivable sadhanas. Among these, some are for the *yab,* or male aspect, and others are for the *yum,* or female aspect. While many vast collections of extensive sadhanas exist, they can be condensed into the sadhanas of the Three Roots, the lama, yidam, and dakini. The lama is the source of blessings, the yidam is the source of accomplishment, and the dakini is the source of activities. The dakini carries out the activities for the lama and yidam. The ultimate view of the tantras, in both the new and old schools, is that the blessings from the male are received more quickly through the female. Once you obtain the blessings and achieve the accomplishment, you need to make use of them; enacting them is called the activity. In other words, the virtue of blessings and accomplishment is the activity, which is the dakini. Buddhists and Hindus alike say that the female deity is swifter than the male deity in bestowing blessings and accomplishments.

The ultimate yidam for the Kagyüs is Chakrasamvara in the male aspect and his consort Vajravarahi in the female aspect. Most Kagyü lamas have received the blessings based on Vajravarahi and attained accomplishment through her. The Indian Pandita Naropa, the Tibetan Lotsawa Marpa, Jetsun Milarepa, Dakpo Dawa Shunnu, and others received the extraordinary blessings of inner heat, *tummo,* and attained the coemergent state of Mahamudra based on Vajravarahi.

Practitioners do the recitation-meditation for Chakrasamvara during the development and completion stage practices. At the time of the extraordinary practices, they do the outer, inner, and secret recitations of Vajravarahi. After finishing those, they train in the *Six Doctrines of Naropa:* tummo, illusory body, luminosity, dream yoga, bardo, and transference of consciousness, *powa.* Accomplishing the vital point of these and attaining the supreme accomplishment of Mahamudra are based on Vajravarahi.

According to this tradition, the ultimate wisdom is realized by relying on the example wisdom. If you want to practice the path of great bliss, based on the power of the channels, winds, and essences, then the skillful means of the female aspect is the vital point. In other words, the practice connected to the vase empowerment is the male aspect, while the more profound parts—the secret and wisdom-knowledge empowerments—are connected to the female aspect of sadhana, which is Vajravarahi in the Kagyü lineages. As it is taught, although Milarepa and his disciple Gampopa had various yidams, they attained accomplishment primarily through Vajravarahi practice connected with the second and third empowerments.

In the Sakya tradition, one of the principal yidams is the male Hevajra, whose female counterpart is Khechari (*Kachoma*), a form of Vajravarahi. The Sakyas practice the path and fruition tradition, *Lamdre,* transmitted by the great mahasiddha Virupa, through a golden chain of masters. However, in this lineage as well, receiving the blessings and attaining extraordinary realization in this life or in the bardo relies on consort practice based on Khechari. A rain of *sindura,* flowers, and consorts will accompany awakening. All the realized masters of this tradition have practiced in this way. One of the great Sakya masters, Sachen, attained accomplishment through receiving the blessings of Khechari. For instance, at the time of death, he did not leave a corpse behind but went directly in his body to the celestial realms. This mode of departure is depicted as climbing a staircase that descends from above. I'm not exactly sure what that looks like and how it functions, but it definitely works. Having attained this siddhi, he received a lot of pith transmissions through Khechari. The Gelugpas also practice a form of Vajravarahi.

The Nyingmas have a red form of Vajravarahi and a black one, Tromo Nagmo. This black form is the exalted deity of many past vidyadharas, who practiced a sadhana revealed by Nyang Ral Nyima Ozer. The biography style supplication to Jamyang Khyentse Wangpo recounts that when he did the retreat of the black Vajravarahi, his skull cup started to blaze with fire, becoming so hot he couldn't touch it. A large number of sadhanas are now based on Troma Nagmo. *Yumka Dechen Gyalmo,* revealed by Jigme Lingpa, also has a form of Vajravarahi.

Kurukulle belongs to the family of Vajravarahi and Arya Tara. For Arya Tara, the dharmakaya is the Great Mother, Prajnaparamita; the sambhogakaya is Arya Tara; and the nirmanakaya is the infinite manifestations, as stated in the Tara tantras. There are 108 main Tara sadhanas.

Within these, the outer emanation is Kurukulle, Lhamo Rigzinma, and the inner emanation is Lhamo Uma. Within the Tara emanations, the inner aspect is the magnetizing female deity, Kurukulle, Lhamo Rigzinma.

Other dakini sadhanas belong to a cycle of six dakini practices known as *Zursa,* the personal practice of the princess of Zur. She was Prince Damdzin's consort when Padmasambhava was in Tibet. These six practices include the outer Tara, the inner Vajravarahi, the secret Sangwa Yeshe, the most secret Mandarava, and *thatness* Yeshe Tsogyal, as well as a guru sadhana.

Additionally, the *Rinchen Terdzö* contains the Padma Khandro practice of Rongzom Mahapandita, an emanation of Vairochana, which Jamyang Khyentse Wangpo rediscovered, and the *Seven Profound Teachings* on Kurukulle, the terma of Chokgyur Lingpa. These are the most well-known in the Nyingma tradition. One of Tertön Sogyal's terma also has a Padma Khandro sadhana that is practiced in Serta, in eastern Tibet. In short, in Tibet, both the Kama and Terma traditions have Padma Khandro sadhanas with unbroken lineages and great blessings that are still practiced today.

Among the various treasure revealers, very few have dakini sadhanas. As I have heard it said, this is due to the dakini practices being very profound and the dakinis being kind of stingy with their teachings. They don't really want to let go of them that easily. Some auspicious coincidence has to fall into place perfectly before they're willing to pass on such teachings, and that doesn't happen so readily. Most tertöns have experienced a lot of trouble with trying to land a dakini terma, and they are rarely successful.

For instance, Chokgyur Lingpa was predicted to go to Karpo Drak, the White Cliff in Bhutan, where he was to reveal a very grand terma called the *Khandro Gongdü, the Embodiment of the Realization of All Dakinis.* If he had succeeded in doing this, it would have ensured that all his activity would have reached completion; however, somebody interfered, so he wasn't able to, and a big obstacle to his life arose as a result. In the prophecy, it also said that there's a connection between the *Khandro Gongdü* and his other Dzogchen terma called the *Dzogchen Desum, The Three Sections of Dzogchen*. It says that if he had established the *Dzogchen Desum* in writing, it would have become possible to also decode the *Khandro Gongdü,* and if both of them had been brought into this world at the same time, a huge number of people would have attained rainbow body.[37]

Chokgyur Lingpa's daughter, Mayum Könchok Paldrön, had a parchment from her father with one of the dakini scripts that had never been decoded. After she died, her son Tersey Tulku inherited it. When Tersey Tulku met with Dilgo Khyentse Rinpoche,[38] he asked Rinpoche to decode it. This turned out to be the sadhana for the eight dakini consorts of the eight herukas. It was eventually written down, but then the lineage was broken. Some years ago, when I went back to eastern Tibet, I got hold of the text, but the empowerment lineage no longer exists.

What is the purpose and benefit of dakini practice? It has outer, inner, secret, and innermost ways to magnetize. The outer way is to magnetize those with and without form—humans and nonhumans. For humans, the three categories of male, female, and neuter all need to be brought under control. The males subdivide into five families, or as in the Indian system, castes of kings, brahmins, businessmen, workers, and untouchables. The females also group into five families: padma, conch, elephant, drawing, and deer. Many beings live in the three planes of existence—the gods above, the nagas below the ground, and the nonhumans in between—and these make up the eight categories of haughty spirits. We magnetize them all. In addition, we magnetize the five primary elements.

Based on controlling the outer elements, we inwardly magnetize the inner elements, the five aggregates, and the sense organs. When we gain control over the five elements outwardly and the five aggregates, sense organs, and inner elements inwardly, then we subdue the five poisons, which transform into the five wisdoms. This is the inner way to magnetize.

Secretly, when we gain mastery over the moving winds, the arranged channels, and the blissful bindus, the wisdom of the three vajras arises. Innermost magnetizing means gaining mastery over mind. Mind is what we are trying to control, and right now we do not have this mastery. As for the fruition of magnetizing, I will not tell that now. However, the reason we practice a magnetizing deity is to attain this power of magnetizing.

It is essential to know that you need to dissolve duality in order to accomplish any deity. To attain this within the structure of a sadhana practice, you progress through the stages of approach, close approach, accomplishment, and great accomplishment. This is in the extensive way, which you can condense into approach, accomplishment, and activities. The aspect of approach means the deity is very close. Accomplishment occurs when you recognize that you and the diety are inseparable; this is called "realizing one taste." Once you accomplish the deity, you can enact the infinite activities related to pacifying, increasing, magnetizing, and subjugating.

In the Kurukulle sadhana in particular, the vital point is to fulfill the activities. The work, or activity, of the deity is the display of enlightened body, speech, and mind. Individuals who cannot benefit from peaceful and increasing activity can be helped by magnetizing and subjugating activity, which is unique to the unexcelled Secret Vajrayana. The other vehicles do not have magnetizing and subjugating activity. Many methods are available for enacting peaceful and increasing activities. However, for completely unruly beings, or ones with great desire, anger, impure perception, or no faith, only the Secret Mantra activities of magnetizing and subjugating can tame them.

Kurukulle enacts the magnetizing activity that brings profound benefit rapidly. You need to accomplish this sadhana practice, and to do this you need the empowerment. As it is said, "Without the empowerment, you cannot attain the accomplishments." In short, dakini practice expedites the process of attaining supreme and common siddhis. It is also especially effective for clearing samaya damages. As I mentioned before, once you receive the blessings through the guru sadhana and attain accomplishments through the yidam practice, you make use of those by engaging the activity through the dakini practice.

Magnetizing Practice[39]

When you receive an empowerment, it is necessary to do the practice for that empowerment. The lineage empowerment is first, followed by the path empowerments, which altogether authorize disciples to do the practices. The path vase empowerment is for the practice of the development stage. The path secret empowerment is for the practices of channels, winds, and essences as well as mantra recitation. The path wisdom-knowledge empowerment utilizes the emptiness of the example wisdom to encourage the ultimate wisdom being to arise in your experience. The secret and the wisdom-knowledge empowerments correspond to completion stage with and without characteristics, respectively. The precious word empowerment authorizes you to practice Dzogchen, primordially pure Trekchö and spontaneously present Tögal. The best disciples will maintain an unbroken flow. Immediately upon receiving this empowerment, they will instantly be undeluded and undistracted in practicing the path. The middling ones will maintain awareness six times in a day. Those with lesser capacity will hold this awareness at least one time each day. This is the process of receiving the four empowerments for yidam practice. You must practice until you truly actualize the result of the path, without breaking the continuity of the deity.

After you receive the lineage empowerment, utilize the deity empowerment and do not abandon sadhana practice. If you practice the deity after receiving the lineage empowerment, you will ultimately become enlightened and temporarily receive the fruition empowerment. The fruition empowerment bestows all the qualities of the three kayas of buddhahood. At that point, you will effortlessly benefit innumerable sentient beings as vast as the sky. I have given this condensed explanation of empowerment so you can understand. Merely receiving empowerment from a lama has a bit of benefit, but without practicing, you will not become enlightened.

Enhancement

With the vase empowerment, you recite the mantras for the outer, inner, and secret practices. You visualize the deity and maintain that visualization with vivid presence. Once you have accumulated the appropriate numbers, you should have made a connection with the practice. Jamgön Kongtrül Rinpoche wrote a commentary on how to do retreat on Kurukulle, which you can follow if you want to do a retreat.

Anyway, if you have made a connection with the vase empowerment, everything you see with your eyes can be magnetized or brought under control.[40] You do that by thinking, "I am Padma Khandro." Visualize that clearly. You can engage in the enhancement for this by meditating on a red syllable OM in each of your eyes. As these red om syllables radiate light, the wisdom of great bliss blazes supremely. The blazing light from your eyes pervades all appearances. This light radiates outwardly, clearly illuminating everything it touches, like the light from the sun. All appearances become the light of great bliss, which flows back into the OM syllables in your eyes. The outer objects and the inner subject are magnetized inseparably. The eyes bring all forms under control.

In order to bring all sounds under control, imagine that red SHANG syllables are in your ears. As before, red light rays of great bliss radiate outwardly from the SHANG syllables. They permeate all sounds, which become light and dissolve back into the SHANG syllables in the ears; all sounds are magnetized. Similarly, from the nasal area, red KHAM syllables radiate red light rays of great bliss that permeate all smells. Once touched by this light, the smells are transformed into the light of great bliss, which returns and dissolves into the KHAM syllables in the nasal area. All smells are magnetized or brought under control. In the same way on the tongue, a red RAM syllable sends out red light rays of great bliss that reach all the different tastes, sweet and sour. Again they melt into light and the red light returns and dissolves into the ram on your tongue, whereby all tastes are brought under control or magnetized. In the forehead, a red sum sends out light rays of great bliss that reach all the tactile sensations, which become red light permeated with great bliss. This light returns to dissolve into the red SUM syllable in the forehead. In the middle of the heart is a red HANG syllable. Red light of great bliss blazes forth from this HANG, permeating all mental fixation on phenomena. All appearances dissolve into the red light, which reabsorbs into the HANG syllable in your heart.

These are the six syllables pertaining to sensorial objects and mental phenomena. If you meditate on these gradually and sequentially, the objects of all six consciousnesses and the subject, the six consciousnesses themselves, will become one taste, and you will gain mastery over them.

Meditating like this, you will attain the fruition, realizing that all appearances, sounds, smells, tastes, and palpable things are empty. Furthermore, you will realize that all knowable things, all mental phenomena, are empty bliss. The two truths are indivisible, and you will remain in a state of experiencing all as illusory. At the same time that you visualize the syllables, you also chant each of them.

Do this practice to gain powerful mastery over all the appearances of the six consciousnesses. Sometimes think of yourself as Kurukulle, without a consort in the outer and inner practices and with consort Lokeshvara in the secret practice. Visualize the yab and yum with vivid presence. Like the deity dissolving into the deity, all appearances dissolve into the deity, and you develop stable pride. When you gain control over appearances, you have received the vase empowerment.

Think about these teachings. First, to practice this, you need to have clear visualization, vivid presence, and pure recollection of Padma Khandro. Otherwise, you will not be able to follow this path. Once you are able to clearly visualize yourself as Padma Khandro with stable pride, then you can continue on to reciting the syllables, starting with OM in the eyes. OM radiates rays of light, permeating all forms. The light rays dissolve into the forms, which become red light, and that light slowly merges back into the OM syllables in your eyes. Once they dissolve, you gain control over all forms, which are sealed with emptiness. Then you continue with the visualizations for the other five consciousnesses. This is how to train. During this practice, you need to maintain the clear visualization of yourself as the deity. Do not separate from that.

In short, the main aspect of the vase empowerment is developing the deity. The second empowerment is connected to Anuyoga's practices with the channels, winds, and essences. The last two empowerments relate to Atiyoga. Having received the empowerment of Padma Khandro, you need to keep these ordinary and extraordinary samayas: treat women with the greatest respect and kindness, maintain the mudra and mantra recitation uninterruptedly, and do the practice. Just receiving an empowerment and listening to teachings are not the most important things. The most vital is to practice and accomplish what you receive. Once you follow the

Vajrayana path—where you receive empowerments and teachings and practice development and completion—it will not be long before you attain the state of buddhahood. Practice is essential.

One important element of practice is the tradition of the great accomplishment, drubchen. In *Lama Gongdu,* Padmasambhava said that one week of drubchen practice is the same as seven years of retreat. When you perform a drubchen, the life force of the sadhana is the mantra. Through the recitation, you connect to the wisdom mind of the deity, enabling you to receive the blessings and accomplishments. In a drubchen, the recitation is unbroken. There is power in the great accomplishment practice.

Application

This Kurukulle cycle has sadhanas for outer, inner, and secret practices, and each of these has a different visualization and recitation. This cycle also contains a Three Roots practice, and the Kurukulle practice is a branch of this. In the outer practice, you meditate on yourself as Padma Khandro, who has a retinue of eight dakinis that are exactly the same as she is. At the four doors, there are another four female gatekeepers.

In Vajrayana, you need to think about the meaning of the words you recite and meditate on them. You can easily do the short daily practice and recite the mantra, which is the wisdom mind of the deity. The daily practice begins with taking refuge, generating bodhichitta, and reciting the Seven Branch prayer. Based on the three samadhis, you instantaneously visualize yourself as the deity. It is good to have a photo of the deity as a samaya support for your self-visualization. Based on this samaya support, you visualize yourself as the deity and think that you are one and the same, which will give rise to seven experiences, as it is said in the tantras.

Buddha nature is present in all sentient beings. The ultimate point of Vajrayana is to ascertain that all phenomena have the nature of the three kayas. It is not a question of your being inadequate; it is only a matter of not realizing this view. Habitual tendencies obscure this view, and in order to train in purifying them, you must practice deity yoga. To accomplish a deity, you need to know that it does not come from outside of yourself. When realizing this view, you authentically accomplish the deity; therefore, practice sadhana.

Meditating on a deity requires vivid presence, seeing all the different attributes, down to the white and black of the eyes, as images reflected in a mirror. There is nothing the mind is not capable of thinking. Our core, the buddha nature, is pure and the deity is pure. You need to give up the discursive thinking that the deity is good and you are bad and that you need to accomplish the [outer] deity. Stable means it is not something you need to conjure up, as though it didn't already exist. Stable pride is knowing *what is* to be *as it is*.

Pure recollection is knowing that, ultimately, you and the deity and the mantra to be accomplished are the expression of emptiness. These come from nowhere else, and in the essence of emptiness, there is nothing. However, to say everything is emptiness is not that easy to explain. Since many of you have received pith instructions on Dzogchen, this is training in rigpa, which has been introduced. In short, sometimes train in pure recollection, sometimes in stable pride, and sometimes in vivid presence. When pure recollection has dissolved, train in the empty aspect. Practice all three of these indivisibly.

This is how to practice the development of a deity. For the practice of the enlightened speech of the mantra recitation, follow the daily practice. The mind accomplishes the enlightened body and speech. If you can remain in the nonconceptual samadhi, you will accomplish the completion stage of enlightened mind. If a yogi practices the vajra body, speech, and mind of the deity, the impure aspects of ordinary body, speech, and mind become purified; the purity wisdom is realized; and the enlightened body, speech, and mind are actualized. Truly, you transform into the vajra body, speech, and mind, and the qualities and activities are spontaneously accomplished. This is how you are going to try to practice with your body, speech, and mind. Whatever I have explained is in accordance with the oral instructions of the vidyadharas. Studying and hearing teachings are a lamp for clearing away ignorance, so understanding is a vital point. Nonpractitioners do not need to receive teachings.

Four Doors

A crucial point in Vajrayana is the four doors of Secret Mantra. The first of these is the ultimate clarification based on the "door of words." This door refers to the sadhanas, the means of accomplishment, which remind you of the ultimate essence, the basic state. This is the first of the four doors to be entered. Entering and realizing the ultimate clarification rely on your doing the sadhana from beginning to end, from refuge through the aspirations, with each word reminding you of the meaning.

In the recitation and meditation of the Secret Mantra, you recite the words with your mouth and meditate on the meaning with your mind. The crucial meaning of the words is the mudra of the vidyadhara lineage. Slowly, you sing the melodies and tunes. The benefit of repeating the words and thinking about the meaning is that after a long time you grow accustomed to them. My hope is that you will be able to enter this door. With sadhanas, it does not matter how elaborate or short they are; the ultimate meaning is mostly the same. So, this is the first door.

The second door is the heart-vow, the sacred pledge of the recitation, the "door of the mantra." What is that heart-vow? It is that you and the deity are not separate. You are not accomplishing something better than you. The heart-vow, the sacred pledge, equalizes you and the deity. There are the three recitation intents: approach, accomplishment, and the activities. Once you enter this door, you accumulate the mantra.

The third is the "door of the one-pointed mental visualization samadhi." Through concentration, you need to maintain the samadhi of the visualization. This relates to the essential point of pith instructions of the four nails or the four stakes that bind the life force of the practice. These teachings are extremely important, and if you do not know these four stakes, then you do not know the condensed, crucial points. The final stake is that of the unchanging wisdom mind. So, this is the third door.

Lastly, you have the "door of the mudra of what needs to be done." At the time of meditating on the deity, visualize the three doors sealed by the three vajras and yourself crowned by the victorious ones. Invite the wisdom beings and make offerings and praises. All of these are the door of the mudra of what needs to be done.

These correspond to the tantras' references to deity, mantra, samadhi, and mudra. If even one of these four doors is missing, they are incomplete. In Vajrayana, if you practice the development of Mahayoga, then during great accomplishment, you need to enter these four doors. Once you enter the four doors, you will see the precious wheel of the mandala. These four doors are extremely important.

Since beginningless time up until now, sentient beings have been wandering in samsara. The vital point is that we have not examined our minds. Why have we not examined our minds? Buddha nature pervades all sentient beings; the mind is buddha. However, the essence of buddhahood has been obscured by inexhaustible thoughts, like the ripples on the surface of water. The thoughts arising like ripples on water are endless. For hundreds of thousands of lifetimes, we have not been able to end thoughts. So how do you reach the point of ending them? You do that through a lama's pith instructions, which direct you to investigate your mind. The teachings that show you how to examine your mind are the beginning of the end of thoughts.

One way to end thoughts is to employ them, by visualizing the deity, reciting the mantra, and remaining in samadhi. You have received the empowerment, [are trying to] maintain the samaya, and are training in deity yoga. At the time of practice, keep your body, speech, and mind focused one-pointedly. Concerning body, speech, and mind, the main one is the mind, which needs to be undistracted. If you just keep your mind in an ordinary way, following after different thoughts, you are distracted. According to Mahayoga, *nondistraction* means clearly visualizing the deity. Doing this destroys ordinary thoughts. Once you destroy ordinary thoughts by developing this vivid presence, then you train in the vajra pride, thinking, "I am the deity." When vajra pride arises within your stream-of-being, you recognize the buddha nature, the ground of buddha; thus, you have empowered yourself. At the end of your practice with vivid presence and stable pride, you will obtain the blessings of the deity. Obtaining blessings means that ordinary thoughts have ceased; there is only the purity of the deity and the display of wisdom, and these are the blessings. When your own appearances are pure and you no longer have any impure experience, you can slowly bring others under control. With these three, all appearances become the form of Padma Khandro. If you have visualized clearly and hold the stable pride of being the magnetizing deity Padma Khandro, it truly becomes so. On the basis of these, you receive blessings. Then thoughts of the three times—past, present, and future—become like drawings on water. They dissolve into basic space and are liberated, wherein you gain mastery or control over your mind. All thoughts are naturally purified, and you attain the blessings and the power, or strength. To increase the strength of the blessings within this samadhi, recite the mantra. When the samadhi is like a fire, the recitation is like the wind. When the fire of samadhi blazes, the wind makes the fire even greater. Similarly, to increase the samadhi, recite the mantra.

Recitation

Your recitation should not be either too loud or too soft; your chanting should be heard by your own ear. Pronounce each syllable clearly and sometimes sing the mantra. This singing increases the power of samadhi and the offerings. The lamas, yidams, and dakinis are pleased, and evil deeds and obscurations are purified. Like that, the four activities of the four recitations are accomplished, and the male and female protectors are enjoined. For the practitioner of Dzogchen, all forms of the deity and all thoughts that arise are not beyond primordial purity. Maintaining that awareness decisively renders deity, mantra, samadhi, and mudra the display of dharmakaya. Just remaining like that is the meditation and this is all right.

There are nine aspects of mantra recitation that are common to all mantras. The deity and the mantra are not separate; they are the same. Be certain of that and decide on it. Know that the recitation of the mantra accomplishes the deity. The first aspect is to know the deity and the mantra to be the same.

In reciting one mantra of OM KURU KULLE HRIH SOHA, you can accomplish the mandalas of all the victorious ones. The second aspect is to know the mantra to be the mandala of the victorious ones. The recitation of the mantra, the lights emanating and reabsorbing, and the offerings bring the mandalas of all the victorious ones closer. The third aspect is to know the mantra to be the offering garland.

By reciting the mantra, you accomplish experience, realization, wisdom, and all blessings. The fourth aspect is to know the mantra to be the blessings. In the recitation of the mantra, you can accomplish the supreme siddhi, buddhahood. You can obtain the common and supreme siddhis, all the enlightened activities, and the eight accomplishments. The fifth aspect is to know the mantra to be the siddhis.

Mantra recitation accomplishes infinite activities, including the peaceful, increasing, magnetizing, and subjugating activities as well as power and long life without sickness. The sixth aspect is to know the mantra to be the activities. For example, when someone recites a mantra and blows on a sick person or blows on water, the sick person can be healed by receiving that breath or drinking that water.

Fixation on solid reality can be destroyed and emptiness can be realized by reciting the mantra. The seventh aspect is to know that the mantra reveals emptiness. Simply by reciting ah you can come to realize emptiness. In the recitation of mantra, all breakages, obscurations, and evil deeds can be purified from the root. The eighth aspect is to know the mantra to be purification. By reciting the mantra, all wishes are accomplished. It is like a wish-fulfilling jewel. When a Buddhist supplicates a wish-fulfilling jewel, everything desired is granted. I am not sure that these exist today, but reciting the mantra can accomplish all things. The power of mantra is inconceivable. The ninth is to know the mantra to be a wish-fulfilling jewel.

Since in a drubchen [or a sadhana], you will recite many mantras, it is good to know the ultimate meaning of mantra. Otherwise, just sitting there with your eyes closed and accumulating mantras, without knowing what you have said, will have no benefit. On the other hand, knowing this and reciting with the correct visualization, you will derive great benefit. It is important to understand and repeatedly remind yourself of the meaning. As it is said, when you practice Secret Mantrayana, and in particular the profound treasure Dharma [terma], these practices are easily applied with little hardship and great benefit.

The visualization for the recitation of this activity practice is as stated in the text, and I will talk more about that later. The activity is to magnetize, and it is up to each one of you to decide what or whom you want to magnetize. There are three kinds of beings: nagas, spirits, and humans—and there are many different types of humans.

Through respect and devotion, magnetize a master.༔
Through swift learning and reflection, magnetize the sacred Dharma.༔
Through carefulness, magnetize the three gates.༔
Through compassion, magnetize all sentient beings.༔
Through a mudra, magnetize your own mind.༔
Through great bliss, magnetize primordial wakefulness.༔
Through primordial wakefulness, magnetize all the victorious ones.༔
Through blessings, magnetize the dharma protectors.༔
Through the expression of awareness, magnetize all that appears and exists.༔
Through majestic splendor, magnetize kingly rulers.༔
Through samaya, magnetize the dakinis.༔
Through renown, magnetize all countries.༔
For the benefit of the teachings, magnetize the Mahayana sangha.༔
For the benefit of beings, magnetize gods, nagas, and humans.༔
For the benefit of affluence, magnetize food, clothing, and wealth.༔

*For the benefit of dominion, magnetize attendants, disciples, and followers.*ༀ
*Magnetize harmonious companions, fame, and abundance.*ༀ
*In short, magnetize all the splendor of samsaric existence and nirvanic peace.*ༀ

To accomplish Padma Khandro, you need devotion. If you have devotion, you can magnetize the lama. If you magnetize the lama, then you will receive all the blessings. If you are practicing Padma Khandro, your great intelligence will expand. Having magnetized the learned and accomplished teacher, you will receive many instructions, and through listening and reflecting, your learning and contemplating will increase. Through learning and reflecting, you magnetize the sacred Dharma.

If you practice Padma Khandro, your mind will become more relaxed and careful. If your mind is careful, you will bring your three doors of body, speech, and mind under control. You will refrain from doing or saying things you shouldn't. You will have no need to be thoughtless.

If you practice Padma Khandro, great compassion will naturally arise, and everyone will like you. People do not like someone who lacks compassion, even if it's a lama.

Magnetizing through a mudra refers to taking a consort. To increase wisdom of the ultimate meaning in your stream-of-being, in order to bring your own mind under control, you need to take support of the wisdom mudra. This gives birth to the wisdom of great bliss. If the wisdom of great bliss arises, then the wisdom of ultimate meaning ensues, based on the example of great-bliss wisdom. If this [is a correct experience of] wakefulness, you will accomplish all the victorious ones and all the yidams. If you accomplish all the victorious ones, by their blessings, you will accomplish all the protectors.

The victorious ones are not deluded. All of mind's different discursive thoughts are the expression, or display, of dharmakaya awareness. If you decide that there is nothing other than the display of the dharmakaya, then you gain control of all that appears and exists. If you gain control of all that appears and exists, then you become Padmasambhava. If you do not achieve this, but gain control over yourself, it is a bit good and you will magnetize kings and presidents.

By practicing Padma Khandro, you will amend your samayas, especially all broken samayas with the dakinis. If your samayas are pure, naturally, you will magnetize the dakinis.

When you practice Padma Khandro, you become famous, for better or worse. Once famous, you magnetize all countries. When a famous person comes out with a new movie, we flock to it. Becoming famous is a big pursuit these days, with advertising, web pages, movies, magazines, and books. Any fame that you garner should be for the benefit of the teachings, magnetizing Mahayana practitioners.

To benefit sentient beings, magnetize gods, nagas, and humans. Never magnetize to harm, but only to benefit. The best benefit is to bring beings to the Dharma. If the Vajrayana practitioner does not have any means, it is difficult to do anything. Even for the sambhogakaya in the Akanishtha Buddhafield, there is much abundance and enjoyment. They live in palaces of variegated jewels and are also adorned with many gems and silks. That is an example of the great abundance. When we practice and make offerings, it is like the space treasury without end. In short, *sambhoga,* enjoyment, means "substances and wealth." Also, great power is needed in order to do vast things. With great power, you magnetize vast wealth, attendants, and students, people who follow you. Also, on the political level, you need to have power.

Magnetize harmonious companions, people with whom you have a good connection, which is not easy. Even a spouse with whom you have been living for many years and have had many children can be difficult. Couples argue, complain, and separate. Stay together with harmonious companions, until you reach enlightenment. Jamyang Khyentse Wangpo and Chokgyur Lingpa were together as father and son for thirteen different lifetimes. This started with King Trisong Deütsen and his son Murub Tseypo. Padmasambhava and Yeshe Tsogyal are still together in infinite buddhafields. Don't magnetize just anyone, but someone who can accomplish things. To condense it all to the essence, there is nothing in samsara and nirvana that Padma Khandro cannot magnetize.

If you do not wish to magnetize during the activity practice, you can do so during the recitation: Visualize yourself as Padma Khandro, with the HRIH syllable in your heart center and the mantra coiled around the seed syllable. As you recite OM KURU KULLE HRIH SOHA, lights radiate out and make offerings to the victorious ones. Gather back the blessings and accomplishments within you. This is the intention of the radiating, and it is all right, according to the commentary by Jamgön Kongtrül.

If, however, you do want to magnetize, then follow these instructions in the text and practice that way:

The HRIH *syllables situated on the sun discs in the heart centers of the goddesses radiate red rays of light in the form of hooks. By merely touching the heart centers of whomever they wish to magnetize, those beings are brought under their power—just as a magnet gathers together all iron filings—and dissolve into the* HRIH *in the heart centers of the goddesses.*

Do this visualization repeatedly, and during the recitation, sometimes remain without focus. Once again, do the visualization, and then again remain without focus; this is how you should train. If you practice in this way, by the power of deity, mantra, and samadhi, you will surely bring things under your control, just as ice placed in the hot sun cannot remain frozen. This is the intention of the outer practice.

Practical Advice

Concerning samadhi, you need to meditate, and Westerners really like to meditate. For meditation, nothing surpasses Dzogchen and maintaining rigpa. If you really know the meditation of Dzogchen and can sustain rigpa, you don't need to practice a deity. However, if you are merely counting discursive thoughts, that has no benefit.

You need to do the mudras. Some people are doing them but most people sit with their hands inactive, which is the same as having no hands. You cannot really say that you cannot do them; you simply need to imitate someone doing them. There is nothing embarrassing about this. On the other hand, not knowing how to do them after practicing sadhana is embarrassing. So, you must do the mudras. Doing just one mudra, like the opening lotus one, is more precious than doing one hundred thousand prostrations when taking refuge in the Mahayana vehicle. The movements of mudra in Vajrayana are great bliss. If you cannot do them well, you can improve. The benefits of mudra require so much explanation, in terms of the arranged channels, the moving pranas, and the essences, or tigles. The whole eighteenth chapter in the *Guhyagarbha Tantra* is devoted to explaining everything about mudra.

A *ngakpa* is a male yogi and a *ngakma* is a female yogini, which you are. A yogi is someone who, having received empowerment, is practicing the three yogas. Dilgo Khyentse Rinpoche would sign his name as the yogi, doctrine holder, Mangala, with no fixation at all in his mind; and *mangala,* good fortune, is Sanskrit for his Tibetan name Tashi Paljor. A yogi needs to know that he or she is a yogi. The yogi needs the view, meditation, and conduct. You need to perform a sadhana at least once a day.

There are many samayas for having received an empowerment. The most important samayas are the five buddha family samayas. For the jewel family, the samaya is to have a vajra and a bell and use them. All Dharma practice is unifying skillful means and wisdom, illustrated by the vajra and bell. It is said that you need to hold the vajra and bell perfectly.

You also need a good mala with the right characteristics. If you do not have a vajra and bell and a good mala, this indicates you are not a good practitioner. For food, you need to eat *mendrub,* lama medicine, every single day. To be a good practitioner of the Vajrayana, you need to first gather all the different necessary substances for practice, getting the objects with the right characteristics. This is easier than meditation. What I have spoken is the wisdom intent of the tantras.

Fruition

Yesterday, we finished the drubchen of magnetizing activity. Today, how are you? Have you really investigated that? It is good if you do so. There are many things to gather under your control, to magnetize, to bring into your power. Here, I am talking about bringing your mind under control. Yesterday, you finished receiving the accomplishments. This morning, if you, the practitioners, have had your mind pointed out according to Dzogchen, and have recognized the nature of mind—if while remaining in rigpa, your rigpa was more stable, clearer, and sharper—then you definitely accomplished the magnetizing activity. This only occurs through your own individual experience. When you examine, you know. It is not something learned. That is why it is very important to investigate this. If you are someone who does not practice this or does not rest in rigpa, then I have nothing to say to you.

If your mind has truly become more clear and stable, then the prana becomes calmer. Then, naturally, mind's thoughts will be self-liberated. That is what "bringing under control" means. First, inwardly, you gain control over your mind; then, outwardly, all phenomena is brought under control. Once you completely control your own mind, male and female friends, lamas, and sponsors will be brought under control or magnetized. Thereafter, delusion no longer has any power over you. But if that is not the case, then you will fall under the power of deluded perceptions.

This is why I wanted you to examine what happened this morning. I thought that I needed to talk about it. All supreme and common accomplishments can be obtained. If you attain the supreme accomplishments, you automatically attain the common ones.

The water inside the vase is normally saffron water, but everyone was given alcohol. Also, inside the skull cup, there was beer. Once you drink this, the taste permeates your channels, and this happens in order to bring the mind's thoughts under control. If a practitioner gets a little drunk from alcohol, then rigpa becomes stronger, and coarse thoughts reduce, their strength diminishes. The small thoughts disappear. Due to the strength of alcohol, when you are a little drunk, the prana goes into the central channel. Since you received the siddhis yesterday, I wanted to talk about this. So, I would like you to examine your mental state since waking up today, and see if you were able to rest in rigpa. If this happened very well, then you have attained magnetizing power. Once you have controlled your own mind, slowly, you will be able to bring outer things into your power.

Drubchen Framework[41, 42]

It is incredibly good fortune to receive teachings and empowerments from qualified masters and to ripen the fruit of receiving such empowerments by joining in a drubchen, even if it is only for seven days. To get such an opportunity doesn't come easily. If it were easy, everybody would already avail themselves of such, but the fact is that only a few people ever acquire such merit. So you really should make all the necessary efforts to receive the teachings and be able to fully practice them. Now those of you who are here, rejoice that you have made the commitment to practice in a drubchen and realize the preciousness of this occasion.

Yeshe Tsogyal said that to receive terma teachings and to be able to practice them is a sign of incredibly good karma and the result of the aspirations that individuals have made in the presence of Guru Rinpoche himself. Also, Guru Rinpoche said that to practice for seven days in a drubchen is equal to staying in retreat for seven years.

In order to assure that everything is auspicious during the practice, the drubchen text states that each day we should bathe, wear fine clothing, recite the Hundred Syllable mantra, and pay homage to the deities. This is important when practicing Vajrayana, particularly during the invocation and the descent of blessings, when it is said that we should dress in the very best clothing we have, in order to emphasize the magnificence. It is also important to be wide awake, to bring forth the clarity of rigpa. Everything originates interdependently, so we need to make sure that we carry out all our actions in the best possible way, especially during the practice.

The Ritual Framework text explains:

> From amongst my tens of millions of inconceivable hidden heart practices, the *Dispeller of Obstacles: The Guru's Heart Practice*

> *and Guru's Ocean of Attainments*[43] or the *Wish-Fulfilling Guru Mahāsukha* are specifically intended to dispel obstacles and obtain all spiritual attainments, respectively, in order to accomplish the infinite three bodies and the infinite Three Roots. Now and in the future, those known as my followers must prioritise these two paths exclusively. In so doing, the way for a yogi to arrange his or her practice and facilitate achieving the common and supreme attainments is explained in the tantras as follows:
>
> Taking up a site with perfections,
> A Vidyādhara achieves supreme attainments
> By means of approach, close approach,
> Accomplishment, and great accomplishment . . .

When you perform a drubchen, first, you have the ritual practice for consecrating the land. For that, you need to examine whether the place where you are planning to perform the drubchen is suitable or not. Instructions for determining suitability include these specifications: openness to the east, a grassy plane to the south, a rocky mountain to the north, and a pass to the west. There are also guidelines for the way the water flows and the wind blows. Moreover, different types of lands are recommended for varying types of activity—each has its specific characteristics, depending on the activity that is to be accomplished, whether it is pacifying, enriching, magnetizing, or subjugating. Previously, I spoke about the different sciences of astrology and mathematics. One tradition came from China and another from the great Bodhisattva Manjushri. These traditions give indications for how to know the different types of land and their qualities. It is said that if a place has been blessed by buddhas, great bodhisattvas, Guru Rinpoche, or previous realized vajra masters of the lineage—or if it has been the residence of an awakened master—then that is a suitable place.

There are actually a lot of reasons for that. When inner realization is fully developed, as an outward sign of attainment—this occurs outwardly, due to having become accustomed to all appearances being the mandala of the deities—this power transforms the external elements into the five female buddhas, blessing the outer environment. This happens, in particular, through the power of the descent of blessings and the training in samadhi. Based on these practices, the lamas, yidams, and khandros always dwell in such places. According to the traditional analogy, it's like when you leave a piece of meat out; the flies will immediately gather around it. Similarly, the deities are always gathering in such a place,

As another analogy, a place full of blessings is like fire. If you get close to a fire, you feel the heat; likewise, when you are in a place that has been blessed on a number of occasions, you receive the blessings and gain accomplishment very quickly.

When Jamyang Khyentse Chökyi Lodrö went on pilgrimage, he said that the great masters of the past were able to bless those pilgrimage places, the entire environment, out of their realization. They could expand their realization to bless the external environment. He said, "Myself, I'm not at that level, and so I'm just going there in order to actually receive, or draw, these blessings back into me, so that I don't have any obstacles, sicknesses, and problems for a long life."

As for arranging the text in terms of the four branches of approach and accomplishment: the preliminaries are approach and close approach; the main practice is accomplishment; and the concluding practices, including the ending, are great accomplishment.

As the text states:

I. The Approach

First, in order to dispel adverse circumstances and develop a mass of merit, purify the defilements of body, speech, and mind and read the sūtras in the four directions from the practice hall. For the offering of torma to the four kinds of guests—having earlier made charitable gifts in whatever way is possible, whether extensive or condensed—start with the following:

A. The Ritual of the Ground, Which Has Four Sections

1. Requesting the Ground

Clean the foundation upon which the maṇḍala will be constructed and arrange flowers on it in a single mass. In front, place the white offering torma and serkyem. Around them, starting in the northeast and beginning with the flower, arrange clockwise the two waters and outer offerings. In front of the pre-

siding master, assemble the damarus, bells, and all the other material requirements of the practitioners. When everyone is on their seats, start with the Seven Line prayer, the lineage prayer Trödrel dechen…, and the individual lineage prayers. Then begin the preliminary practice of the Tukdrub Barchey Künsel or the [opening of] the sādhana of the [Tukdrub] Yizhin Norbu, *repeating three times each the refuge, bodhichitta, and the [two] accumulations.*

Think:

In a single instant, I take on the form of the Great Guru
Overwhelming All with Splendor.

Then, make an offering of oblation that you cleanse with:

RAM YAM KHAM ༔

Purify with the mantra of the pure inherent nature:

OM SVABHAVA SHUDDHA SARVA DHARMA SVABHAVA SHUDDHO HAM

From within emptiness, the torma, the nature of amṛita, emanates inexhaustible cloud banks of sense pleasures that fill the entire realm of space.

Bless it with:

OM AH HUNG ༔

Think:

From my heart, light rays emanate like iron hooks, instantly summoning the earth goddesses and the lords of the region.

BHUMI PATI SAPARIVARA VAJRA SAMA JAH ༔
BHUMI PATI SAPARIVARA PUSHPE DHUPE ALOKE GANDHE
NAIVIDYA SHABDA PUJA HOH ༔
BHUMI PATI SAPARIVARA IDAM BALINGTA KHA KHA KHAHI
KHAHI ༔

Saying this three times, offer them the torma. To request their activity, say:

Hung༔
Sovereigns of precious lands of the thousandfold universe,༔
And in particular of Jambudvipa,༔
Earth goddesses, Tenma sisters,༔
Earth lords, and kings, ministers, subjects,༔
And owners of the place and region—༔
From all snow mountains, spring-fed pools, groves,༔
Lakes, and ponds,༔
With a peaceful and hopeful mind,༔
I request you to come here!༔
Accept these five kinds of purely prepared sense pleasures,༔
Offering tormas, golden drink,༔
And excellent land.༔
Previously, before our teacher༔
You made this promise.༔
In order for me to practice in this place,༔
In accordance with the secret teachings and texts of our teacher,༔
Grant me this place of practice.༔
Increase conducive conditions, virtue, and auspiciousness!༔
Accomplish the four activities!༔

Think that, at this request, they say, "You Awareness-holders, happily use this land!" After granting their permission, they joyfully depart to their own abodes.[44]

With the music of peaceful cymbals, offer the torma and serkyem outside. Gather up the heaps and offerings.

2. Taking Possession of the Ground

In front, set up an acacia phurba with an eight-inch red silk ribbon.

From my heart as Guru Overwhelming All with Splendor, a blazing red HRIH syllable emanates. Dissolving into the phurba, it becomes Hayagrīva, red in color, holding a lotus club and skullcup filled with blood; his lower body is in the shape of a dagger tip.

While striking the earth, recite this mantra one hundred times:

OM VAJRA KRODHA HAYA GRIVA HULU HULU HUNG PHAT ༔

Light rays radiate from it,༔
Pervading the earth.༔
All appearance and existence is brought under my power.༔

3. Purifying the Ground

From my heart as Guru Overwhelming All with Splendor, the embodiment of all the families,༔
RAM YAM KHAM emanate—incinerating, scattering, and washing away all faults and defects of clinging to the container and contents as real, and purifying them into emptiness.༔

Concentrate on this instantaneous visualization:

Within emptiness, everything that appears and exists is the guru's buddhafield,༔
The play of timeless awareness, the essence of great bliss,༔
Perfected as the world and contents of the Akaniṣṭha realm, the Great Lotus Net.༔

Recite:

OM SVABHAVA SHUDDHA SARVA DHARMA SVABHAVA SHUDDHO HAM ༔

Consider that the five fingers of your right hand are a five-pointed vajra. Rotate your hand and touch the ground.

Next, to do practice somewhere, you need to also have the owner's authorization to use that land. From an ordinary perspective, if the land belongs to somebody, then you need to go to that person and ask for permission to practice there. If the person wants money, you offer money. If the landowner is not happy, that will create obstacles. This concerns a physical person, but there are also invisible beings, local deities who own the land. You need to also request authorization from them to use the land, which you do by offering them a torma and a serkyem, tea offering. If you have attended a drubchen, you might have noticed that before establishing where the mandala is going to be erected, we place a specific white torma as well as a serkyem offering. The accomplished vajra master blesses those offerings and then summons the landowner spirits, makes the offering, and requests their permission to do the practice. He says, "We would like to do a drubchen here, erect a mandala, and do the great accomplishment practice. Would you agree to that?" Then he makes this offering.

Then the landowning deity appears. It's like the upper half of the deity appears and says, "Yes, this is fine. You can do whatever you wish and practice the way you wish on this land." In this way, he or she grants authorization for us to do this practice, in this particular place. The offering is given, then the deity dissolves and that's the moment where the music is played.

4. Protecting the Ground

Start by offering the torma to the obstacle-makers and commanding them, according to the individual text in question. With gugul incense and hexed mustard seeds, use fierce threats to banish them far away. To plant the boundary phurbas, wrap ten metal or hardwood phurbas marked with the mantras of the ten wrathful herukas from the mantra list, or marked with HUM, *in packets along with white mustard seeds. Arrange them in front, without mixing them up.*

> Light rays emanate from the heart of myself as the wrathful Guru Heruka,༔
> The assembly of all families, manifesting as infinite cloud banks.༔
> Piercing the container and all contents, while considering the ten points of all apparent existence as a blazing wheel,༔
> Summon the ten guardians to all cardinal and intermediate directions as well as above and below.༔
> They are seated.༔
> Once more, ten hung syllables emanate from my heart.༔
> Dissolving into the phurbas, they become blue-black forms of the ten great wrathful ones holding vajras and skullcups filled with blood.༔
> Their lower bodies are phurba points, blazing with raging fire,༔
> Stabbing the hearts of obstructors of the ten directions.༔
> From the ten wrathful ones, innumerable tiny wrathful deities proliferate,༔
> Becoming a vajra-tent in all cardinal and intermediate directions.༔

After taking possession of the site, you need to gain control with sandalwood phurbas that are planted in the different directions. The master, who has the vajra confidence of being the deity, does this. Reciting the mantra, he plants the ten sandalwood phurbas. The phurbas are actually Hayagriva. Through the three neighs of his horse head, Hayagriva gains control over the entire world and the place that has been given. This is the way to take control of the place. It's like when you've bought land, you immediately go and take possession of it; that's the process.

Once you've taken possession of the land, you need to purify it. Therefore, the vajra master now takes the vajra in his right hand and places it on the land, as he recites the OM SVABHAVA mantra seven times, purifying the environment into emptiness. At this point, you've [successfully] bought or borrowed the land and taken possession of it. Next, you need to clean and start to arrange it. These actions correspond to the earth ritual.

After that come the sections of protection, which have outer, inner, and secret ways of being done. If you do an elaborate drubchen, you would leave the practice for about a day or two in order to be able to do *shabten*.[45] Once you finish that, before starting the protection practices, you need to perform *the geg tre,* expelling obstructors and eliminating negative forces or influences. All the practitioners wear the hat and assume the vajra confidence of being Hayagriva. Then they summon all the obstructing forces and bless the torma offering—*the gektor,* the torma offering for obstructing forces—with RAM YAM KHAM and OM AH HUNG. Before giving the torma, the practitioners ask them to leave through peaceful means. The obstructing forces that don't leave when asked nicely are next subject to the wrathful approach. The vajra master recites the words of the sadhana and summons these forces. Different substances, such as *gügul* and *tun*,[46] are used as weapons against them. The vajra master circumambulates the mandala three times. The first time, he is wielding the vajra; the second time, he is throwing those tun seeds as weapons; and the third time, he is performing the wrathful dance. At the end of this, all the obstructing forces have been chased away. They're outside and now the protection is established.

This practice is done with ten phurbas, which are the ten wrathful ones. The practitioners actualize each of these ten phurbas, [the ten wrathful ones] together with their mantras. They summon the protectors of the ten directions: the four cardinal directions, the four intermediary directions, as well as the zenith above and the nadir below. The ten phurbas are planted in the ten directions, in the presence of the protectors of the ten directions, who have been invoked. These ten wrathful ones have the upper body of the wrathful ones, while the lower part of their body is a phurba. The protectors of the ten directions are the ten kings who safeguard each of the directions. Fixed with the phurba, they cannot move their body, speech, and mind. They will remain present, guarding the practice, from that moment at the beginning, until the very end, when the phurba is removed and the vajra master performs a dance. That's for the protection.

B. The three sections of establishing the boundaries, so that obstacles do not carry the siddhis away are:

1. Establishing the outer boundary

Place images or mantra lists of the four great kings on the fours sides of the hall, with offerings in front.

In the east for Dhṛitarāṣhṭra—the practitioners should gather with musical instruments.

In the south for Virūḍhaka
In the west for Virūpākṣha
In the north for Vaiśravaṇa

After that, the vajra master draws the boundaries. The outer boundary is drawn by entrusting it to the care of the four great kings. Outside of the practice place, you erect the palaces of the four great kings, one in each direction, and you establish a seat for each of them. Visualizing this, you invoke them, offer the torma, and entrust them with the activities. This practice is called *gyalto,* the practice of laying out the seat, or marking the boundary, for each king of the four cardinal directions.

2. Establishing the intermediate boundary, which has two parts:

a. Suppressing the samaya violators (*damsi*)

Trap effigies of the damsi in iron chains, with the mantra written at their hearts.

Clean the serkyem by saying,

RAM YAM KHAM ༔

Bless it by saying,

OM AH HUNG ༔

Request the great beings to bear witness:
Summon and immobilize the samaya violators by reciting, again and again:

The suppression of the samaya violators occurs in the intermediate space between the outer and the inner boundaries. There are two classes of samaya violators to be suppressed: damsi, the outer karmic demons, and inner samaya breakers. For the actual suppression, an effigy replete with required dharanies and symbols needs to be properly drawn and washed. The samaya violators are then summoned, or hooked, [by the vajra master], separated from their protection, *lha-ye,* [their protections are lesser spirits who accompany them, a kind of security detail] and banished [absorbed] into the effigy, which is subsequently folded and placed within a dog's skull. The skull is then wrapped in a special black cloth and tied with red and blue thread. The knots of the threads are to be sealed with the face of a wrathful deity [at best]. The skull is then buried in the ground.

The vajra master visualizes himself clearly as a deity and emanates an inconceivable number of weapons from his heart, which pervade the very reaches of space itself. In particular, this [the visualization] can cause the ground [before the master] to crack open. The damsi demons are summoned and bound [as above, and are then placed] in the *hung kung.*[47] He offers a serkyem to the deities [of the Three Roots and dharmapalas to request their assistance in the ritual of suppression by reminding them of their vows] and puts the damsi in the ground.

The vajra master then tells the damsi that they will remain bound in the ground until they give rise to bodhichitta.[48] He then seals and buries them under the four elements and the sky, as well as Mt. Meru, a crossed vajra, and black tsa tsas [of stupas]. There are various hand gestures that accompany the ritual of suppression. Thereafter, the vajra master, his regent, and all the assembled lamas walk over the suppressed demon, performing the wrathful vriyual ajra dance of suppression—in its peaceful, increasing, magnetizing, and subjugating forms. That is the practice for the intermediate boundary.

b. Preserving the blessings inside and keeping the obstacles outside

After that, in order to prevent the blessings inside the practice environment from being lost and going outside, you entrust that activity to the deity Amrita Kundali. In order to prevent the obstacles outside from entering the practice place, you entrust this activity to the deity Yamantaka. You prepare their seats, visualize the samaya deities, invoke the wisdom deities to come, merge indivisibly, and make offerings. A torma is offered and these activities are entrusted to them. Say, "As long as we'll be doing this practice, until the end of this practice, remain here in order to prevent the obstacles outside from entering and to prevent the blessings inside from leaving."

This boundary is established through the protection circles. Visualize five circles of different weapons surrounding the practice place, as well as fences of fire and fences of vajras. Emanate male and female wrathful deities that surround the practice place as well. The male wrathful deities face outward and the females face inward. Use the protective circle text for whichever drubchen sadhana you are practicing. You create the secret boundary by realizing the inherent emptiness of whatever you believe needs protection, the act of protecting it, and the one accomplishing the protection. In this way, the secret boundary is established.

In the interval between creating the outer boundary and the inner boundary, the practitioners cannot come inside the practice place. When they do, they have to be purified through fire, water, and tun.

3. Establishing the secret boundary

To liberate Matam and establish the secret boundary, place an image of Matam Rudra on his back, with his head facing southeast, on the ground where the mandala is to be erected. The practitioners should don wrathful garments and recite:

MAHA GURU SHRI HERUKO HAM

To really make the secret boundary, you need to suppress Matam Rudra. To render the obstructing forces incapable of causing any destruction in the practice, you must completely suppress the king of obstructors, Matam Rudra. If you are able to liberate the king in the palace of practice, all the other thousands of minor obstructing forces and spirits will never be able to cause harm. You then arrange the effigy of Matam Rudra in the practice place. Invoke the actual Matam Rudra to come and dissolve indivisibly with the effigy. Matam Rudra appears clearly with all his characteristics: three heads, six hands, four legs, wings, the ten ornaments of the wrathful ones, and the eight adornments of the charnel ground. Then the vajra master, with the vajra confidence of being the glorious heruka, and supported by the two wrathful ones under his arms, approaches Matam Rudra.

Through specific movements of dance, the vajra master takes a trident, whose three spokes represent the three poisons, and plants it in Matam Rudra's heart. The three poisons are, thus, transformed into the three kayas, and the vajra master expels him toward the dharmadhatu, so he is liberated. The limbs and head of the Matam Rudra are cut and dispersed in the four directions. Then the palace of the belly is cut open with a specific mantra. Uttering HUNG HUNG HA HA OM PHAT, the vajra master makes three circumambulations around the mandala.

This is establishing the boundaries. These last aspects of the practice are probably things you've seen when you attended drubchens. In the elaborate practices, the Horse Dance is done at this point.

II. The Close Approach

This has five sections: doing the preparatory ritual, building the mandala, integrating the practitioners, investing them, and receiving the descent of blessings.

A. The preparatory ritual has four sections: preparing the deities, the vases, the materials, and the disciples.

1. Preparation of the Deities

Begin by inviting the deities, sprinkling alcohol and five amritas in a skull cup.

The next phase of the practice is drawing the mandala. First, you need to request authorization from the deities to draw the mandala. The vajra master is in the center, surrounded in the four directions by the four vajra regents, the four umdzes, and others holding the different offerings for each of the individual families. They first start with the East, making the request in the eastern direction, and then do the same in the South, West, and North. The vajra master, in the center, invokes the buddhas of the five families and asks for the authorization to draw the mandala, He asks, "Can you grant us permission to draw the mandala?" The deities reply that they authorize the mandala to be drawn, as desired. The vajra master again dons the hat. Informing the students that the deities have granted permission to draw the mandala, the vajra master tells them to do so, according to the correct indications and instructions. The vajra master and the retinue chant HUNG several times, rejoicing at having received this authorization. They circumambulate, turning to the right of the place where the mandala is going to be drawn. This is the drawing of the mandala.

2. Preparation of the Vases

In order to accomplish the deities, you do the vase practice, in which the main purpose is to grant empowerment. The best way to do that is to have as many vases as the deities in the mandala. For example, the *Tukdrub Barchey Künsel* has fifteen deities, so ideally you would have fifteen vases. These vases have specific characteristics for the base, the round middle part, and the spout. If you're not doing this elaborately, you can follow the middling way, where you have at least one vase for the main deity and one activity vase.

First you need to eliminate the obstructing forces, by means of the *geg tre,* and for this you use the torma, the gügul, and the tun. The vase is purified into emptiness with the OM SVABHAVA mantra, and then water is poured in. As I explained before, this water possesses eight qualities. Also, it needs to be brought from a place where there's a constant flow of water, not a place where water flow is intermittent. The one sent to fetch the water must be somebody who still has both parents and is of a good family. He or she needs to bring the exact amount of water; otherwise, you will have to pour it out, as there shouldn't be any remaining water. When taking the water, the water bearer washes his or her face, drinks the water, and then pours it, having taken the exact amount, so nothing needs to be thrown away. With each different substance that is put into the vase, there is an accompanying mantra. There are five different collections of five—including precious materials, medicinal substances, grains, and so on—which add up to twenty-five ingredients that are put in the vase.[49] There are ten extra unsurpassable substances you can add, if you have them; so you could have thirty or thirty-five types of ingredients.

The vase needs to be two-thirds full, not completely full. Wrapping a cloth around it, you say, *ting sa lakar*. Then you put on the top ornament. For most of the vases, the top ornament is made of kusha grass and the wood of a fruit tree. But for a Dzogchen empowerment, you need a peacock feather as the top ornament of the vase. Then you attach the vajra protective cord. Preparation for both the elaborate and unelaborate vases is the same up to this point.

From the outside, the vases appear to be vases. However, the inside of each vase is the palace of the deities and the substances are the deities. To develop the deities of the vase, you make offerings and praises and recite mantras. When reciting, visualize yourself as the deity. From your heart center, light rays emanate and enter into the vase water. The deities in the vase are pleased, and their blessings and wisdom mix in one taste with the vase water. That was the explanation for the main vase. For the activity vase, the activity deity is Hayagriva. Through the same process, you invoke the wisdom mind of Hayagriva, so that all the activities may be accomplished without any hindrance or obstacle. The vase deities basically depend upon the practice you're doing; each is different. Sometimes it is Hayagriva, other times it is Amrita Kundali, and so forth. That is the preparatory practice for the vase.

3. Preparation of the Practice Materials and Ritual Instruments [and the Accomplishment Substances]

4. Preparation of the Students

The final preparatory phase concerns getting the students ready to do the practice and receive the empowerment. The process for empowerment includes the preparation stage, the preliminaries, and the main part—and on top of that, receiving the blessings.

Next, there is the preparatory consecration connected to the deity. For this, you arrange a mandala, placing heaps on top of it in connection with the different deities. You visualize the deities, invite them, and make offerings and praise. After this, you chant a specific mantra, as the deities are elevated into space and the mandala is drawn below.

B. Erecting the Mandala and Arranging the Support of the Accomplishment and the Ornaments

To draw the mandala, first you cleanse the ground by sprinkling water. Then you sprinkle different substances: the five ingredients coming from the cow, the five nectars, and so on. The vajra king or regent goes to the eastern direction, and the vajra guard goes to the western direction. Then the process of drawing the lines of the mandala begins. To render the lines straight, you need to use threads, which must first be blessed. The tantras contain many details about those different threads.

The vajra master rolls the threads in his hands. The process of drawing the lines starts with the vajra guard visualizing the vajra master as the male deity and the vajra guard as the female deity. They are in union, and the nectar of bodhichitta coming from their place of union draws the line in space. Before you draft the lines on the ground, the lines are rendered in space. There are specific ways of moving around the mandala, facing in different directions, according to the pith instructions.

They draw the eight major lines. First, the wisdom lines are drawn in space, and as a reflection of that, the lines on the ground are arranged. These lines provide the structure for delineating the mandala. Then the drawing of the mandala starts, with placement of the different colors, which have been blessed before as the five buddha families. If you are unable to complete the sketch of the mandala in one day, then at the end of the day, place a kapala upside down with a vajra on top of it, in order to prevent the obstructing forces from entering. There are many instructions on drawing and coloring the mandala.

Once the mandala has been drawn, there are many ways to check whether the auspicious circumstances are present. It is said that if the mandala has been rendered very clearly, without mixing, then the practitioners will accomplish the deity. If you are not in a position to create a mandala using colored sands, then once you have drawn the wisdom lines in space, you can arrange an image of a mandala on the ground, provided you choose one that is allowed. It is said that the best kind of mandala is made of colored sand and the middling kind is drawn.

To consecrate the mandala, practice supports are placed inside. The main practice support is the kapala marked with the wheel of life. Then, the vases that have been consecrated are arranged as supports for the empowerments. Next, the representations of body, speech, mind, qualities, and activities are laid out.

As a support for the enlightened body, place a statue of the deity, a card representing the deity, or a thangka. The support for speech is the volume of the tantra connected with that particular sadhana; as instructed, it should be written in gold. As a support for the enlightened mind, place a vajra and a bell bound together by red and white silk as well as a stupa, mirror, and crystal. *Chulen* pills—pills from extracting the essence practice—are the support for the enlightened qualities. A consecrated phurba supports the activities. First, eliminate the negativities with mustard seeds, then cleanse with rakta, and purify with gügul, applying the means of deity, mantra, mudra, and samadhi. Finally, the long-life arrow and long-life tormas, *chung,* and pills uphold the longevity practice.

These are the main things that you place in the mandala for a drubchen. However, there are also other substances, offerings, and supports—such as men, torma, and rakta—which you can arrange according to your need. These shouldn't be of poor quality. You want really great substances, magnificent offerings, full of blessings and endowed with all the impeccable qualities, as described in the practice instructions. They should have all the perfect measurements and characteristics, according to the instructions given in the teachings.

Once you have established the mandala in this way, if you know that it has been accomplished perfectly, that's ideal. However, if you know that the result is not so good, you make a fire offering, a *jinsek,* and all the practitioners recite the Hundred Syllable mantra to purify the breakages of samayas.

After building the mandala, you immediately do the practices for placing the various adornments. Once again, you need to eliminate the obstructing forces through the ritual for expelling them and purify the adornments as well. Before placing the ornaments, the vajra masters and the practitioners put on their hats and try to appear as beautiful and impressive as possible. As it says in the tantras, at this point, the practitioners need to wash with the five nectars, groom themselves, dress well, and wear the different bone and jewel ornaments. There are actually five specific fragrances, according to the tantras. The monks now put on the *chö gö,* the yellow outer robe, and hats. The chö gö is from Buddha Shakyamuni, who gathered pieces of cloth and sewed them together in order to form a shawl.

To review, we have erected the mandala and placed inside it the different supports of the enlightened body, speech, mind, qualities, and activities. Around the mandala, we placed the various ornaments: pendants, victory banners, swords, arrows, and so on, each of which has a symbolic meaning. Now is the moment where the protective cord from the mandala is bound around the vajra and handed to the vajra master. This is done to indivisibly unite the life force of the visualized front mandala with the self-visualized mandala.

At this point, there is a lecture with instructions, and the next step is to entrust the different practitioners with their respective jobs. The vajra master and regents are enthroned and the different actors in the practice are delegated their seats, offered *chang,* and told what to do. Ideally, the vajra king would sit on a lion throne, with his consort on a throne of flowers next to him. There is also a throne for the vajra regent, as well as thrones in the four directions for the deities of the four families—karma, ratna, padma, and vajra. Finally, there are thirteen lower thrones and vajra seats. In brief, you have the vajra throne—the lion throne of the vajra king in the middle—then the female practitioners to the left and the male practitioners to the right. At that point, you sprinkle a little beer. Since the participants represent the deities, you should formally sprinkle a little beer for each participant, requesting them individually to take a seat. Once this is done, you cannot move seats; having been given a particular seat and function, you need to stay there. Then, to be able to perform the activities, the practitioners will be invested with the peaceful and wrathful attires, depending on which activities they are supposed to accomplish. They're given the corresponding signs and marks that relate to these activities. If you are supposed to meditate on a deity, you are given attire that corresponds to the aspect of that deity. Each person should really practice assuming the vajra confidence of being that particular deity.

C. Mixing and Integrating the New and the Old Practitioners

D. Investing the Practitioners

Empowerment/Enthronement: Empower the Practitioners and Arrange Them on their Seats, So They Engage in the Activity of the Group Practice Correctly.

As soon as these steps have taken place, all the practitioners are brought together as one. Thus, older practitioners who are accustomed to this practice are brought together with the newer ones. From this point on, consider that there are no differences between these groups of practitioners. Before this is done, the older and newer practitioners are in separate places. The newer ones, who are on one side, come in front of the vajra master in order to be initiated and introduced into the mandala. The vajra master eliminates all the obstacles, meditates on the protective circle, gives transmission of the Dharma, explains the teachings, clarifies the samayas, and asks the newer practitioners if they feel like taking these pledges. If they agree, ritual implements—bells, vajras, and malas—are placed before them. Through this practice, they become the same as the older practitioners. This is sealed by rejoicing, wherein *chang* is offered to everyone. Through this, the beginners become a suitable vessel for the practice, just as the older practitioners are. After that, they are mixed together.

In most of the drubchen framework texts, this aspect of the practice—making the beginners suitable vessels for the practice and mixing them with the older students—takes place before the entrustment of the different practitioners. However, here, it is given in this sequence, so I just followed that and explained it in this way.

According to the Chökling tradition, eleven blessings are bestowed at the beginning of the practice: blessing the practice place, the master, the hand, the vajra, the bell, the mala, the symbols, the phurba, the drum, the food, and so forth. That's the extensive approach. The vajra master places tsampa and butter on the tray and presents them to the different practitioners, saying, "Now enjoy all the desirable objects as the great tsok offering." Each of these has great significance. When the vajra master goes around blessing with the mala, he's reciting the mantra and saying to the students, "Continuously recite the mantra." For the drum, he tells them, "Always meditate and follow the drum of enlightenment." The middling approach is the five blessings.

E. Receiving the Descent of Blessings

For the descent of blessings, the practitioners—donning their hats, dharma robes, and the like to generate brilliance—should arrange themselves surrounding the mandala. You hold multi-colored tossing streamers and burn fine smelling incense. Accompanied by cymbals and a melodious tune inspired by intense faith and devotion, first perform the Seven Line prayer three times and then the descent of blessings, as it is found in the particular ritual manual. At the conclusion, circumambulate the mandala and sing the melody of the mantra recitation three times. Complete the preliminary phase by performing the dissolution and re-emergence, dedications, and aspirational prayers.

These are the preparatory stages of the practice. For the main part, the wisdom deities—who are present in space above the mandala—need to descend into the mandala, which is the descent of blessings. With this, the preparatory and preliminary stages of the practice are concluded.

III. The Main Part

The Accomplishment of Becoming Indivisible with the Deity

Do the main practice of the activity manual and encourage the enlightened mindstream through recitation.

The complete practice consists of seven preliminary sections; seven sections of the main part, which starts with the three samadhis; and the seven concluding sections.

A. Conducting the Rite and Enjoining the Deities' Heart through Recitation

The main part of the practice will last for seven days. During this time, the actual sadhanas are repeated three times during the day and three times at night. During each of these sessions, you also expel the negative forces and request the blessings to descend. The most important aspect of engaging in a drubchen is to maintain the actual life force of the practice, the mantra recitation, uninterruptedly during the entire practice.

Throughout the practice, it is crucial to understand the three statements: all appearances are the deity, all sounds are mantra, and all thoughts are samadhi. *All appearances are the deity* means that throughout the drubchen, you need to maintain the recognition that you are the deity. You do not just do it once when reciting the lines of the visualization; you need to continually recognize this fact. If you get distracted and forget, you must recall it again. To realize all appearances, including your own body, as the deity, you must practice unifying the three aspects of visualization—sustaining the visualization clearly, remembering the purity, and having vajra confidence—altogether as one.

During practice, it is important to have clear visualization, vajra pride, and recollection of the purity; in addition, you should rely on the four nails that bind the life force and also offer feast. Six times during the day and six times at night (thus, twelve times), we do practices to tame the twelve *jungpos* through the manifestation of the twelve wrathful deities with the twelve wrathful substances. These expel the *nuley* demons. In those twelve times, there are also twelve different deities who give the accomplishments. That is why we perform *The Descent of Blessings*. From the moment you commence the practice until you conclude, sustain the continuity in which you perceive all appearances as the mandala of the deity, all sounds as mantra, and all thoughts as the dharmata. Maintain that throughout the practice.

All sounds are mantra simply means that whenever you hear a sound, it is mantra. While reciting the mantra, you also emanate rays of light, purifying and making offerings. As you draw them back in, where they dissolve, you receive the siddhis and accumulate merit. There are also four phases of recitation: the moon with the garland of stars, the whirling firebrand, the king's emissaries, and the beehive that has broken open. During the drubchen, the most important is the last one. Just as all the bees buzz and swarm around a beehive that has broken open, all the syllables of the mantra are buzzing with their own sounds. For example, each of the twelve syllables of the mantra OM AH HUNG BENZA GURU PEMA SIDDHI HUNG resound over and over again, creating a droning buzz of all twelve together.

All thoughts are samadhi means you shouldn't let ordinary thoughts—which are related to past, present, and future—invade your mind; instead, remain concentrated in samadhi and focus on the practice you are doing.

These three can be summed up simply, by saying, "Do not let your body, speech, and mind fall under the influence of delusion." Of course, it is impossible for beginners to be completely free of delusion, but you should do your best to diminish deluded appearances and to increase pure appearances. Maintain the continuity of the mantra and samadhi throughout the drubchen, and do not allow the ritual activities to dissipate into ordinary behavior. Relate to all that you do in an extraordinary way; for example, regard your clothing as the ornaments of the deities and your meal as a ganachakra feast offering.

It is said that if everyone, from the vajra king down to the vajra sweeper—the person who cleans up the temple—maintains the continuity of actualizing the deity, an incredible power is generated.

The text also includes many less important instructions, which detail what you need to do, such as making large tsok offerings as well as offering many butter lamps and tormas. As it also says, if good signs manifest, you need to receive the accomplishment at that time. However, if negative signs arise, you should practice confession by reciting the Hundred Syllable mantra and doing the Horse Dance.

Now for the signs of accomplishment, the results from doing this practice are mentioned very clearly in the text. I have also spoken about this in the past, so I don't need to say it again. If signs of realization and qualities arise in your mind, I cannot determine them, but if you flew in the sky, I could see that! In Kathok Monastery in the past, when they were doing drubchens, a number of people attained rainbow body, and such signs were seen by others.

There are several approaches to receiving the blessings: through the path of union, from the deities, and from the vajra protectors. Once again, I have spoken about this in the past and I cannot say anything more than is already in the commentary.

IV. Great Accomplishment

The great accomplishment: after having perfected the practice, take the actual accomplishment.

A. The Actual Taking of the Accomplishments

The first part has three subsequent parts: the arrangement of the materials, the preliminary ritual, and the actual ritual.

1. The Arrangement of the Materials

2. The Preliminary Ritual

For the preliminary ritual, or procedure, conduct the rite according to the text, in the early hours before sunrise. After completing the mantra recitation, confession, verses of offering and praise, and so on, according to the given text, release the previous continuum of approach (i.e., the mantra melody) and, instead, add the following to the heart mantras to receive attainments:

> Kāyasiddhi OM, vākasiddhi AH, cittasiddhi HUNG, guṇasiddhi TRAM, karmasiddhi HRIH, sarvalokajñānasiddhiphala HUNG ༔

First, to receive the siddhis from the deities, arrange the substances that are mentioned in the text. When you are about to receive the accomplishments, you do a self-visualization of the mandala of the deities. The main things to do, before receiving the accomplishments, are to sincerely wish to receive them and to rejoice at that prospect. There is a mantra to recite at that point, which you attach at the end of the mantra of the deity you've been practicing. You see all the wisdom deities in union, and from their point of union, the nectar of bodhichitta flows down, ready to emanate rays of light containing the blessing. Everybody is full of joy and satisfaction.

> HUNG! In this non-abiding, innate wisdom mandala,༔
> Obstructive spirits who steal attainments,༔
> Obstructors who disturb me—gods or demonic forces—༔
> Do not stay here; go elsewhere.༔
> If any sinful being is to go against ༔
> The secret word of the vajra,༔
> May his brain be splintered into a hundred pieces!༔

Also, at that time, all the siddhi substances are incredibly beautiful, blazing, and magnificent. The butter lamps are bright, the nectar is overflowing, the rakta receptacle is completely full, and so on. All the deities are smiling, and you see all that vividly, as if they were really there in front of you. At this point, before receiving the accomplishments, we need to once again eliminate the obstructing forces and perform the descent of blessings. There is a danger that robbers will steal the blessings, and these practices prevent that.

This is the point where you are just about to receive the siddhis. As you go through the lines of the text to be granted the siddhis, you sincerely wish for the siddhis to be bestowed.

Recite fierce mantras, play music, and toss white mustard seeds. Burn gugul. To create a boundary, recite:

HUNG ༔
In the mandala of the primordially manifest deity,༔
The vajra body, speech, and mind are inherently complete.༔
Self-arising insight, wrathful gathering, dome of weapons ༔
Cut the boundary in unfabricated, luminous space.༔
HUNG BENZA RAKSHA DHRUM ༔

Recite this while cultivating the protection circle. Conduct the consecration from the particular text as you burn incense, play music, and wave the ribbon. Then, for the consecration of the practice materials, recite:

HUNG HRIH!༔
From the magical display of the awakened mind,༔
Which is the heart of innate wisdom, fire, water, and wind,༔
Destroy the aeon of grasping to things.༔
Inside the skull palace, an abode of establishing purity,༔
The five ambrosias emerge from OM HUNG TRAM HRIH Ah.༔
The five meats emerge from MUM LAM MAM PAM TAM.༔
From the five elements, which have the identity of the five innate wisdoms,༔
And by means of the application of fire and wind produced from the magical display of awareness,༔
The materials melt into the state of bliss and emptiness,༔
The inseparability of the basic space and awareness.༔
Inconceivable light rays of the five innate wisdoms emerge ༔
And collect the pure essences from both saṃsāra and nirvāṇa,༔
Transforming them into the five buddha families.༔
They join in union and dissolve into bodhichitta,༔
The materials swirling as the ambrosia of innate wisdom.༔
OM AH HUNG SARVA PANCHA AMRITA HUNG HRIH THA༔

Repeat this mantra and consecrate.

Confess discord:

HUNG HRIH!༔
Denigrating others, I have fallen under the influence of ignorance༔
Of the primordially pure nondual dharmakāya.༔
Results of pleasure and pain variously ripen.༔
Despite having taken up the victors' commitments in order to avert this,༔
Within the unobservable basic space,༔
I request forgiveness for everything that—under the influence of laziness—has gone against these commitments.༔
Granting forgiveness, I request you to bestow attainments!༔

Recite the Hundred Syllable mantra.

3. The Actual Ritual

For the actual ritual, or procedure, gather the accomplishments:

HUNG HRIH!༔
In the nondual basic space-awareness,༔
From the place of union of the deities of great bliss,༔
Limitless light rays emerge, pervading the sky.༔
Offered to the victors, they purify the obscurations of beings.༔
Gathering all of the supreme and common attainments,༔
They dissolve into me, spontaneously accomplishing all desires.༔
Dissolving into the materials, they create an ocean of ambrosia.༔

Thus enjoin and focus. At the end of each deity's heart mantra, add the following and repeat one thousand each:

SARVA AMRITA KUNDALI SARVA SIDDHI HUNG HUNG༔

Enjoin from the core:

By countless light rays in the shape of red hooks that emerge from my heart centre, gurus, vidyādharas, the victors along with their sons, the peaceful and wrathful bliss-gone ones, ḍakinīs, and dharmapālas arrive, like a violent blizzard, and dissolve into me, the being who holds the sacred commitment.

Hung Hrih!༔
Gurus, vidyādharas, victors, and your children,༔
Peaceful and wrathful sugatas, ḍakinīs, and those bound by the sacred commitments,༔
Arise from Akaniṣṭha, the basic space, and be installed in this maṇdala of sacred commitments.༔
I request that you accept this nondual homage and these ambrosia offerings of the materials of sacred commitment.༔
I request that you grant the supreme and common attainments.༔
If you, sugatas, do not bestow attainments in this place,༔
Would that not contradict your powerful prior commitments?༔
Therefore, please bestow attainments immediately.༔

Thus enjoining, repeat one thousand times the heart mantra with the following attached to it:

Samaya vajra samaya༔

Then you receive the blessings, by again reciting a specific mantra and appending with samaya vajra samaya.

The enjoining for accomplishments:

Hung!༔
O hosts of the guru maṇḍala, gathering of vidyādharas,༔
Who are present in this great sambhogakāya paradise,༔
Which does not waver from natural basic space—༔
First, covered by the thick darkness of ignorance,༔
I did not see your face, even though you reside inseparably within me.༔
By the kindness of the lama,༔
Through the lamp of the profound pith instructions,༔
I saw the self-illuminating, self-awareness deity and maṇḍala.༔
In the interim, by the yidam who is worthy of refuge, as the object of worship,༔
I practised and accomplished by perfecting the approach and close approach.༔

My body, speech, and mind have matured into awakened body, speech, and mind.ཿ
Now, O supreme deity, you and I are inseparable.ཿ
The dawn of Vajrasattva is breaking.ཿ
In the vast expanse of the sky, the embodiment of all the sugatas,ཿ
The sun of compassion shines forth, wherein ignorance self-vanishes.ཿ
The time has come for accomplishments.ཿ
I beseech you to quickly bestow the desired result!ཿ

Recite the verses for receiving accomplishments found in the ritual manual for the particular heart practice you are doing and touch the practice supports to your three places. Take up the mantra repetition as a melody and, starting with the master, distribute the materials to all vajra brothers and sisters. Apply drops of ambrosia to your three places. Enjoy the substances while maintaining an experience of bliss and emptiness. Think:

I easily obtain all the supreme and common accomplishments upon this very seat.

Then, if required, you should now conduct an empowerment for the sake of others, in whatever manner is most appropriate—extensive, moderate, or condensed.

Your visualization when receiving the blessing is the same as when receiving the four empowerments. The deities are blazing and emanating different colored lights from their place of union. The white light enters your forehead, granting the blessing of the enlightened body. The red rays of light enter your throat, conferring the blessing of speech. The blue light dissolves into your heart, bestowing the blessing of the enlightened mind. The yellow light for the qualities and the green light for the activities also dissolve into you, after which you imagine that you have received the siddhis. There are three components involved here: the deity that gives accomplishment, the siddhis that are bestowed, and you as the one who receives those accomplishments. If you can rest in the one taste of those three, you have received the accomplishments, the siddhis.

At that time, people who already have an established practice will see it improve greatly. Practitioners who have understanding will gain a taste, an experience, and those who have an experience, will gain a realization, and those who have a realization, will see their realization increase. Then, we take the accomplishment substances and place them at the different points—forehead, throat, and heart. In this way, you receive the empowerments. At that time, eat accomplishment substances that are edible and drink those that can be drunk. See them as the nectar of accomplishment and receive them in this way. As the nectar enters your mouth, it penetrates your entire body. As a result, you experience supreme bliss and gain the supreme, ultimate accomplishment. If you are a meditator who has taken part in the drubchen, you will see some improvement in your practice once you receive the accomplishment.

It is said that when really doing the great drubchen practice, if you have reached supreme accomplishment of the vidhayadhara level of Mahamudra, you receive accomplishment through the path of union or through the path of liberation. For us, when we're doing drubchen practices, we are just emulating that approach. It is said that it is fine to receive the accomplishment from the deities when practicing more at that aspirational level. When receiving the accomplishment through the path of union, monks and nuns can also participate, if they have really mastered the practice and are able to not generate any desire. Otherwise, there is the danger of breaking their vows.

B. The stage of the activity of the conclusion . . . and the concluding ritual connected with the mandala

At this point, the other activities for concluding the drubchen are performed. In the context of the practice of the *Kagye*—for example, Yamantaka or Vajrakilaya—this is the point of the accomplishment of the higher activities of enlightenment and the lower activities of eliminating enemies and obstructing forces. This is the time when those are done in the practice. They entail a more elaborate type of approach, which is not required.

The remainder offerings have been kept from the beginning of the practice until the taking of accomplishment, the siddhis. They are kept so that the deities and the protectors enjoy these offerings and stay around to protect the mandala. After the siddhis have been received, the remainder offerings are taken outside. The offering for the protectors is given next. If necessary, the *zor* weapon torma, which is an averting torma, is also thrown at that time.

In the same way that we established the boundaries with the four kings at the beginning, we go out and bring down the boundaries of the four kings as well as the two protections at the doors. After that, we take out each of the ten phurbas sequentially, starting with the one at the base and concluding with the phurba at the top. They all dissolve back into the one at the zenith. The tip of each of the phurbas needs to be cleansed with milk. Playing the bell and actualizing that everything is truly emptiness, the colors of the mandala are dispersed.

We make many mistakes when doing drubchen practice, which is why, at this point, we request forgiveness for every one of them. Then we dissolve the mandala and arise again as the deity. Finally, we seal the practice with dedication and aspiration prayers. When it says that we need to seal with dedication and aspiration prayers, the aspiration prayer that we make here is the *Marme Mönlam,* the lamp offering aspiration prayer. During the Marme Mönlam, the vajra master chants first. After the Marme Mönlam, we seal with the dedication of all the virtues and the words of auspiciousness.

For three days, you celebrate without going far. It is said that when you first leave the drubchen place, it is important that you don't meet samaya breakers. You try to maintain the practice that you've been doing for seven days, so that the accomplishments will mature. If you can, prolong that for seven days. We continue to do the practice for seven days, to receive the full maturation of it.

It is said that the benefits of the drubchen practice are such that a practitioner who does seven days of drubchen practice accomplishes what a practitioner would achieve during one-pointed solitary retreat for seven years. Being part of the drubchen practice is the same as holding the innermost essence of the heart blood of Guru Rinpoche, as he stated. Even people who've committed the gravest of the grave negative actions—the five negative actions with immediate retribution—are able to completely purify those evil deeds and reach the level of a vidyadhara, if they genuinely confess and purify those heinous actions and do the drubchen practice. Such is the power of the mantras.

It is also said that in these degenerate times, in particular, circumstances will become more difficult and beings will encounter outer, inner, and secret obstacles to the reflection of the teachings and its practice. For these times, Guru Rinpoche—out of his great skill in means and compassion—gave these incredible pith instructions, which were hidden and preserved by the dakinis and later revealed as termas. At this time of degeneration, the great skillful means of the drubchen practice should be done. If people do drubchen practice, they'll reach the vidyadhara levels, and, basically, have no need to worry.

Through these practices, in one lifetime, you'd be able to progress through the four levels of the vidyadharas. It is said that even if you're not able to progress through those four levels of realization of the vidyadharas, at the moment your breath stops at death, you will immediately go to the Zangdok Palri pure land, where you will receive direct teaching from Guru Rinpoche and progress through those four vidyadhara levels without the slightest obstacle.

It is also said that even people who attend a drubchen without actually doing the practice will sever their bond with samsara. Guru Rinpoche said that the benefits of drubchen practice are inconceivable. More than a hundred great tertöns have come, and all these tertöns revealed drubchen practices in their termas.

It is a truly incredible opportunity to participate in such a profound practice as this, and you should rejoice when you have such an opportunity. The Dharma is not just a bunch of theory to discuss and ponder; you need to actually practice it. Spending your entire life receiving teachings but not really practicing them, and instead continuing with your ordinary worldly tasks, will not result in much benefit. Yet, if you take just seven days to be diligent and joyful while engaging in a drubchen, great benefit can be attained, not only for you but for all beings everywhere as well.

Vajrasattva Drubchen[50]

As the Vajrayana teachings are present and we have met them, we need to practice them. The essence of the tantras is the sadhana section, which is to be practiced. There are four sections of [development stage] practice: approach, close approach, accomplishment, and great accomplishment. Now we are doing a drubchen, and the tradition of drubchen first started here—at Mount Malaya, in English known as Adam's Peak, Sri Lanka—and slowly reached to King Jah and other places. Through the practice of drubchen, great accomplishment, one can progress through the stages of the four vidyadhara levels and reach enlightenment.

In a drubchen, there's a lot to do; it's an elaborate practice, with many details. In the past, there were times when they would do great accomplishment practice and the entire country would join in. For each feast offering, they would offer one hundred thousand measures of gold. Being such a great, elaborate practice, it also makes the results come quickly. It's like the difference between doing something by yourself and doing it with one hundred people. With one hundred people, it can be done immediately. This is a tradition of practice that went to India, to Uddiyana, to the lands of the Muslims, and also to Tibet. However, the way it's done now in Tibet is just a reflection; it kind of looks like it, but it's not the real way, because we're not able to do it exactly as it should be done. So, we're doing the best we can to emulate that, and as a mere resemblance, we practice for seven days. Still, this has enormous benefit; the teachings explain how incredible the benefits of such practice are.

The very essence, the core, of all the tantra and sadhana section teachings is Vajrasattva. In the tantra teachings, it is the essence of Vajrasattva that manifested all the deities, the mandalas, and the teachings. The root of all the sadhanas is Vajrasattva, who gathers into one family the three, five, and one hundred families. They all come down to the one single family of Vajrasattva. The ultimate fruition is to reach the state of Vajrasattva. The great emptiness, the great purity, free of all stains and obscurations, is Vajrasattva. This is the drubchen that we're going to do, the practice of Vajrasattva called *Mindroling Dorsem,* which brings together the essence of all the tantra and sadhana sections.

We need to accomplish Vajrasattva. You all have entered the path of Vajrayana already; now you have no choice. It is something to think about carefully beforehand, before doing it, because it is dangerous. If everything goes well and you keep your samayas, you reach enlightenment very quickly. If everything does not go well and you break your samayas, then you will end up in the worst hell, which means an enormous amount of suffering. Those are the only two options. The main aspect is empowerment. Whether you enter the path of Vajrayana depends on whether you have received empowerment or not. You do have the freedom to decide whether you are going to receive an empowerment or not. Tibetans don't have the slightest doubt; when an empowerment is given, they flock to the empowerment place and receive the empowerment. Many of you Westerners have received empowerment already.

The life force of the empowerment is the samaya. There are samayas of body, speech, and mind; there are the twenty-five samayas and one hundred thousand samayas. Having gotten an empowerment, some people sometimes say, "Oh, don't talk about the samayas, because people will be freaked out." That is the worst thing I've ever heard, because that's a one-way ticket to hell, for sure. About samayas, we don't keep most of them, actually. In general, that's the situation; we actually break more samayas than we keep. That is why Vajrasattva gave this Hundred Syllable mantra, which is the most powerful way of restoring samayas. Vajrasattva, himself, said that if you recite the Hundred Syllable mantra one hundred and eight times without distraction, then all the negativity, all the samaya breakages you may have done, will all be cleansed and purified. Vajrasattva is not a liar. That means that reciting this mantra has enormous benefit. However, first, you need to be able to do it well, correctly. What is difficult is to be undistracted—which basically means you recite the mantra, visualize the deity, think of the meaning, and leave the mind undistracted. If, on the other hand, you recite the mantra and you're just thinking of all sorts of things, that's when the mind is distracted.

You need to be undistracted, and that is how to do the drubchen as much as you can. Practice the self-visualization, the front visualization, and the vase visualization. Actualize body [appearances as the deity], speech as mantra, mind in samadhi, the emanating, and reabsorbing. After that come the fulfillment and confession practices, in which you apologize and repair by fulfillment, which has four sections. Following that is the self-empowerment, through which you stabilize the wisdom you received at the time of the empowerment. First you receive the empowerment from the lama and every day you restore that through the self-empowerment. Next comes the feast offering. When you do all these practices, you should be undistracted, because if you are distracted that won't bring much result. Think well about this.

Now, actually, when teaching about drubchen, one needs to talk about all the aspects of development stage practice. There are many sections in development stage practice; there are the preliminaries, the main part, and the concluding sections. I've taught quite extensively about this in the past.[51] Now is the time to put all these into practice, and the way to do so boils down to sights, sounds, and samadhi. All appearances manifest as the deity, all sounds as mantra, and all thoughts as awareness. Do this for seven days; however, the nail[52] of unchanging wisdom mind, is not something that we are able to keep for seven days. Again and again renew it, [rest in the nail of unchanging wisdom mind]; it gets lost and repeatedly bring it back. To put it concisely, ordinary thoughts decrease and development stage practice increases.

If you don't know the practice, you need to bring in the four powers. The drubchen starts later today, so think, "Before beginning this drubchen, for countless aeons, I have accumulated bad karma, evil deeds, and negative emotions; things have not turned out well. I really need to have regret." Of course, you could think, "I haven't done anything negative," but you are still in samsara. We are deluded and every instant we accumulate so much negativity. In particular, we forget about the vows of individual liberation, the greater vehicle trainings in bodhichitta, and the Vajrayana samaya precepts. There are also the ten unvirtuous actions we have done. And it is not just you, but all sentient beings have done that. We need to develop regret, and we are not going to lose anything by doing it; just have that sense of regret.

First is the power of regret. Once you have generated regret, it is necessary to confess those negative actions. You also need to purify them through confession. For the confession to work, you need to have regret, because otherwise it becomes like the way Westerners say sorry all the time, but don't really mean it. To have regret without formal confession practice is fine, but you can't have confession without regret. When offering confession, we need a support. For the drubchen, we've established the mandala of Vajrasattva, indivisible from Vajrasattva as the support. Actually, the glory of Vajrasattva appears, wherever you want it to appear, because the body of Vajrasattva is the space-like wisdom body; like space, it is absolutely everywhere. That is the support for confession, this elaborate mandala we've erected. Then you need to make the pledge not to make future negative actions and do the best you can. This benefits a bit. Westerners have the expression, "I did my best!" So do your best. However, just to say it is not good enough; really think well about doing it.

The key point is that you meditate on the deity Vajrasattva and the mandala, make the offerings, engage in the ritual, and invite the wisdom deity. With this support, confess negative actions and make the pledge that in the future, [you will not do them]. This will ensure that negative actions are purified, based on these methods. Really be able to decide that this is so. You need to have stable devotion. Whether your devotion is stable has to do with whether you've been able to decide clearly or not. Decide definitively that through the power of the deity, mantra, and samadhi, then all negativity has been purified. Otherwise, if you are unsure, then you are fooling yourself. If you are fooling yourself, what benefit is there? You need trust; that is the most important point, so think well about this.

Whether there's benefit for you or not basically has to do with your mind; the Dharma is about the mind. Even if physically you are unable to put in much effort, at least, if you put effort into your mind and apply these points, there will be some benefit. If not, if you just come to all the sessions, stay for the night sessions, and exhaust yourself, all the while thinking about all sorts of things, that is a waste of time. It would be better to stay in your bed and sleep!

Now comes a brief explanation on how to engage in this practice. Ultimate bodhichitta is emptiness, one's own mind, beyond thought, word, and expression. Based on emptiness in Vajrayana, the clarity of the empty mind arises as the deity. There is body, speech, and mind. Body is apparent, speech is semi-apparent, and mind is non-apparent. The body that is appearing now is our ordinary body, and we need to meditate on the pure body of Vajrasattva, as described in the text.

The text says,

OM MAHA SHUNYATA JNANA BENZA SVABHAVA ATMA KO HANG.ꞈ

These are the words that establish emptiness. All things of samsara and nirvana are emptiness. Within emptiness, all phenomena of samsara and nirvana unfold: *From the very beginning, all the phenomena of samsara and nirvana are the sphere of unborn emptiness.* Then the text leads to the three samadhis. This is a very vast topic that I do not have time to go into here. In short, they are the samadhi of suchness, the illuminating samadhi, and the samadhi of the seed syllable, which you need to meditate on. The third samadhi is the samadhi of the seed syllable; here, it's the letter HUNG. As you progress through the text, there is the outer world and the inner contents of beings; the outer world is the palace, and within the palace is the seat. All of this is indivisible from your own mind. The letter HUNG descends onto the seat and transforms into a vajra, from which light radiates out, making offerings to the buddhas and reabsorbing as blessings. Once again, light goes out and the vajra transforms into Vajrasattva. Vajrasattva is very clearly described in the text. If that is too complicated, each of you has a photo of Vajrasattva that you can study. Vajrasattva is the lord of all families. It is the one family that includes the nature of all families. If you accomplish Vajrasattva, you accomplish all deities, as when you turn on the main switch, all the lights go on.

When meditating on Vajrasattva, you need vivid presence, stable pride, and pure recollection. Visualize Vajrasattva in union with his consort, skillful means and wisdom inseparable; that is the meditation. Keep following the text, which says, *By rays of light arising.* It is necessary to begin with a self-visualization. In the Nyingma tradition, there is no division between self-visualization and front-visualization; they are together. Here, first do a self-visualization and after this is finished, you, the samayasattva, then invite the wisdom being. After the wisdom being takes his seat, you make offerings and praises. These are all the different aspects of a sadhana. When we do sadhana, we need the mudras and the samadhis. It is easy to see others doing the mudras and imitate. Now we have our ordinary, impure body, and these are all methods of purifying.

Next comes the speech-recitation section, as in the text: Within my heart as the samayasattva, is *the wisdom being, in a form identical to mine.* In the heart of the wisdom being, or jnanasattva, is a vajra, which is the samadhisattva, with a HUNG inside it, encircled by the mantra. Light rays go out, make offerings, and bring back the blessings and siddhis. All four recitation intents are here: the moon with the garland of stars, the firebrand, the messenger of the king, and the beehive broken open; nothing is left out. While reciting, think about these. The condensed mantra is

OM BENZA SATO AH. OM BENZA SATO SAMAYA and so on, is the extensive mantra. For the meaning of the Hundred Syllable mantra, you can study Jamyang Khyentse Wangpo's[53] explanation of this mantra. The mantra is in Sanskrit, and if you do not know Sanskrit, you can recite many times but not know the meaning. The Hundred Syllable mantra itself is not most important. What is important is the meaning; it is good to look at the meaning. But if you still cannot understand that, then supplicate Vajrasattva; invoke the wisdom mind of Vajrasattva.

When reciting the Hundred Syllables, we are performing the speech aspect, and through recitation, we realize vajra speech. At the time of recitation think, "All appearances are the deity, [enlightened body]; all sound is mantra, [enlightened speech]; and all thoughts are the display of unchanging wisdom mind. Everything—the three realms, the container and contents, beings—is the nature of enlightened mind. So, like this, the sadhana is a self-visualization, then there is the dissolution and re-emergence. The words are as follows:

> Rays of light from my heart center strike the mandala circle.
> Melting into light, it dissolves into me, the samayasattva,
> who dissolves into the jnanasattva, who dissolves into the
> samadhisattva, who dissolves into the hung. The hung gradually
> dissolves up to the nada, which dissolves into the nonconceptual
> state, radiant emptiness; I then rest in meditation.

Then rest in that and when a thought arises, do not regard it as an ordinary thought; it is your re-emergence as Vajrasattva. The text says, OM BENZA SATO AH. This brings forth the clear visualization of Vajrasattva again.

There is a front-visualization, which is more detailed. The self-visualization is the terma text itself, revealed by Terdak Lingpa, who expanded on the terma with the more detailed visualization. What might have happened is that students were unclear about the shorter text, so he added all the details. For example, the palace is explained, with its pillars, doors, and decorations. Also, in the front visualization, each ornament on Vajrasattva is listed, where the ornaments are merely mentioned in the terma text. The offerings are more elaborate. However, the practice is the same. Now, we have reached the self-visualization and the front-visualization in this practice. During recitation, rays of light radiate from the self-visualization and go into the heart of the front-visualization and emanate. The main effort involves the front-visualization.

Next is the blessing of the vase. Meditate on Vajrasattva inside the vase and recite the mantra. From the self-visualization, light rays dissolve into the vase; these light rays are like sweat. Finally, Vajrasattva turns into light that dissolves into the amrita [in the vase]. Now we have completed three visualizations, self, front, and vase, which are the same. There is not a big retinue, only Vajrasattva; there aren't many different mantras, just the Hundred Syllables and its essence mantra, OM BENZA SATO AH.

We have arrived at the self-initiation; it is an empowerment. From the dharmakaya Buddha Samantabhadra until our own root guru is an unbroken lineage, which is the lineage empowerment. The path empowerment needs to be taken every day, as to not deteriorate and to revitalize the lineage with the lama. When we become enlightened, in the future, we will have the fruition empowerment. In this practice, there is the path empowerment, the self-empowerment. The tradition in India is that before you do any work, you need to wash, like washing your hands before eating. Likewise, before receiving the self-empowerment, we need to cleanse. We also need to offer a mandala, which is extremely important. Then we request the yidam to bestow the empowerment followed by refuge, developing bodhichitta, and the Vajrayana vows. Unless we think, "I am going to keep the vows," we cannot get the empowerment. Lately people want the empowerment but do not want the samayas. So, commit to the samayas.

The empowerment begins with the view and descent of wisdom, the most important part. You visualize yourself as Vajrasattva in union with a consort and invoke many wisdom beings, who dissolve into you. Request the wisdom beings to remain until you become enlightened and seal it by placing the vajra on your head. Next comes the request for the four empowerments, so once again offer a mandala. We are following the intent of the tantras. The four empowerments are the vase, the secret, the wisdom knowledge, and the precious word empowerments. The vajra master, inseparable from the main deity of the mandala, bestows the empowerment on the students, who recognize this. You receive all four empowerments and even though you have received the lineage empowerment before, to prevent degeneration, renew and stabilize that transmission. Think this and have the confidence that it is so. Once you have taken the four empowerments, vow to keep the samayas. The life force of the empowerment is the samayas, and if you do not keep them, then the life force is severed.

Once again, we offer a mandala—not just a mandala, we offer everything, our body and our possessions. This represents how the Dharma is greater than anything else. In worldly terms, we value things that are the most expensive. By offering our body, possessions, and all our merit, we show how precious this is. Afterwards, we dedicate. This is one cycle of the sadhana practice. According to the Nyingma tradition, the best way to do a drubchen is to do the sadhana three times in the day and three times in the night, six times. If not possible, then at least do four times, two times during the day, and two times during the night. That is what we will do here, because foreigners will have trouble going as quickly as the lamas and monks can.

Progressing through the sadhana, we arrive at the confession, *Yeshe Konchok*. There are many extensive confessions: for example, for body, there are prostrations to the hundred peaceful and wrathful deities; for speech, there is the definitive *Confession of Rudra*; and for mind, there is confession of the view. Offering confession for the body, prostrate; for speech, say the Hundred Syllable mantra; and for mind, meditate. All of this is included in *Narak Kongshak*, whereas in the *Mindroling Dorsem*, the confession is the general confession of *Yeshe Konchok* and the one following that. Once finished with confession, we make the pledge, in order to keep this purification stable. When we are sick and have finished taking the medicine, we apply methods to not get ill again. It is said in the tantras that there are twenty-eight commitments that we need to keep. These are quite scary; reading them makes me afraid. We have to one-pointedly make these pledges, and commit to them by holding the vajra at our heart, which is a way to stabilize our vows. After that, there is a short pledge as well. Next come the four fulfillments. The first is in accordance with the view. Thereafter, they are fulfillments of amrita, rakta, torma, and butter lamps. These have incredible meaning. If, in this life, we can truly enact fulfillment, then all broken samayas and transgressions are purified.

Vajrasattva is the lord of the one family, which when expanded is the hundred families. The five poisons are transmuted into the five wisdoms. The peaceful ones abide purely and the wrathful ones transform [from this]. First the peaceful ones abide as naturally pure, [primordially pure] and the wrathful ones are transformed from them, and connected with this are two fulfillment prayers. So, each day, from the confession down through the fulfillment, we recite these verses without break. Best is to do them twice daily. In short, the confession and the fulfillment are extremely important. The Mindroling tradition does not recite the *Narak Kongshak,* but we do. The reason is that we wish to attain enlightenment and we have taken empowerments, and to keep the samayas, we need to confess and fulfill, considering that we are constantly fighting amongst ourselves. There is benefit in doing these.

The root of empowerment is samaya, as I have said, and there are two categories, the root and subsidiary, or branch, samayas. There are fourteen root samayas. The first is not to go against the vajra master,[54] not to upset or disobey him. The lama is the vajra master. The vajra master can be endowed with one, two, or three kindnesses. The first kindness pertains to the master who bestows empowerment. Having given empowerment, the master with the second kindness also explains the tantras. A master who points out the nature of mind is endowed with the third kindness. We need to cherish the master endowed with the three kindnesses, more than our own hearts. It is your choice whether you cherish the lama or not and whether you need to do so. It is necessary to check the master before you receive teachings from him or her and that is merely about any teachings. Regarding empowerments, it is more critical to check the teacher; you need to make sure that he or she has the proper lineage. To be introduced to mind's nature, in Dzogchen, then you really need to investigate the master giving these teachings.

When receiving the vows of the lower vehicle, you are like the child and the abbot who imparts them is like your father. Buddha Shakyamuni said this in the Vinaya. When you receive the trainings of Mahayana, the lama is like a doctor and the student is like a sick person. If you do not take the medicine and the doctor's advice, you die. For an empowerment, you need to see the master as indivisible from [the main deity of] the mandala, which is the way to receive the empowerment. If not, you will not really get the empowerment. To truly receive the pointing out instruction, you need to see the master as the Buddha. If you see the teacher as the Buddha, you can be introduced to the mind as the Buddha. This teacher is the most precious and important. Then there are the samayas of the three kayas, and if you go against them, you break them. So, the second root samaya is to abide by whatever instruction the teacher gives you.

The third root samaya concerns the dharma friends,[55] and there is a lot to say about this. In fact, buddha nature permeates all beings; we all have the same *gyu* basis. Merely harming even one sentient being is a negative action. That is the larger dharma community; a smaller group would be the students of the same teacher. Even closer are those with whom you receive empowerment in one mandala. It becomes increasingly tighter as you receive not only an empowerment but teachings together as well. Then there are those with whom you receive Dzogchen teachings and they are truly your vajra siblings. They are very important and to be treated with respect; there are many texts that explain this. It says that you need to consider each one of them as the lama, and it explains why you should avoid fighting with them in any manner, not even holding negative thoughts about them in your mind. There are many details and if you do not keep these, you will go to hell. Actually, you will go to the worst hell. In sutra it is called Avichi Hell; in Vajrayana, it is called Vajra Hell and you will stay there a very long time, an immeasurable length of time.

These days, people do not respect these [samayas] at all. They do try somewhat to keep the samayas with the lama, as long as there are no difficulties. Mentally, you probably think negative things about the lama. But there is no consideration whatsoever for vajra siblings, and that is only the third one, so you can imagine the rest!

What do you do when samayas are broken? There are several levels: damaged, transgressed, and broken, according to time. The quicker you can purify it through confession, the better. Time matters; it matters how long it has been damaged, whether it is a month, days, or weeks. We have the way to confess as illustrated here in this drubchen practice.

We have come to the feast offering, which is the supreme way to purify breakages and remain clean. We need to accumulate both merit and wisdom, and feast offering increases these. We, therefore, make offerings to the Dharma protectors, first. We then follow the text all the way to the residual offering, followed by offering the covenant, the *tenma*, and so forth. To prevent obstacles that steal the siddhis from arising, we liberate the *nyuley*[56] spirits. In an elaborate fashion, we would do this liberation offering to the nyuley twelve times, corresponding to the twelve different times in the day that the twelve different types of nyuley appear. To liberate each one of them, we need to invoke a specific deity, with a specific mantra, and specific substances to liberate each one. Here we do it more essentially, at the end of each session. If we do not liberate them, the siddhis could get lost.

Having done that, we request the blessings from the deities during the descent of blessings practice, which comes next. At this particular time and place, we are doing the *Descent of Blessings of the Great Sacred Places (Nas chen Jin beb),* a very extensive descent of blessings invocation, from the sacred places and the beings associated with those places. At a precious site like this, confessing breakages restores the blessings of the site. Quite honestly, this place is a buddhafield; before, it was impossible to even come here, without high realization. But these days the blessings must have declined, as even tourists have arrived.

In this world, the most important, sacred places are those that the nirmanakaya buddha, Shakyamuni, went to: Bodhgaya, Varanasi, Kushinagar, and so forth. The one thousand buddhas will go to those places in this kalpa. In the buddhafield of Akanishtha, the most precious and sacred place, the sambhogakaya manifested and then came and taught the secret Vajrayana for the first time here. This was an emanation of Vajrasattva who taught the Vajrayana to those five extraordinary beings. He turned an inconceivable wheel of the teachings for them at this very place.

In order to restore and stabilize the blessings here, at Adam's Peak, we perform this detailed descent of blessings, at the end of the evening session. We invoke all the wisdom deities, yidams, dakinis, the Dharma protectors, Guru Rinpoche, and so on to send their blessings. This benefits the doctrine to remain, because if the doctrine is firm, then sentient beings are benefited. This is accomplishing enlightened activities for sentient beings.

When circling the mandala, all the yogis need to wear their ornaments. Actually, they should dress in charnal ground attire, just like the picture of Jamyang Khyentse Chökyi Lodrö dressed that way. If we are not able to wear all those ornaments, at least we don the hats, the yellow Dharma robes, and brocade cloaks. The benefit is that this auspicious connection arranged in the body brings realization to the mind. It is like when we see a Sri Lankan monk dressed in the yellow robes, we know he is a Theravadan monk. As we are in the tradition of Guru Rinpoche, then we wear the crown of Guru Rinpoche and the red Dharma robes with golden patterns; when we see this, we see Guru Rinpoche. Actually, seeing all the beings in the three realms of existence, we see them as Guru Rinpoche, as they are students of Guru Rinpoche. We recite the mantra and think about the meaning of the prayer. To symbolize the descent of the five wisdoms, we wave streamers of five colored silks. It is a symbol, like the traffic light; when we see red, we stop, and green, we go. The multicolored streamers are an invitation to the five buddha families to arrive and send their blessings. We hold the vajra and the bell to show that we are practitioners of Vajrayana, because Vajrayana practice is the unity of skillful means and wisdom, symbolized by the bell and vajra. We also chant loudly, play the bell and damaru, and sound the trumpets at this point in the ritual. We offer incense and burn gugul. These are the special substances that we use. If we do this at a place like this, so precious to the Vajrayana, it will not only bless this place, it will also extend out to the other twenty-four sacred places and help the Vajrayana doctrine to remain there and be of benefit, as Dakpo Rinpoche explained to me.

I have explained the practice; there are many key points; it is difficult. For the Buddhadharma, it is not enough to just think about it—you need to really contemplate upon it. The teacher teaches and the student thinks very well about the teachings. You really need to reflect on them, and to be able to do this, you need to be intelligent. These days, there are not that many smart people. One of the first things to do to be able to understand the Mahayana teachings is to pray to Manjushri to increase intelligence. To understand the Buddhadharma requires great intelligence, and the Buddha taught that in the beginning, intelligence is needed for the path.

These days most people are quite dull, like being asleep or drunk; people cannot think. For the secret Vajrayana, there are secret and hidden points that need to be uncovered. No matter how much they are explained, most people do not understand them. If you understand well, buddhahood is very close, and you will be taken away from samsara. Once you understand, you need to experience and then realize it. If you realize it, you are a siddha. This understanding brings you very close. So, what do we need? We need merit. In these degenerate times, only people devoid of merit come to the teachings. However, those who have come here to participate in this drubchen do have great merit. In the whole world, you have the most merit. The person with the most merit was the Buddha; no one has more than he does. Yet, this is not easy. For both Mahayana and Vajrayana, you must not separate from the view, meditation, and action. We think that we need to unite these and we do not do it. Now we are here in this place for seven days. It was not easy to come and it is hard to know how many future opportunities like this will again arise. However, this is even better than going to a party, because we need to dress up to go to a party, talk to different people, get a bit drunk, and spend a few hours, which is a worldly way. But here, we are at a great party, where we will be together for seven days practicing. We will meditate on the deity, mantra, mudra, and samadhi.

The mandala we set up is not the real mandala but a resemblance. There are the actually present offerings and the mentally created ones. I am not sure how much of the mentally created ones we can do, but we will make sure that we have the actually present ones. If we do this correctly, practice with deity, mantra, mudra, and samadhi, then a kalpa of obscurations and negative deeds will be purified. Also, we will accumulate a massive amount of both merit and wisdom. That is what we are doing here, and in the end, we will conclude with the butter lamp prayer. I do not know how much of the supreme and common accomplishments we will receive, but at least we will have a great time partying, rejoicing together! This is very good and beneficial.

Sangchö[57]

The detailed version of the cleansing smoke offering, which pleases all divinities ༔
And is meant to establish an auspicious coincidence, ༔
Should be learned from elsewhere, ༔
But the condensed daily offering and giving is as follows. ༔

In a clean place, upon a stand, ༔
Put jewels, grains, medicines, brocades, ༔
And the best part of your food and drink ༔
Into a fire fueled by various kinds of nectar-filled woods. ༔

KYE! ༔
Within nonarising primordial purity, unconstructed space, ༔
Unceasing spontaneous presence manifests as five-colored light.
From the magical display of this effortless capacity, ༔
I invite guests, all possible forms of existence and peace, ༔
To this site of offering and giving. ༔
Come here in the flash of a single instant, ༔
Like a rainbow appearing in the sky, ༔
And remain upon whichever seat pleases you. ༔
SARVA SAMAYA JAH JAH ༔

RAM YAM KHAM ༔
All things, the magical reflections of awareness, ༔
Are purified of all impurities, the habitual patterns of confusion, ༔
Into emptiness, being burned, scattered and washed away ༔
By the fire, wind, and water of great wisdom. ༔

Within this empty state, the space of the five consorts,༔
From the utterly perfect offering-cloud of cleansing smoke,༔
Appears a treasure of unexcelled sense pleasures,༔
Which becomes a sky-treasury cloud bank.༔
Om ah hung༔

Hung༔
In the radiant mandala of self-existing empty cognizance༔
Is a blazing fire of nectar-filled woods.༔
The smoke of burning sense pleasures and affluence༔
Showers a rain of myriad divine offerings.༔

Forms, sounds, odors, tastes, and textures—like gathered clouds—
Auspicious articles and signs, and the seven precious royal possessions,༔
Food, drink, clothes, ornaments, grains, medicine, horses, and so forth,༔
Proliferate, as the infinite wealth of existence and peace.༔

With this inexhaustible, great Samantabhadra offering cloud,༔
Completely filling the realm of the sky,༔
Unfailing Three Precious Jewels, whom we rely upon as refuge until enlightenment,༔
Accept this cleansing offering.༔

Lords of all blessings, siddhis, and activities,༔
Assemblies of gurus, yidams, and dakinis, accept this cleansing offering.༔
Samaya protectors, you who watch over good and evil,༔
Ocean of outer and inner teaching guardians and vow-holders, accept this cleansing offering.༔

You who relieve the anguish of poverty and shower a great rain of desirable things,༔
Yakshas, wealth gods, and treasure lords, accept this cleansing offering.༔
You who are endowed with abilities to benefit or harm and move by miraculous power,༔

Hosts of *jungpos* of the three-thousandfold universe, accept this cleansing offering.༔

In particular, *nyens* protecting the land of Tibet on the Jambu continent,༔
Virtuous devas, nagas, and local deities along with your retinues, accept this cleansing offering.༔

Gurlhas of the King, *kyelhas* of the subjects,༔
And successions of worldly gods of creation, accept this cleansing offering.༔
Mentsünma, chief guardian of the land of Tibet,༔
Five sister-emanations and your retinues, accept this cleansing offering.༔

Par and *me*, lords of the years, months, days and times, and others,༔
Elemental gods of the sciences, accept this cleansing offering.
Innate and temporarily appointed gods,༔
Gatherings of *dralhas*, who increase positive conditions, accept this cleansing offering.༔

Naturally dwelling or temporarily present,༔
Adversaries, obstructors, and karmic creditors, accept this cleansing offering.༔
Objects of compassion, who since former lifetimes have been my mothers,༔
All guests from the six classes of beings of the three realms and three worlds, accept this cleansing offering.༔

In short, may the outer vessel, the realm of all-encompassing purity,༔
Be cleansed into being the never-ending adornment wheels of inexhaustible sense pleasures.༔

May the inner contents of all living beings, the mudra deities of the Three Roots,༔
Be cleansed into being the great indivisibility of space and wisdom.༔

I cleanse you by making this restorative offering with the smoke of nectar-filled woods;༔
May all the defilements of the veils of broken samayas be purified.༔

I make you this offering of an ocean-like cloud of sense pleasures;༔
Entrust me with the supreme and common siddhis and the activities of the four karmas.༔
Precious Ones, guests of honor, I offer you the best part;༔
Bring forth the brilliant splendor of blessings, empowerments, and compassion.༔

I mend my heart samaya with all protectors, the guests of virtue;༔
Dispel all obstacles and increase positive conditions and goodness.༔
I dedicate this to all guests who are obstructors and karmic creditors;༔
If you are pleased and satisfied, fulfill my wishes for benefit and happiness.༔

I make an all-pervading gift to the six classes of beings, the guests of compassion;༔
May they be free from all suffering and possess happiness.༔

At this auspicious and delightful place of virtue,༔
Through my deeds of making a cleansing offering and giving nectar,༔
May the prosperity and goodness of the world and its inhabitants,༔
Of the infinite realms of the ten directions of samsara and nirvana,༔
Be brought under my command.༔

Three times a day, may auspiciousness shine forth like sunlight.༔
Three times a night, may auspiciousness glow like moonlight.༔
Throughout the entire day and night, may there be auspiciousness and goodness,༔
And may the auspicious coincidence of everything excellent be spontaneously perfected.༔

Perform this daily, especially༔
When commencing an important task༔

Of spiritual or secular deeds.༔
If you perform this in order to arrange the right coincidence,༔
All samaya-veils and discordant factors will be pacified,༔
Positive conditions and everything excellent will effortlessly multiply,༔
Good years and cattle will increase and offspring will flourish,༔
The dharma lineages will last long and their position will be heightened,༔
All the goodness of the world and its inhabitants will be magnetized,༔
And auspiciousness, goodness, and excellence will take place.༔

Ultimately, by perfecting the gathering of merit,༔
The supreme wisdom will dawn without effort.༔
This profound instruction should, therefore,༔
Be regarded as important by everyone in common.༔
Samaya. Seal, seal, seal.༔
May virtuous goodness increase!༔

A Brief Explanation of Sangchö

Teachings on the condensed cleansing offering according to Tukdrub Barchey Künsel

Sang is the Tibetan word for smoke offering. According to the Hindu tradition, Brahma is the creator of the world and the sang ritual originated when Brahma fell asleep and created the world in his dream. According to this account, the sang ritual is used to awaken one from that dream.

In our Buddhist tradition, the five elements are the result of two factors: primordial purity and spontaneous presence, which represent means and knowledge (prajna and upaya). Everything is composed of these five elements, including the ingredients of the sang offering, which are not man-made, but occur naturally. The pure aspect of the five elements is called the five wisdoms. [As you see in the first two lines chanted.]

> KYE!ཿ
> Within nonarising primordial purity, unconstructed space,ཿ
> Unceasing spontaneous presence manifests as five-colored light.ཿ

When King Trisong Deütsen wanted to create the great temple complex of Samye, both divine and mundane spirits interfered. He discussed the situation with his ministers, and they decided that in order to dispel obstacles and overcome hindrances, they should invite Guru Rinpoche from India. On the hill above Samye known as Hepori, Guru Rinpoche built a small sang temple, where he performed the smoke offering for all the local spirits of Tibet. This first type of sang was for the pacifying activity. Afterwards, in order to tame those spirits that were not pacified by peaceful means, Guru Rinpoche manifested in the wrathful form of Dorje Drollö. Thus, it is now the tradition that whenever commencing a great task, you always make a sang offering before beginning the actual work. For instance, you always perform a sang ritual before constructing a temple, consecrating a shrine, beginning a drubchen, or getting married. The main purpose, or benefit, is to clear all hindrances in order to successfully accomplish the task.

In sang and *sur* rituals, as well as for *Chö* practice, there are four types of guests who are the recipients of the offering. First are the respectable guests of virtue: the Three Jewels—the Buddha, Dharma, and Sangha. Second are the protective guests of qualities, which include the yidams, Dharma protectors, dralhas, dakas, dakinis, and so forth. Third are the guests of compassion, the six classes of sentient beings. Fourth are all those obstructors to whom you owe a karmic debt, including various spirits, obstructing forces, and the like. You offer the gift to all four types of guests at the same time.

The opening of the text states:

> *In a clean place, upon a stand,*༔
> *Put jewels, grains, medicines, brocades,*༔
> *And the best part of your food and drink*༔
> *Into a fire fueled by various kinds of nectar-filled woods.*༔

You should never put the ritual ingredients on the ground, rather on a table or platform above the ground. *Jewels* refer to precious and semi-precious stones and *grains* are any of the numerous kinds available, though in Tibet, there were only five. You should also include the five main medicinal plants as well as brocade, the best food and drink that you have, and pure water.

To do the offering, prepare a fire using proper types of wood. Since the five elements are the identities of the five female buddhas, this is a natural mandala of the female buddha Pandara Vasini, who is the essence of fire. You should put branches from different trees containing the five types of nectar, namely juniper, into the fire. If you do not have these five specific types, you can choose from among the one hundred and eight other types.

As you put the wood into the fire, smoke appears; imagine the smoke as taking the form of cloudbanks of desirable objects, including the eight auspicious emblems and all kinds of wonderful things.

You utter RAM YAM KHAM to sanctify and increase the offering articles, so they become an inexhaustible sky treasury. RAM is for fire, to consume all offerings in fire; YAM is for wind, to scatter everything away; and KHAM is for water, to wash away any remaining ashes. Uttering OM AH HUNG increases, multiplies, sanctifies, and makes unexcelled sky treasury offerings to the body, speech, and mind of all the victorious ones.

The main part of the ritual begins with the line *HUNG§ In the radiant mandala of self-existing empty cognizance.§* In your mind, you present all the offerings to the respectable guests of virtue, the Three Jewels. Due to this, the smoke turns into beautiful offerings and you receive their blessings. You next make offerings to the protective guests of qualities, mending any breaches of samaya. Then you offer to all classes of sentient beings, satisfying any needs they may have. Finally, you offer to those with whom you have karmic debts, thereby pacifying any grudges they may have. Those are the four main guests. Here the text makes an explicit reference to specific protectors and guardians of the Tibetan tradition for Buddhism in general and for discreet subjects—such as the protective divinities who guard the teachings, termas, sacred places, and so on, as appointed by Padmasambhava. Next come the five Tseringma sisters, who are the main guardians of the *Tukdrub Barchey Künsel*. Special gifts are then given to the lord of the vicinity, the five spirits who accompany you from the moment you are born until you die, and the dralhas. The benefits you hope to achieve are all listed after this, and four lines of auspiciousness mark the end.

The final outcome of making gifts to all of these guests is to increase your chances of success, known as "windhorse," or *lungta* in Tibetan. As all matters, whether spiritual or secular, are mainly based on your attitude, an increase in lungta benefits any task or aim you might undertake. Simply put, when this attitude, which is mind, improves, it is known as spirituality; when it worsens or turns in a downward direction, it is known as a mundane pursuit, which is samsara. Thus, there are the two aspects of mind, known as samsara and nirvana. For instance, let's talk about three states of being: divine, human, and hell. Heaven, or the divine state, simply put, means getting whatever you want at any moment, without effort or the least bit of pain; that is what we call "heaven," isn't it? The human level alternates between pleasant and unpleasant, and sometimes it's a mixture of the two. On this level, when the lungta is inadequate, even a pleasant situation feels unpleasant. The other way around is also true: you may perceive someone to be in a dreadful state, when actually their mind is at ease and they are very happy. For example, when you encounter someone who has been poor, and perhaps sick, for many years, imagining what they must be experiencing, you feel spontaneous pity. Whereas, as a matter of fact, if you were looking at that person from inside, he or she may be fine and worry free. In that case, there's merely a semblance of suffering, but not suffering in actuality. That is how it is for human beings; they have a blend of joy and sorrow. What we call "hell" is when a sentient being suffers intensely from hunger, thirst, heat, cold—everything is wrong, so there is no pleasure whatsoever. Nonetheless, all these levels are only states of mind—nothing more.

An attitude, or state of mind, is like a horseman riding on the wind of karma. You could say that the wind blows the attitude from one state to the next. *Ta* means "horse" and *lung,* meaning "wind," can be of various types: wisdom wind, karmic wind, and so forth. Increasing this lungta brings a lot of benefits. In the age of degeneration, just by default, marriage is down and lungta is also on the decline. You can clearly see this when people try to achieve something that is strongly on their minds—and they want it so badly that they try everything they can think of—but still they are unable to accomplish it. Even good things like achieving the circumstances to accumulate merit do not just come together. When it comes to accomplishing the smallest task, it seems so difficult, as there are so many obstacles. So Padmasambhava emanated the forms of the dralhas to take care of those things.

Think about the example of meditation training: whether or not you succeed is not really in your own hands. It is not just by wanting to be successful that it happens; something else is required. For instance, if your lungta were at its peak, then immediately upon beginning meditation, you would already arrive at the fully awakened state of dharmakaya, which is the unchanging dharmakaya citadel. On the other hand, if something vital is missing, no matter what practice you are doing, you may totally misunderstand and use every kind of practice, including development stage and completion stage, to confuse yourself, hallucinate, and go down a completely wrong track. A very simple example is when sitting down to begin a session, you start out very nicely, as a real Dharma practitioner, but by the end, you are no more than an ordinary person at best. What it really comes down to is something vital in your attitude, which is mind.

Increasing lungta, windhorse, has to do with controlling, guiding, or steering the attitude, the "wind" of mind, as if you were reining a horse in the right direction. In other words, as soon as a negative frame of mind arises, you are immediately able to take the reins and guide it in a positive direction. Otherwise, without lungta, there is a possibility that one moment you have virtuous, noble-minded attention, thinking, "I want to do good. I really want to help many beings." Then in the next moment, a nasty, selfish thought takes over and hijacks the good intention. In other words, your attitude is completely unstable and easily changed. This is why the buddhas have skillfully and compassionately provided various methods and why Padmasambhava has given this specific method of sangchö to increase lungta.

To summarize: good and evil are simply a mental attitude, which can change from one moment to the next. The capacity to direct that change is connected to the wind energy known as lungta. Phrased differently, when the lungta energy increases, there is also an increase in the basic wakefulness, which has a sharp strength capable of consuming or burning away any emotional turmoil like flames consume firewood. That is the basic principle of sang.

The condensed cleansing offering known as Sangchö, is extracted from the basic scripture of *Tukdrub Barchey Künsel* known as the *Sheldam Nyingjang, Essence Manual of Oral Instruction*. The actual title is Detailed Version of the Cleansing Smoke Offering That Pleases All Divinities. It comes from the subsidiary activities connected with Kyepak Rigdzin, one of the twelve manifestations. The longer, detailed version is called Dögü Gyamtso. There is another even longer version as well.

This was a very short explanation.

Pilgrimage[58]

The Dharmakaya buddha is the most precious—so where is the dharmakaya buddha found? Dzogchen teachings say that this is our own mind. This precious dharmakaya buddha is primordially pure and undeluded. The primordial buddha, who is the source of all the buddhas, possesses infinite qualities, as stated in *The Treasury of the Dharmadhatu.* All of these amazing qualities of the primordial buddha, as mentioned in the Dzogchen texts, are inherent within each of our minds and that is amazing.

When the Dzogchen teacher gives pith instructions to the student, at the time of the *Rigpai Tsal wang,* the empowerment for the expression of awareness, and shows the individual his or her mind—the dharmakaya buddha: direct, unfabricated, not sullied by ordinary thought—that is the introduction to [mind's nature]. By saying *phat,* or giving the introduction using symbols, the lama shows that the disciple's present mind is the buddha. Anyone who has received the introduction to the nature of mind in different ways is familiar with what I'm talking about.

Individuals who are able to remain in the unaltered state of present mind and maintain the continuity of the recognition of mind's nature don't need to go on pilgrimage. However, we are not exactly the same, so we are here on pilgrimage, and I am going to explain the various ways to go on pilgrimage and how to get the greatest benefit out of this experience.

The dharmakaya buddha, never wavering from that pure state, still appears for the benefit of taming beings, manifesting the sambhogakaya buddhas and the buddhas of the five families. The sambhogakaya buddhas of the five families can be expressed varyingly as: the one family of Vajrasattva, the three families, the five families, the one hundred families, or an inconceivable number of buddhas that arise. These are the expression and display of the dharmakaya buddha. Like that, saying that mind is the buddha and being introduced to the dharmakaya, you understand that the spontaneously present expression is the sambhogakaya buddha.

The dharmakaya and sambhogakaya buddhas do not appear to the ordinary beings who need to be trained. Therefore, to benefit beings in an ordinary form and tame them, a nirmanakaya buddha manifests in this world. When a nirmanakaya buddha comes to the world and enacts the twelve deeds, it is for the benefit of sentient beings. To benefit beings, the nirmankaya buddha needs to be in harmony with the perceptions of the beings there. If not, then, buddhas may as well only manifest as sambhogakaya and dharmakaya. The main deed to benefit beings is to turn the wheel of the Dharma. Turning the wheel of the Dharma needs to be in accordance with the mind and disposition of sentient beings. If not, the dharmakaya buddha need only enact the mind-to-mind transmission possessing utter purity, turning the pure wheel of wisdom, from within the great equanimity, where all dharmas are perfectly pure. The twelve Dzogchen teachers and the one thousand buddhas all received transmission via the mind-to-mind transmission possessing utter purity, the Dharma wheel turned from within the great equanimity. We are unable to understand this [type of transmission]. This is the perfectly pure Dharma, without the mention of any impurity whatsoever.

The sambhogakaya buddhas teach according to symbols, turning the wheel of the Dharma in the fourth time of great equality. In the buddhafield of Akanishtha, endowed with the five perfections, they turn the wheel of the Dharma based on symbols. For example, the buddhas of the five families appear in symbolic forms. Their mere appearance is turning the wheel of the Dharma. The five poisons, completely purified, are the nature of the buddhas of the five families. This is completely pure Dharma. The wheel of Dharma is turned during the fourth time, which is the time of the great equality, meaning that there is no time when the teachings are not taught.

We are unable to see or comprehend the dharmakaya and the sambhogakaya. We can, however, understand the nirmanakaya buddha. The Buddha accomplishes the benefit of sentient beings by having enacted the twelve deeds. As mentioned in the Vinaya, he descended from the Tushita heaven, took birth, lived the life of pleasure in the palace, and then renounced that life. Thereafter, he went to practice the ascetic conduct, reached enlightenment, turned the wheel of the Dharma, and passed into parinirvana. The fact that a nirmanakaya buddha has come and beings were able to meet such a nirmanakaya buddha requires an enormous amount of merit. Only those who had extraordinary merit were able to meet him.

It also says that the words of the Buddha, his teachings, are something extremely rare in this world. When a nirmanakaya buddha comes to the world, there are places where he enacts these twelve deeds. We are able to know about these places, such as where he turned the wheel of the Dharma, and the kind of teachings that he gave, the three turnings of the wheel.

When we go on pilgrimage, we need to relate to the nirmanakaya buddha and know who the Buddha is. The dharmakaya and the sambhogakaya buddhas are endowed with inconceivable qualities, beyond anything our minds can conceive or understand. As it says in the *Prajnaparamita,* "Beyond words, beyond thought, beyond description, prajnaparamita." When it comes to the qualities of this nirmanakaya buddha, it is said that even the Buddha cannot describe all the qualities of a nirmanakaya buddha.

It's not that the Buddha lacks the capacity; the problem is the time it would take—you wouldn't find anyone that could listen to it. In short, there are thirty-two major marks and eighty minor signs, which are the qualities of the enlightened body of the Buddha. The qualities of his enlightened speech are the sixty aspects of melodious voice, as they are called. The quality of the enlightened mind of the Buddha is the wisdom of the prajnaparamita. The teachings of the Buddha are true and authentic.

Each one of the major signs of the enlightened body of the Buddha—for example the ushnisha—came about for a particular reason. Long ago, kalpas and kalpas ago, the Buddha performed acts, such as paying homage to the teacher. Whatever positive deed he enacted became the cause for a particular sign to manifest when he reached enlightenment. It is similar with everything we do. When we put our mind to something, the result will ripen in accordance with our motivation. These results are not made but arise based on the cause. When the cause is there, the result will come to be.

In any case, to put it in a nutshell, the Buddha has that extraordinary radiance and charisma that come from his great merit. Since the Buddha has this enormous merit, greater than anyone else has, if we go to the places where he accomplished the twelve deeds—bringing to mind the Buddha's qualities at each place and doing circumambulations and pilgrimage—then, through the strength of the Buddha's merit, we as pilgrims will be able to receive the blessings. That's why we go on pilgrimage.

The way to go on pilgrimage is the same for practitioners of the lower yanas and for Tibetans. When going on pilgrimage, you remember the qualities of the Buddha, bring forth faith and devotion, and keep the Buddha in mind. In this manner, negative actions can be purified within your mindstream, and you will be able to take blessings from the places. Kalpas of merit increase even further and further in so doing. Think like this.

Why does this benefit come? The reason is that the Buddha has extraordinary merit; the blessings from this merit and your own devotion in remembering the Buddha mingle, and this purifies your mindstream. You receive the blessings and accomplishments and purify negative actions and disturbing emotions. That is how it is. This means that you need to bring that purity to your mind. If you just go around with a camera taking pictures as a tourist, having a good time, it's not going to work. Of course, there will be a little bit of benefit.

For example, let's say you see a statue of the Buddha made of wood or stone and you think, "This is the actual Buddha!" In this way, making offerings to that buddha, you will receive blessings. The great master Nagarjuna said that even if you see a representation of the Buddha made out of ordinary wood and think, "This is the Buddha," that is fine. You don't receive the blessings from the wood; you receive the blessings from the wisdom of the Buddha. Similarly, the *Guhyagarbha Tantra* says that you can get blessings from a buddha made out of clay or wood. It is 100 percent certain that if you go on pilgrimage thinking like that, in those places where the Buddha accomplished the twelve deeds, you will surely receive blessings.

If as a follower of the bodhisattva path you go to the places where the Buddha trained for three countless aeons in the conduct of the bodhisattvas, practicing the six paramitas—if you perform acts of generosity where he perfected generosity, your generosity will be perfected. If you develop patience where he perfected patience, your patience will be perfected. That is how powerful those sacred places are. By means of the six paramitas, for the benefit of beings, the Buddha generated the precious mind of enlightenment, incredibly vast like an ocean.

In Bodhgaya, when the Buddha was about to reach enlightenment, the king of the maras, Gargi Wangchuk, claimed that the seat of enlightenment rightfully belonged to him and not to a mortal. Mara's demon soldiers cried out together, "I am his witness!" Mara challenged the Buddha, saying, "These soldiers speak for me. Who will speak for you?" Then Buddha reached out his right hand to touch the earth, and the earth goddess spoke, "I can count the number of atoms in Mount Meru and in all the realms, but I cannot count the number of times that this bodhisattva gave his head to help sentient beings, perfecting the paramita of generosity. I bear witness!" Mara disappeared. The places where the Buddha accomplished the twelve deeds were also places where he perfected each of the paramitas.

When we practitioners of the Mahayana go on pilgrimage, we generate the precious mind of enlightenment as followers of the bodhisattva path. We think of all sentient beings and generate the incredibly vast, ocean-like mind of enlightenment. We try to cherish all others more than ourself; even if unable to do so, at least we can make the wish. We rejoice at the thought of bodhichitta and aspire to have that bodhichitta, to be able to lead all sentient beings to enlightenment. Like that, you wish to give birth to the mind of enlightenment, thinking, "May my conduct be the same as that of all the buddhas and bodhisattvas of the past." That is the aspiration. Truly, when you make the vow to behave in accordance with the six paramitas—and actually practice generosity, discipline, patience, forbearance, concentration, and intelligence—you have entered the bodhichitta of application. With the two aspects of bodhichitta, aspiration and application, you go on pilgrimage.

These days, when people go on pilgrimage, they take their mala and pass it over stones, stupas, and statues. They also touch these sacred representations with their head, which is not the way to receive the blessings. You're not going to reach enlightenment like that. If you really want to receive the blessings of the Buddha, basically, you need to become a buddha.

If you want to become a buddha, you need to follow in the footsteps of the Buddha, doing the same things that the Buddha did to become enlightened. How do you do that? As it says in the Buddha Shakyamuni practice written by Mipham Rinpoche:

> Out of great compassion, you took care of this world of degeneration and strife
> And made five hundred great prayers of aspiration.
> You are praised as a white lotus; whoever hears your name will not return to samsara.
> Compassionate teacher, I submit obeisance to you!

Those lines show exactly what the Buddha has done to become a buddha, and this is what we need to emulate.

In our case, even though we do not have the great compassion of the Buddha, we need to start with small acts of compassion. Begin by considering others to be more important than you. If you're unable to do that, at least think that others are equal to you. If that proves too difficult, at least try to generate a little bit of compassion for them. Based on that, you need the two types of bodhichitta: aspiration and application. If you have those two, the bodhichitta of aspiration and the bodhichitta of application, the benefit is quite vast. You accumulate an enormous amount of merit from having those in mind.

Within these two, the bodhichitta of aspiration is very important—it's crucial, and the basis of this is prayer. When you make prayers to be able to accomplish those wishes, you need a support, and what better support could you have than the holy places of the Buddha, like the Bodhi Tree. You make prayers under the Bodhi Tree to reach enlightenment.

You need a support, a witness. In the worldly sense, when you do something important, you need witnesses. When you get married, you go to city hall. Likewise, as a follower of the Mahayana, when you go on pilgrimage, you need to generate the supreme mind of enlightenment and also engage in the six paramitas. If you go on pilgrimage doing that, it will make your path to enlightenment much swifter. If you have generated the precious mind of enlightenment, bodhichitta, just taking one step has enormous merit. First remember the qualities of the Buddha; next, generate the vast, ocean-like mind of enlightenment, bodhichitta. After this, going on pilgrimage will have enormous benefit.

The negativity that's been accumulated for kalpas and kalpas can be purified in one instant. For example, the *Bodhicharyavatara* as well as many other sources say that you can purify so much negativity by going on pilgrimage, in the way that has just been explained. You need to know how to receive blessings from sacred places.

Even superior to this, as *nakpas,* tantric practitioners, we have received empowerments. The way to go on pilgrimage as followers of the Vajrayana is different. We need to abide by the indivisibility of purity and equality. Vajrayana practitioners on pilgrimage often do tsok, or feast, practices with all the dakas and dakinis, enjoying the great offerings with the dakas and dakinis in those sacred places. To do that, you need to maintain constant awareness that all appearances are the forms of the deity, all sounds are the sound of mantra, and all thoughts are the dharmakaya. To know this to be so, read the life stories of the great mahasiddhas of India and of great masters like Jamyang Khyentse Chökyi Lodrö.

We are also following in the footsteps of such great masters and try to imitate them. We buy a lot of food that we place in front of the Bodhi

Tree. The benefit of one tsok offering cannot be described. For the great practitioners, it's like a blazing fire, an enormous, gigantic fire of wisdom, power, realization, and experiences. When we do tsok offerings, all the dakas and dakinis of the three planes of existence—those who live in space, those who live in the ground, and those who live under the ground—all of them attend by the hundreds of thousands. All the dakas and dakinis of the outer, inner, secret, and thatness mandalas will gather.

Wherever the nirmanakaya Buddha was enlightened and enacted the twelve deeds, he also emanated the sambhogakaya—the Kalachakra, Hevajra, all the deities of the Sarma and the Nyingma schools. In respect to Vajrayana, wherever he manifested the mandalas, they remain there. When the Buddha reached enlightenment, he radiated the mandala of Akanishtha. The Akanishtha buddhafield was manifested by the Buddha and does not go anywhere. This is why, when Jamyang Khyentse Chökyi Lodrö went to Bodhgaya and saw the Buddha Shakyamuni statue, he saw that externally he was the Buddha Shakyamuni; internally, his heart as the samayasattva was Vajradhara; and secretly, inside Vajradhara, the samadhisattva was Samantabhadra. That is what he saw every single time he went to Bodhgaya. In his collected works, there is a guru yoga practice of that.

These are the kinds of things you should discuss when you go on pilgrimage. You need to decide for yourself which of those three approaches you feel you want to apply. Basically, you need to do the one that works best for you. Of course, there is a way to go on pilgrimage according to the Dzogchen approach, but I am not going to go into that now.

I do need to mention a bit about the history of each of these places. We talk about the four great places of the Buddha: Lumbini, where the Buddha was born; Bodhgaya, where he reached enlightenment; Varanasi, where he turned the wheel of the Dharma; and Kushinagara, where he passed into parinirvana. Actually, not only Buddha Shakyamuni but also the other thousand and one buddhas of this kalpa will all accomplish those four activities, those four great deeds, in the exact same places.

The fifth buddha will be the buddha of the future, Maitreya. He will come and do the same deeds at the same places. This will be so, down to the last of the thousand and two buddhas of this kalpa. All of this is clearly stated in the sutras.

Amongst these four great places, Bodhgaya is where the Buddha attained enlightenment. As Buddhists, we consider Bodhgaya the center of the world. When the universe first formed, the element of wind spiraled around and created a momentum that appeared in the form of a crossed vajra. That happened below Bodhgaya, below the Vajra Seat. Then, progressively, on top of that the other elements piled up and the ground came to rest on them. At the center of this crossed vajra, the Bodhi Tree grows right in the middle of that exact point. This crossed vajra has seven qualities of the vajra.

Since Bodhgaya is considered the center of the world, it has very special qualities. Truly, the vajra-like samadhi arises there. The vajra-like samadhi is when emptiness becomes a vivid or direct experience. Vajra refers to that, to emptiness. Much is said regarding emptiness in the different teachings of Mahamudra, Dzogchen, and Madhyamika. In any case, this is the place of enlightenment, and after having reached enlightenment, Buddha acted for the benefit of sentient beings.

When reaching enlightenment, there's no need to be in a particular building or house. This is something that happened under the Bodhi Tree. The place where the Bodhi Trees grow is where Buddha Shakyamuni and the three buddhas before him reached enlightenment upon the Vajra Seat, under the Bodhi Tree. As each of the thousand and two buddhas of this kalpa will have a different name, likewise, the tree also will change names. Here, at the time of Buddha Shakyamuni, we call it the Bodhi Tree, but when the buddha of the future, Maitreya, comes and reaches enlightenment, at that time it will be called the Naga Tree.

There is a story about the Bodhi Tree. The qualities of the Bodhi Tree are basically the same as the qualities of the buddhas and bodhisattvas. The only difference is that the tree cannot talk. The Bodhi Tree, the Tree of Enlightenment, has the capacity to bring the Dharma to incredibly vast numbers of sentient beings. It is also mentioned that when the winds blow through the Bodhi Tree and the smell of the Bodhi Tree enters your nose, or when you feel the wind that touched the tree, it has the capacity to stop ordinary thoughts, so you may have an experience of enlightenment. There are many examples like that.

Under the Bodhi Tree, buddhas come to reach enlightenment. Externally, they sit in meditation; inwardly, their minds experience emptiness, and they attain enlightenment. At that time, the power of blessings is quite extraordinary; buddhas bless the environment. It is said that at the end of the final kalpa, when the seven fires destroy the entire universe, Bodhgaya will remain; it won't be destroyed.

To reiterate, I have spoken about three approaches to going on pilgrimage: to remember the qualities of the Buddha with devotion, as in the Theravada vehicle; to develop bodhichitta, as in the Mahayana vehicle;

and to sustain pure perception and performance of ritual, as in the Secret Mantra, Vajrayana. Whichever of these ways you can generate, accordingly, go on pilgrimage

The Buddha himself repeatedly said, "For those who did not have the great good fortune to meet me in person, if they visit these four great places—where I was born, where I reached enlightenment, where I turned the wheel of Dharma, and where I passed into parinirvana—and remember me, remember my noble qualities, and pray to me whole-heartedly, my blessings will enter them.

For example, all these pilgrims from Sri Lanka, saffron-robed monks from Burma, and ones from other places, when they come to pilgrimage places, they remember the Buddha and aspire to really receive blessings. That is the purpose of pilgrimage. They come to remember the qualities of the Buddha and to receive his blessings. It is said that just remembering the Buddha, or even having the mere thought of the Buddha for a moment, if that enters your mind, you accumulate tremendous merit. Of course, if you go to these places and make praises that will gather more blessings.

Followers of the Mahayana, like those in the Tibetan Buddhist tradition, always say, "Just as Buddha dedicated merit, developed bodhichitta, and strove to attain enlightenment for the benefit of beings, may I too follow in those same footsteps and attain enlightenment for the benefit of beings." The motivation is vaster, and that is the element of bodhichitta. Think, "I, too, will follow in his footsteps for the sake of all beings, accumulating merit and attaining enlightenment as he did. May it be so." Aspire and pray that way. Therefore, if you go on pilgrimage in that way, you will not only be accumulating merit, you will also be accumulating wisdom; wisdom and merit are the two accumulations. In this way, you will be able to purify the two defilements, including habitual inclinations.

Then on top of that, for followers of Secret Mantra, Vajrayana, try to go on pilgrimage in accordance with the wisdom mind of Jamyang Khyentse Chökyi Lodrö, who never had the slightest ordinary perception. He saw everything purely, in the ultimate realm of pure perception—that is most remarkable!

Accomplishment[59]

To truly practice development and completion stages and teach them, you need to recognize and stabilize the view. The great dharmadhatu is free of center and edges, coming and going, outer and inner. Resting in the equanimity of rigpa, from this great emptiness, the unimpeded display, the great compassion, appears as the deity, empty but apparent—indivisible, complete, and luminous yet empty. From this unified empty luminosity, all the characteristics of the deity appear, completely perfect. The appearance is the deity; the mantra is the self-resounding sound; the deity and resounding sound unfold from the non-grasping mind, which is recognized devoid of solid reality. A realized being knows that it is not appearing from outside but from the nature of mind, without elaborations. The deity is the empty essence and the cognizant, clear, and luminous nature; it is non-existent, like an illusion, free of concepts, and liberated upon arising. The mind—free of elaboration, empty in essence, and luminous in nature—is the completeness of the deity. This form unimpededly manifests as empty appearance, from the state within which all phenomena arise. From within this state, the great display unfolds, and the mantra is recited.

The crucial point of the Nyingma teachings is that first the view is ascertained. In the new schools, the view is of the great purity but it is considered inconceivable, as according to Rangzom Pandit's commentary *Ascertaining Appearances as the Deity,* or the various texts of Longchenpa. First the view has to be established, according to the Nyingma way, which is very profound and precise. In the new schools, if the view of the great purity is not ascertained, then what does not exist needs to be created, and that is complicated.

All that appears and exists is the great primordial purity, from the beginning; do not grasp after the words, recognize the meaning. The expanse of the great purity is seeing things as they are—all appearances are the display of the deity. There is nothing to visualize, but merely know things to be as they are. For you as the practitioner, the deity and you are the same; there is no big or small, good or bad. For the intellectual, the Dzogchen view just does not fit in their brains. But if it does, that is the way to practice a deity. Vajrayana begins with pure perception, the purity of all. However much you can experience that will determine the extent of the blessings. It is pure phenomena, free of any dualistic grasping. However, impure perceptions obscure this, preventing you from experiencing pure phenomena. Some can talk about this but not really know it. The ultimate view in Vajrayana is pure perception. The basis is the buddha nature, where there is no mention of pure or impure; it is completely pure. If you think that you and the deity are separate, that the deity is pure and you are impure, then with this duality, there is no way to accomplish a deity. All duality needs to be dispersed, and once that happens, then you can practice deity yoga. The whole root of deity practice is realization of nonduality. That is the way to practice.

APPENDIX

The Mind Ornament of Padma

An Explanation of the Vajra Verse Supplication[60]

Kyabje Dudjom Rinpoche

Om svasti

Having paid homage to the lord guru,
The wish-fulfilling jewel, who dispels our misery when we think of him,
I will let my words open up a small understanding of the meaning
Of the Vajra Verse supplication.

The supplication is stated in these words:

Buddha of the three times, Guru Rinpoche,༔
Lord of all siddhis, Great Blissful One,༔
Dispeller of all obstacles, Wrathful Tamer of Mara,༔
I supplicate you; please bestow your blessings.༔
Pacify the outer, inner, and secret obstacles༔
And spontaneously fulfill all wishes.༔

I will now clarify a little of the meaning of these vajra words of Guru Rinpoche himself, the quintessence of all supplications revealed in the profound treasures of Orgyen Chokgyur Lingpa, by explaining it in accordance with the regular teachings of Kunkhyen Lama Dorje Siji Tsal, from the oral instructions of my family lord, Gyurmey Ngedon Wangpo.

Buddha of the three times, Guru Rinpoche,ꟾ

Externally, this means the precious Buddha, among the Precious Ones, because Orgyen Rinpoche, himself, is the master who is inseparable from the three mysteries of all the buddhas appearing throughout the past, present, and future.

Internally, it means the guru, the root of blessings, among the Three Roots, because Orgyen Rinpoche, himself, is the general wisdom form of all the gurus of the Mind, Sign, and Hearing lineages.

Secretly, it means the dharmakaya among the three kayas, because he is primordially present as emptiness endowed with all the supreme aspects possessing the indivisible nature of the kayas and wisdoms.

Lord of all siddhis, Great Blissful One,ꟾ

Externally, this means the sacred, precious Dharma, because all the virtues of the truly high, definitive goodness originate from practicing in accordance with the words of the guru.

Internally, it means the yidam, the root of siddhis, because all the common and supreme siddhis, without exception, originate from Guru Rinpoche himself.

Secretly, it means the sambhogakaya, because he enjoys all the phenomena of samsara and nirvana as unconditioned great bliss in the manner of nonduality without moving away from dharmakaya.

Dispeller of all obstacles,ꟾ

Externally, this means the precious Sangha, because the dispelling of all obstacles on the five paths and ten bhumis, as well as the origination of all virtues, depends upon the sangha, the companions on the path who, again, originate by means of Orgyen Rinpoche.

Internally, it means the dakini and dharmapala, the roots of activity, because they clear away the practitioner's obstacles on the paths and bhumis and accomplish favorable conditions by means of the four activities. They, too, originate through Orgyen Rinpoche, himself, because he is the main figure in all mandalas.

Secretly, it means the nirmanakaya, because he emanates in bodily forms, taming by any means necessary, within the perceptions of the various higher, inferior, and mediocre disciples. He establishes them on the paths of ripening and liberation, after having taught all the essential points of the profound and extensive teachings to suit their intellects.

In this way, he is the one who externally is the nature of the Three Precious Ones, internally is the nature of the Three Roots, and secretly is the nature of the three kayas. Thus, as the chief form of all the buddhas, the source of all the sacred teachings, the crest ornament of the entire sangha, and the great lord encompassing all families, he is the one who holds the secret name:

> Wrathful Tamer of Mara,༔

Why is that? It is because he spontaneously tamed the terrifying four maras, delivered the three secret enemies into dharmadhatu, and liberated himself through realization. Since he has attained mastery over the four activities, he liberates others out of loving kindness by means of the unceasing compassion of eliminating and cherishing. Thus, through his power of great wisdom endowed with the twofold purity, he liberates the two obscurations, along with habitual patterns, into the state of nondual space and awareness.

To the guru who possesses such qualities,

> I supplicate you,༔

Externally, approach the desired aim of quickly achieving the supreme and common siddhis, by supplicating him with the intense power of devotion and longing.

Internally, accomplish Guru Rinpoche's level by acknowledging the fact that, primordially, your three doors are the mandalas of his body, speech, and mind.

Secretly, supplicate by applying the activities and maintaining the unfabricated continuity of self-awareness in its natural state, which is the real means of resolving the fact that the guru is nothing other than your mind-essence endowed with the nature of the four kayas and five wisdoms.

Having supplicated in this way, now request,

> Please bestow your blessings.༔

This means, "Please bless me to accomplish the vajra body, the apparent yet empty body, after having been blessed with the guru's body in my body. Please bless me to accomplish the vajra speech, the resounding yet empty speech, after having been blessed with the guru's speech in my speech. Please bless me to accomplish the vajra mind, the aware yet empty mind, after having been blessed with the guru's mind in my mind."

> Pacify the outer, inner, and secret obstacles ༔

All the conditions adverse to accomplishing enlightenment are called "obstacles." Outer obstacles are the sixteen major fears: the earth fear of pride, the water fear of desire, the anger fear of fire, the envy fear of wind, the lightning fear of thunderbolts, the weapon fear of sharp and piercing things, the tyrant fear of prisons, the enemy fear of bandits and thieves, the ghost fear of flesh-eaters, the wrath fear of elephants, the beast fear of lions, the poison fear of snakes and such, the illness fear of plagues and the like, the fear of untimely death, the fear of poverty and scarcity, and the fear of vanishing sense pleasures. These are the sixteen major fears.

Inner obstacles are the four maras: the aggregate mara of ego-clinging, the klesha mara of desire and attachment, the godly son mara of deception, and the lord of death mara of snatching one's life away.

Secret obstacles are the kleshas of the five poisons: desire, anger, stupidity, pride, and envy.

What do these obstacles impede? They impede the attainment of liberation and the state of omniscience. For this reason, supplicate, asking that all outer obstacles be pacified by the power of realizing that sights, sounds, and awareness are the display of deities, mantras, and dharmakaya; that all inner obstacles be pacified by the power of liberating grasping and fixation into the space of egolessness; and that all secret obstacles be pacified by the power of realizing that the five poisons are the five wisdoms and by taking adverse conditions as the path.

[Thus, with the removal of all obstacles, make aspirations that all wishes be spontaneously fulfilled:]

> And spontaneously fulfill all wishes.༔

TIBETAN SOURCE MATERIAL

Chokling Tersar[61]

Volume KA: Author: Chokgyur Lingpa (*mchog gyur gling pa*)

This volume introduces the texts revealed by Chokgyur Lingpa on the cycle known as *Lamey Tukdrub Barchey Künsel, Dispeller of Obstacles, The Heart Practice of Padmasambhava* as well as the related sadhanas, lineage prayers, and so forth. It also contains commentaries and explanations by other masters of the lineage.

The Essence Manual of Oral Instructions (*zhal gdams snying byang*). This is the basic terma text of *Lamey Tukdrub Barchey Künsel,* with chapters for historical background; sadhanas for the gurus of the three kayas and for each of the twelve manifestations, and so forth; as well as prophesies for the future.

Volume GA: Author: Chokgyur Lingpa (*mchog gyur gling pa*)

The Concise Manual for Daily Practice (*rgyun gyi rnal 'byor bkol byang*). This is the concise daily guru sadhana, according to *Lamey Tukdrub Barchey Künsel.* 179–182.

Vase of Fortune: The Source of Wish-Fulfilling Attainments: A ritual framework for the two branches of The Guru's Heart Practice (*yan lag rnam pa gnyas kya dbub yad bzan dngas grub 'byung b' bum bzang*). 227–294. Authors, Jamyang Khyentse Wangpo and Jamgön Kongtrül.

Volume A: Author: Chokgyur Lingpa (*mchog gyur gling pa*)

Supplication and The Sadhana of the Single Form of Vajrakilaya (*gsang thig snying po'i skor las rdo rje gzhon nu pyag rgya gcig pa'i sgrub thabs ldeb*). 35–42.

Volume Gi: Author: Chokgyur Lingpa (mchog gyur gling pa)

Tara: Outer, Inner, and Secret Sadhanas and Threefold Excellence (*bzhi ba dgongs gter la dgongs gter sgrol ma'i zab tig las slob ma rjes su bzung ba phyi nang gsang ba'i sgrub thabs legs so gsum gyi don khrid rdo rje lung gi nges pa rdo rje srung ma'i mchod byang srung ma'i las tshogs zab mo bcas gter gzhung ldeb*). 267–299.

Chokling Tersar BA: Author: Chokgyur Lingpa (*mchog gyur gling pa*)

The Essence of Magnetizing (*zab bdun padma mkha' 'gro'i gud byang dbang gi thig le gnad byang tshig brgyud ma bcas ldeb*). 293–296.

ENDNOTES

Note Attributions

DKR	Dilgo Khyentse Rinpoche
Ed.	Editor, Marcia Schmidt
EPK	Erik Pema Kunsang
JR	Jokyab Rinpoche
TJD	Tulku Jampal Dorje

1. Four Great Rivers of Transmissions are the rivers of empowerment of yidam, tantric scriptures, spiritual friend, and of the expression of awareness. These four transmissions originate from, respectively, Garab Dorje, King Jah, Buddhaguhya, and Shri Singha, Tantra Section.

    Tantric sections. 1) The four or six sections of tantras. 2) One of the two divisions of Mahayana. The Mahayoga tantras appeared in this world when revealed by Vajrasattva and the Lord of Secrets to King Jah, the ruler of Zahor, who was born 112 years after Buddha's nirvana. Some of the contemporary lineage holders were Uparaja, Kukuraja, Vimalakirti, and Jnanamitra. Subsequent masters were Shakputri, the regent and son of King Jah; King Jah's daughter, Gomadevi; Singaraja; Lilavajra; Buddhaguhya; and Vajrahasya. The following generation of lineage holders included Bhashita, Prabhahasti, and Padmasambhava, the latter of whom also received the tantras directly from King Jah. The son of King Jah was a lineage holder of both Mahayoga and Anuyoga. He is also known as Indrabhuti the Younger and Master Lawapa. [EPK]
2. OTR leaves out the fifth greatness of Nyingma, the greatness of the offerings. This can be found in Padmasambhava's life story, *The Lotus-Born*. [Ed.]
3. The setting was a gathering in the Bay Area, organized by Rigpa. After OTR extolled the virtues of the text, I thought he was going to get up and walk out, but he did not. He felt unworthy to teach such a profound text. [Ed.]
4. Padmasambhava and Jamgön Kongtrül, *Light of Wisdom*, Volume 1, trans. Erik Pema Kunsang, (Hong Kong: Rangjung Yeshe Publications, 1999), 273.
5. Ibid., 208. One list of the five tertön kings contains Nyang Ral Nyima Oser (1124–1192), Guru Chokyi Wangchuk (1212–1270), Dorje Lingpa (1346–1405), Pema Lingpa

(1445/50–1521), and Padma Ösel Do-ngak Lingpa (Jamyang Khyentse Wangpo) (1820–1892). Sometimes the list also includes the great tertön Rigdzin Godem (1337–1408). [EPK]

6. Padmasambhava and Jamgön Kongtrül, *Light of Wisdom,* Volume 1, trans. Erik Pema Kunsang (Hong Kong: Rangjung Yeshe Publications, 1999), 231. The threefold equality means being equal to all the buddhas in having perfected the accumulations, in being enlightened, and in accomplishing the welfare of beings. [JR]

   The Matchless King of the Shakyas is another name for Buddha Shakyamuni. He is called "matchless" because his aspiration was superior to that of others. [JR]

   Padmakara is called King of Victorious Ones because he conquered the enemy, the four maras. Padmakara means "lotus-born." [JR]

7. Ibid., 179–180. Appendix V.
8. Ibid., 231. Note 108. The eight great vidyadhara receivers of the transmissions are listed as follows:

   (1) The receiver of the transmission of Manjushri (Yamantaka) was Manjushrimitra, the vidyadhara of Body.

   (2) The receiver of the transmission of Mighty Padma (Hayagriva) was Nagarjuna, the vidyadhara of Speech.

   (3) The receiver of the transmission of Vishuddha was Hungchen-kara, the vidyadhara of Mind.

   (4) The receiver of the transmission of Amrita Medicine was Vimalamitra, the vidyadhara of Qualities.

   (5) The receiver of the transmission of Kilaya was Prabhahasti, the vidyadhara of Activities.

   (6) The receiver of the transmission of Liberating Sorcery, Botong, was Danasarnskrita, the vidyadhara of Mamo.

   (7) The receiver of the transmission of Maledictory Fierce Mantra, Mopa, was Shantigarbha, the vidyadhara of Fierce Mantra.

   (8) The receiver of the transmission of Loka was Guhyachandra, the vidyadhara of Mundane Worship. [JR] [DKR].

9. Ibid., 44
10. Ibid., 44
11. Ibid., 45
12. Ibid., 45
13. Ibid., 45
14. Ibid., 45–6
15. Ibid., 47
16. Ibid., 47
17. Ibid., 47
18. Ibid., 89
19. Ibid., 88
20. Ibid., 161–6, Appendix I.
21. Ibid., Appendix I.
22. Ibid., 90
23. Ibid., 91

24. Ibid., 91
25. Retranslated by Marcia B. Schmidt
26. Retranslated by Marcia B. Schmidt
27. Ibid., 91
28. Ibid., 91
29. Ibid., 92
30. Ibid., 92
31. The five from others are the facts that: the Buddha appeared, he taught, the doctrine survived, there are teachers, and they have the kindness to teach. [Ed.]
32. Padmasambhava and Jamgön Kongtrül, *Light of Wisdom,* Volume II, trans. Erik Pema Kunsang (Hong Kong: Rangjung Yeshe Publications, 1995).
33. Jokyab Rinpoche, *Light of Wisdom,* Volume 1, Appendix II.
34. See *Powerful Transformation,* trans. Erik Pema Kunsang. (San Rafael, CA: Rangjung Yeshe Publications, 2017).
35. *Color* has an alternate translation, which means "weapon," as denoted by Kyabje Dilgo Khyentse Rinpoche's commentary. Orgyen Tobgyal Rinpoche is using this meaning here.
36. Translated by Erik Pema Kunsang & Marcia B. Schmidt
37. While this was gradually decoded from the yellow parchment, *Das sum, The Three Sections,* which the incarnated, great tertön Chokgyur Lingpa had revealed from the ceiling of the Lotus Crystal Cave, was put into writing by Khyentse Wangpo, the joyful servant of the Lotus-Born Guru. May it be virtuous. Extracted from Jamgön Kongtrül Rinpoche's colophon for *The Heart Tika History,* his historical account of *The Sections of the Great Perfection.*
38. Tulku Urgyen Rinpoche, Blazing Splendor (Hong Kong: Rangjung Yeshe Publications, 2005). And Dilgo Khyentse Rinpoche, Brilliant Moon: The Autobiography of Dilgo Khyentse, trans. Ani Jinba Palmo (Boston and London: Shambhala, 2009), 280 and 284.
39. Retranslated by Marcia B. Schmidt; root text by Erik Pema Kunsang.
40. This teaching comes from a commentary on *Padma Khandro* by Rongzom Mahapandita in the Rinchen Terdzö. [Ed.]
41. He is teaching from the *Ritual Framework text of the Dispeller of Obstacles.*
42. Retranslated by Marcia B. Schmidt
43. *bla ma dngos grub rgya mtsho.* This text was destined to be revealed by Chokgyur Lingpa, but it was not revealed because of a lack of required auspicious conditions. *Wish-Fulfilling Guru Mahāsukha* (*gu ru bde ba chen po yid bzhin nor bu*) is, in a certain sense, its functional equivalent. [TJD]
44. This section of the text was translated by Padmakara Translation Group. Thereafter the text translation is by Ryan Conlon.
45. Various practices of auspiciousness.
46. The substance called *tun,* which probably doesn't have an English translation, is a gathering of thirty-two different substances that are used as a weapon to expel the negative forces. It is also used as a means of purification before entering the mandala.
47. Triangular iron box, whose sides represent the three gates to liberation.
48. The inner meaning of the ritual is that the demon of ego-clinging is being suppressed

until the precious mind of enlightenment is born within their mindstreams. If bodhichitta is born, liberation will occur. Until this time, the suppression remains. [Lama Sean Price]

49. Ryan Conlan, trans., *The Ritual Framework Text* (Boudhanath: 2018). The root treasure text explains as follows:

    It will increase by adding jewels, gold, silver, coral, and pearl.

    Merit will be generated with barley, rice, wheat, peas, and unhusked barley.

    Sweet flag (acorus calamus), early purple orchid (orchis mascula), thorns—i.e., yellow-fruit nightshade (surattense nightshade and fallopia aubertii), and black-myrobalan (terminalia chebula) will pacify illness.

    Salt, butter, honey, molasses, and sesame extract will give rise to innate wisdom.

    White and red sandalwood, saffron, camphor, and cloves will make discipline pure.

    Having thus properly enclosed and blessed these five groups of five, the five illnesses and spirits, the five afflictions and so-on, the five aggregates will be transformed, and one will manifest the attainments of the innate wisdoms of the five buddha families.

50. Retranslated by Marcia B. Schmidt

51. See Tulku Urgyen Rinpoche, Orgyen Tobgyal Rinpoche, and Lama Putsi, *Great Accomplishment,* trans. Erik Pema Kunsang (Hong Kong: Rangjung Yeshe Publications, 2013).

52. Tulku Urgyen Rinpoche, unpublished oral commentary.

    The practice of a particular yidam deity (*lhag pa'i lha*) contains inconceivable benefit. The yidam should be accomplished with the four nails that combine the vital essence of the deity. These are:

    The nail of the deity samadhi (*ting nge 'dzin lha'i gzer*) refers to the proper visualization of the yidam deity.

    The nail of the essence mantra (*snying po sngags kyi gzer*) refers to the mantra recitation of the yidam deity.

    The key point of the radiating and absorbing (*'phro 'du phrin las kyi gzer*) refers to the nail of the recitation-visualization (*dzab dmigs*).

    And finally, but most importantly, the nail of the unchanging wisdom mind (*dgongs pa mi 'gyur ba'i gzer*) refers to the recognition of the essence of your mind.

53. See the website of Orgyen Tobgyal Rinpoche: all-otr.org.

54. Because of weak respect and devotion,༔ 1. I have gone against the mind of the vajra master.༔

55. Because of lacking affection and modesty, I have gone against the minds of my Dharma brothers and sisters.༔

56. Padmasambhava and Jamgön Kongtrül, *Light of Wisdom,* Conclusion, trans. Erik Pema Kunsang (Hong Kong: Rangjung Yeshe Publications, 2013), 84. In general, *nyuley* spirits are presented very clearly in the *Kagye* and in the *Lama Gongdü,* as well as in Ratna Lingpa's *Secret Gathering of the Compassionate One*. Yet the specific approach of the Chokling Tersar is as follows:

    The twelve nyuleys who create obstacles to the practice and wander about meddling at the twelve times of day are given in the original terma in the Practice Arrangement That Gathers the Entire Intent of the Root Heart Practice:

(1) The obstructing nyuleys who create obstacles at sunset are the Shatring daughters cawing like crows; (2) likewise, those who create obstacles in the evening are the black female robbers; (3) at nighttime, the ignorance maintainers; (4) at midnight, the *ranus* of desire; (5) in the middle of the night, the *duntses* of aversion; (6) at the break of dawn, the Hedö daughter of the sun; (7) at sunrise, White Space Dust; (8) in the morning, the black female nagas and rakshasas; (9) at midday, the four families of seals of the nagas; (10) in the late afternoon, the border *terang* demons; (11) in the early afternoon, the female owners of the land who spread epidemics; (12) in the early evening, the maras and damsi demons of samaya-breakers. They are tamed by the twelve messengers who are their antidotes: Ekadzati, Seyijadra, the Great Red One, Dragon-Faced Dakini, the Great Blazing One, Hundred-Headed She-Wolf, Great She-Crow, Blazing-Mouth Crocodile, Great White One, Rakshasi Form, Tsangpa Lingpamo. There are also twelve oppressing substances and mantras.

57. Translated by Erik Pema Kunsang
58. Retranslated by Marcia B. Schmidt
59. Translated by Marcia B. Schmidt
60. Translated by Erik Pema Kunsang
61. Please note, all Chokling Tersar references are from the TBRC editions.